There have been few books about Grey's glorious but ultimately ill-fated West Indies campaign in the early years of the long, terrible Great War of 1793-1815. Yet five of the subalterns in Grey's expeditionary force went on to command divisions in Wellington's Peninsula army, another two commanded the Iron Duke's Royal Artillery, and one – Richard Fletcher – famously, the Royal Engineers.

The tactics used by Sir Charles Grey were as far removed as can be imagined from the traditional image of the two-deep British line delivering massed volleys at point-blank range. The invasions of Martinique, Saint Lucia and Guadeloupe were raids, undertaken by troops instructed to operate in open order, in silence, and at bayonet-point. All attacks went in with unloaded muskets. Most of the heavy-duty fighting was undertaken by converged flank battalions, grenadiers and light infantrymen assembled under hand-picked field officers, and used as storm-troops in every major assault. Here were French Revolutionary War tactics that are largely unexplored and largely undocumented, at least in modern times.

Sir Charles Grey was one of the most aggressive British generals of the era, something his gentlemanly appearance and demeanour did not immediately indicate. Ever cheerful and optimistic, humane and loyal to his friends, his ability to deliver needle-sharp assaults and then harry a defeated enemy – the latter being something at which British generals of the Napoleonic era were distinctly mediocre – makes him one of the more interesting personalities of the early portion of the 'Great War with France'. If he was not ultimately unsuccessful, it was not his fault. He was robbed of the resources he needed at the outset, then given virtually no reinforcements by Horse Guards.

The great killer on this campaign was not the French. It was disease – principally Yellow Fever. Of the 6,200 men who landed with Grey on Martinique in February 1794, some 4,100 were dead by Christmas.

Such then is *By Fire and Bayonet*, an account of a very dramatic period for the British Army in the West Indies. It took many years to learn the lessons presented by the campaign, but for the young officers who survived, it provided some invaluable lessons that put to good use fifteen or twenty years later, in the British Army of a later era.

Steve Brown is the author of *Wellington's Redjackets*, the history of the 45th Regiment of Foot 1807-1815, and has edited and annotated Helion's re-issue of William Brown's *The Autobiography, or Narrative of a Soldier*. He also a frequent contributor to, and book reviewer for, The Napoleon Series website.

By Fire and Bayonet
Grey's West Indies Campaign of 1794

Steve Brown

Helion & Company Limited

Helion & Company Limited
Unit 8 Amherst Business Centre
Budbrooke Road
Warwick
CV34 5WE
England
Tel. 01926 499619
Email: info@helion.co.uk
Website: www.helion.co.uk
Twitter: @helionbooks
blog.helion.co.uk/

Published by Helion & Company 2018. Reprinted in paperback 2022
Designed and typeset by Mach 3 Solutions Ltd (www.mach3solutions.co.uk)
Cover designed by Paul Hewitt, Battlefield Design (www.battlefield-design.co.uk)

Text © Steve Brown 2017
Maps © Steve Brown 2017
Cover: 'The Landing at Martinique' (Painting by Peter Dennis © Helion & Company 2017)

Every reasonable effort has been made to trace copyright holders and to obtain their permission for the use of copyright material. The author and publisher apologise for any errors or omissions in this work, and would be grateful if notified of any corrections that should be incorporated in future reprints or editions of this book.

ISBN 978-1-915070-90-6

British Library Cataloguing-in-Publication Data.
A catalogue record for this book is available from the British Library.

All rights reserved. No part of this publication may be reproduced, stored in a retrieval system, or transmitted, in any form, or by any means, electronic, mechanical, photocopying, recording or otherwise, without the express written consent of Helion & Company Limited.

For details of other military history titles published by Helion & Company Limited, contact the above address, or visit our website: http://www.helion.co.uk

We always welcome receiving book proposals from prospective authors.

Contents

List of Plates		iv
List of Maps		v
Preface		vi
Acknowledgements		viii
Naming Conventions		ix
Prologue		11
1	Never was a Kingdom Less Prepared	14
2	Grey	21
3	Jervis	29
4	Ostend and Back	33
5	The Knife-Edge	42
6	The Capture of Tobago	54
7	A Lock Step Banditti	58
8	Landing and Consolidation	70
9	Falstaff's Corps	92
10	Saint Lucia	114
11	High-Water Mark	126
12	Enter Hugues	141
13	We Have Been Greatly Neglected	157
14	Prize Money	177
15	Daily Expected	181
16	The Cost	187
17	The People	194
Appendices		
I	British Forces in Windward & Leeward Islands June 1793	203
II	Return of Troops Embarked at Barbados 1 February 1794	205
III	French Garrison of Martinique February 1794	207
IV	Returns of British Forces in Windward & Leeward Islands in 1794	208
V	State of Martinique Garrison in November 1794	209
VI	Grey's Officers	210
VII	Royal Navy Squadron at Martinique, February 1794	226
VIII	Royal Navy Squadron at Guadeloupe, April 1794	228
Bibliography		230
Index		238

List of Plates

A typical British infantryman of the era in West Indies tropical service uniform. (Anne S K Brown Collection) — 19

Lieutenant General Sir Charles Grey. Defeated as much by his own superiors and failing health as by the French, he deserves to be remembered as one of Britain's best generals of the era. (National Portrait Gallery) — 27

Vice Admiral Sir John Jervis. A fist of iron in a velvet glove. The naval commander and Grey's best friend. (National Portrait Gallery) — 31

Fort Royal, called République-ville in 1794. (Anne SK Brown Collection) — 43

His family motto was 'To live and die valiantly'; Donatien-Marie-Joseph de Vimeur, vicomte de Rochambeau certainly lived up to his creed commanding the French defence of Martinique in February and March 1794. (Public Domain) — 47

Saint Pierre in 1794 as depicted satirically by Cooper Wylliams. Note the guillotine, and heads on spikes. (Anne S K Brown Collection) — 91

A view across the bay towards Fort Louis on the right (called Fort de la Convention in 1794) with Grey's light infantrymen in the foreground. (Anne SK Brown Collection) — 93

The Royal Navy in action against Forts Bourbon and Louis (République and Convention). (Anne SK Brown Collection) — 96

The valiant Captain Robert Faulknor leads HMS *Zebra* to glory at Fort de la République. His death the following year robbed the Royal Navy of a fine officer. (Anne SK Brown Collection) — 109

The storming of Fort Royal on 24 March 1794. The uniform details are probably incorrect. (Anne SK Brown Collection) — 111

The town of Basse-Terre in Guadeloupe in 1794. (Anne SK Brown Collection) — 133

The beginning of the end. The capitulation of the defenders of Fort Fleur d'Epée on 7 June 1794. Much worse was to follow at Berville and Fort Matilda. (Public Domain) — 144

Lieutenant General Robert Prescott. Undeniably valiant, but one of the most difficult subordinates to ever serve a field commander. (National Portrait Gallery) — 171

List of Maps

1	The West Indies Theatre	x
2	Grey's movements on Martinique, March 1794.	72
3	The Capture of Saint Lucia, April 1794.	117
4	The Capture of Guadeloupe, April 1794.	128
5	The Loss of Guadeloupe, October-December 1794.	175

Preface

Sir Charles Grey's glorious but sadly ill-fated West Indies campaign in the early years of the long, terrible Great War of 1793-1815 is all but forgotten today. The time is right to bring it into the light, and reveal in equal parts the valour and squalor of close fighting in those far-off days. Practically none of the men who fell found remembrance beyond the end of that endless war, let alone white tombstones in grassy parks. Most died from fever, a fate far worse than a musket-ball, and most did die: some two-thirds of Grey's force, a death-rate worse than that ascribed to the so-called 'butcher' generals of 1914-1918.

But the death did not draw me to this story; the legacy of the campaign alone did that. Intrigued to discover that five of the subalterns in Grey's expeditionary force went on to command divisions in Wellington's Peninsula army, that another two commanded the Iron Duke's Royal Artillery, and that one – Richard Fletcher – famously, the Royal Engineers, I saw the conception of careers of ultimately famous men. Upon reading about the tactics used by Sir Charles Grey, which were as far removed from the traditional image of the two-deep British line delivering massed volleys at point-blank range as can be imagined, it was radiantly clear that this story needed to be explained. The invasions of Martinique, Saint Lucia, and Guadeloupe were raids, undertaken by troops instructed to operate in open order, in silence, and at bayonet-point. All attacks went in with unloaded muskets. Most of the heavy-duty fighting was undertaken by converged elite flank battalions, grenadiers and light infantrymen assembled under hand-picked field officers, and used as storm-troops in every major assault. Here were French Revolutionary War tactics that seemed to me unexplored and largely undocumented, at least in modern times, and certainly not associated with the average British infantryman of that era.

Grey's was an army finding a new footing following years of inactivity and disrepute after the disasters of 1781 in North America. Most of his regiments had been untested for fifteen years or more, his battalion commanders bored from years of drill-square inspections, his subalterns callow boys and indigent younger sons of the middle and upper classes. Yet Grey made them into something.

Sir Charles Grey was somewhat of a split personality. His gentlemanly appearance and demeanour disguised his reputation as one of the most aggressive British generals of the era. Ever cheerful and optimistic, humane, and loyal to his friends, his ability to deliver needle-sharp assaults and then harry a defeated enemy – the latter being something at which later British generals of the era were distinctly mediocre – marks him one of the most under-rated commanders of the 'Great War with France'. If he was not ultimately successful, it was not his fault. He was robbed of the resources he needed at the outset, then given virtually no reinforcements. The blame for this rests with Whitehall, which spent 1793 and 1794 throwing the few troops possessed by Britain at every opportunity to harm France which presented itself. The foreign policies of the time were full of knee-jerk reactions and last-minute re-arrangements. Then there was the problem of age; Grey was well into his sixties and spent the latter half of the campaign exhausted and debilitated (as did his naval colleague and great friend, Sir John Jervis). Aggressive warfare in torrid climates needed younger men, and therefore it is unsurprising that, a decade-and-a-half later, Moore commanded in Spain at the age of 47, and Wellington assumed command in Portugal at the age of 39. But these lessons were being learned the hard way.

The ways in which the Royal Navy and Army co-operated on campaign were grand. Grey and Jervis were so close, such good friends, that the two services acted almost as one for the first three months of the campaign. Such routine co-operation over long periods rarely features in Napoleonic era military accounts. The same spirit of cooperation sadly did not exist between Grey and his second-in-command, Prescott. Can any commander ever have had such a quarrelsome and pessimistic subordinate? Equally negatively, aspects of Grey's overt nepotism and greed will shock the modern reader, but were evidently more common in those times, when personal connections counted for everything in the densely arcane world of military and civil affairs.

The great killer on this campaign was not the French, nor even the native inhabitants of those isles. It was disease – principally Yellow Fever. Of the 6,200 men who landed with Grey on Martinique in February, some 4,100 were dead by Christmas. Any modern combat unit is considered to be hors-de-combat before it reaches half of its strength. The notion that regiments might still be expected to serve in the front line with barely 50 or 100 men left is incomprehensible, yet it happened often. In October 1794 Colin Graham found that his garrison at Berville contained 125 fit men left out of the 46 companies of infantry with which he had started.

Such then is *By Fire and Bayonet*, an account of a very dramatic period for the British Army in the West Indies. It took many years to learn the lessons presented by the campaign, but for the young officers who survived, it provided some invaluable experience that they put to good use fifteen or twenty years later, in the British Army of a later era.

Acknowledgements

My thanks go to the staff at the Palace Green Library, Durham University for allowing me access to the Grey Papers; to the British Library; to the National Archives, Kew; and to the Surrey History Centre.

On a more personal level, this book could never have been completed without the love and support of my long-suffering wife Jen, who did not bat an eyelid when I told her I would need to go to the UK for two-and-a-half weeks to rustle through the papers of a general she had never heard of, for a book about a campaign that seemed impossibly obscure. By such love and support is history made.

Naming Conventions

Place-names have generally been used as existed at the time of the campaign in 1794. Most survive to this day, however some clarification is required concerning the names of the principal towns and fortresses on Martinique.

Convention at the time was such that such places were named by the ruling power, and changed names as ownership changed. Thus, the town of Fort Royal (under the Bourbons) became 'République-ville' under the Republicans; by the same process Fort Louis became 'Fort de la République' and Fort Bourbon became 'Fort de la Convention', and later 'Fort Edward' after capture by the British.

In deference to what such places were actually called at the time of the campaign, and in homage to the considerable skill and tenacity of the defenders, I have opted to use the French Republican names for these places. However, wherever a pre-Revolutionary reference is required, or where memoirists have used the earlier Royalist form of the names, I have left them in the older style.

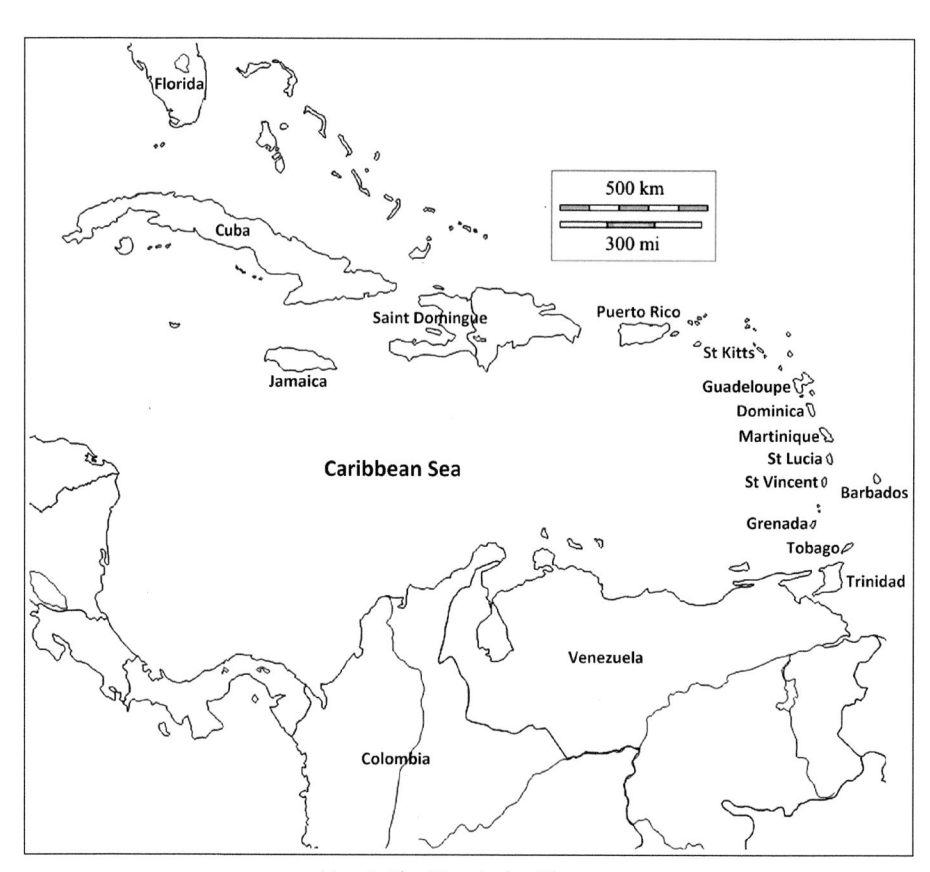

Map 1 The West Indies Theatre.

Prologue
Fort Matilda December 1794

Anyone standing in Fort Louis Delgrès, overlooking the ocean at the southern end of Guadeloupe, might think it one of the most picturesque spots on earth. The fortress once known as Fort Saint Charles, then Fort Royal, then Fort Matilda, overlooks the town of Basse-Terre, a sleepy provincial town of maybe 15,000 inhabitants. Lush green lawns cover yards where colonial soldiers once drilled in the torrid humidity, running like bowling greens between bastions and buttresses. The view from the ramparts is a wide blue ocean to the west, the town itself to the north, and looming, jungle-covered mountains to the east and south – Morne Boudoute and Mont Caraibes, whose thickly-wooded slopes run down to the cerulean sea. A small stream, the Galion, runs past the south-eastern end of the forest and discharges into the ocean. It is a bucolic spot, but one that harbours ghosts.

The fort was built in the sixteenth century, clustered around a house on a hill built in 1650 by Charles Houël, Governor of Guadeloupe. Originally running east to west, perpendicular to the sea, the fort was substantially improved between 1720 and 1750, when casemates, the postern (a small rear gate), and the great magazine were built, safely ensconced behind massive stone walls as part of France's defence of her West Indian possessions. Additional bastions, kitchens, underground tanks, and an officer's quarters were added between 1763 and 1790. Clusters of mature trees crowned the centre of the fort, providing relief against the steamy equatorial climate. But the fort was impregnable to the sea only; like Britain's defences at Singapore in 1942, it provided minimal defence to attack by land, being overlooked by Battery Houëlmont, which commanded the fort, the town, and the bay. In December 1794 the view of the sea and mountains would have been very similar; the town would have been much smaller of course, without the modern port facilities, and plantations rather than houses would have covered the landscape from the edge of the town up the slopes of Morne Boudoute, following and taking nourishment from the course of the Galion and other streams than ran down rivulets to the sparkling Caribbean Sea.

However, the men who occupied the fort in early December 1794 considered it the most detestable place on earth. Within the walls lived a tiny, sickly garrison of British troops, barely 500 men, of whom more than half were incapacitated through fever and other tropical illnesses. The largest contingent came from the 4th Battalion of the 60th (Royal American) Regiment of Foot, mainly German mercenaries with British officers, veterans who had long served in these islands and were better acclimatised than some of their English colleagues. There were parcels of men from various British line infantry regiments – a hundred or so from the 21st Foot, sixty from the 35th, twenty from the 39th, thirty from the 15th, and less than ten from the 33rd. These were the sad remnants of an entire expeditionary force, the survivors. Locally-raised militia, called Rangers, were also present, although in small numbers. Sixteen blue-coated artillerymen and an unknown number of sailors (brought ashore to man the siege artillery) formed a depleted specialist arm. The staff consisted of five Royal Engineers officers and eight officers and aides, and one general officer as commander-in-chief. This lieutenant general had so few fit officers that his second-in-command was a mere captain.

That man was Lieutenant General Robert Prescott, and this pathetic band was all that remained of His Majesty's expeditionary force to capture the French West Indian Windward Islands. This was all the men left from 6,200 or more who had landed on Martinique the previous March, not even counting the reinforcements. Over 4,000 were already dead, mostly from fever, some from malaria, some from dysentery. Barely two months earlier, the other British garrison on Guadeloupe, a camp called Berville, had been surrendered to the Republicans, and sickness had destroyed the garrison there also. Over a thousand men had been taken prisoner on their sick-beds, most not to survive. All French Royalists serving with the garrison had been guillotined, shot, or buried alive. Sensing blood, the victorious Republican commander, Victor Hugues, had sent his 2,000-man army southward, towards this this last bastion of British sovereignty, at the very southern tip of Guadeloupe. His fanatics had burned plantations owned by Royalists as they advanced. One overwhelming attack might have seen Prescott and his paltry band put to the sword. But the big attack had not come.

Prescott's languid cadre had lived in this stone fort in increasing desperation since 14 October, when Hugues' forces had commenced the siege. Only three days earlier, the Republican artillery had finally destroyed the last large calibre gun on the cavalier (the highest part of the fort); food was desperately short; medical supplies were virtually gone; men took their life into their hands to leave the fort to scoop water from the adjacent Galion, a mountain stream running between deep banks on the southern side of the fort and crossed by a single-arch stone bridge. The fort's bastions on the northern and eastern sides were crumbling under impact and were likely to give way at any time. No man could show his head above the ramparts for fear of a musket-ball through his brains. The men threw empty bottles into the ditches around the fort, knowing that the broken glass would slow any attackers, most of whom wore no shoes.

Prescott judged that the cause was lost; he had been abandoned. Countless written requests for reinforcements had produced no result. It was time to cut and run. He constantly looked out to sea, the only place salvation could come from, and scanned the horizon, waiting for each night-fall. Nine months of campaigning, and it seemed to him that the few left must skulk away in the dead of night, reduced to this ignominy by what was, in his eyes, a band of brigands and cut-throats. It must have hurt him deeply.

How had such a major campaign come to this bitter end? It is a story of government over-confidence, mismanagement, and ineptitude. It contains an aggressive commanding officer with his own very personal style of conducting war, bold infantrymen and courageous naval captains; but also lack of resources, sickness, neglect, and ultimately, dismal failure. It kick-started the careers of a number of junior officers who would go on to greater fame under a much later British commander, the Duke of Wellington; for under Sir Charles Grey they first learned the art of war; and they emerged much the stronger for it.

1

Never was a Kingdom Less Prepared

The French revolution of 1789 stirred people's minds profoundly, although it took some time for the after-effects to rumble across the Channel. The execution of King Louis XVI on 21 January 1793 turned those rumbles into seismic shocks. Continental Europe, hostile to Republican France, sought to encircle her. The French, aware that to sit on their hands was to invite invasion, went on the offensive. The First Coalition, a conglomerate of the ancient monarchies and their satellites, had found themselves aligned together after France declared war on 20 April 1792. The Prussians and Austrians (under the banner of the Holy Roman Empire) shouldered the early impact at Valmy and Jemappes, whilst Britain watched from afar, declaring all the while that war was unavoidable unless France gave up her new conquests, especially the Austrian Netherlands. The French had annexed the Austrian Netherlands in November 1792, an action which drove the other European powers into each other's arms as the First Coalition against France. Possession of the Austrian Netherlands gave France control over the vital channel port of Antwerp, a serious threat to British continental trade.

On 24 January 1793, a mere three days after Louis' bloody head had been held aloft in the Place de la Révolution, and sensing that war was close, the War Office in London planned an increase of the army by 16,000 men. On 1 February, Republican France declared war on Britain. The War Office scheme was presented to Parliament ten days later; amongst other measures it involved raising a hundred independent companies, of about 100 men each, and then drafting them into existing regiments. Just over a week later the Secretary at War moved a request to fund an additional 9,945 men, exclusive of the hundred independent companies. Regiments grappled with a new standardised system of drill, introduced in 1792 and therefore still unfamiliar. Brigade drill was virtually unknown. The government was raising new men to feed a deeply flawed and unprepared machine, '…lax in its discipline, entirely without system, and very weak in numbers' as Sir Henry Bunbury famously wrote.[1]

---

[1] Sir Henry Edward Bunbury, *Narratives of Some Passages in the Great War with France, from 1799 to 1810* (London: R. Bentley, 1854), p.vii.

But to make matters more tortuous, the British Army of the day had no Commander-in-Chief. Lord Amherst was appointed General on the Staff on 25 January 1793, a command appointment in fact if not in name. Amherst was 76 years old and in poor health. Once a valiant soldier, particularly in North America, Amherst was by this time in his dotage: mentally and physically unfit for the major exertions required for the new war against France. His influence in the looming war was to be to all intents and purposes nought.

Prime Minister William Pitt and his administration mistakenly believed that the war would be short. They underestimated France's robust sense of patriotic identity, and the enormous esprit de corps of her citizen armies. Their financial measures were based upon short-term thinking, as indeed was British strategic thinking for many years to come. The plan to defeat Revolutionary France rested on three strategic pillars. Firstly, supporting European allies such as Austria, Prussia, Holland, and Hanover with cash and troops. Secondly, using the Royal Navy to capture French colonies. Thirdly, offering practical aid to opponents of the Revolution, many within France itself.

By February 1793, the Austrians were advancing in the north to re-take the Austrian Netherlands. The Prussians and Austrians were pressing the French borders in the east, and the Piedmontese were pushing the French back on the Italian frontier, as were the Spanish in the Pyrenees. There was major civil unrest in the Vendée – by June, it had absorbed 100,000 French troops – and the four major southern cities of Marseilles, Bordeaux, Toulon, and Lyons were unabashedly Royalist. Significant British intervention at this point would have been decisive.

Pitt's response was anything but. On 20 February 1793, the first battalions of all three Foot Guards regiments were ordered to hold themselves in readiness for overseas service. Britain's initial contribution was to be a single brigade, less than 2,000 men. About the same time, 14,000 Hanoverians and 8,000 Hessians were taken into British service. Money and foreign manpower was the answer. Command of the first tiny British expeditionary force was given to Prince Frederick Augustus, the 29-year-old second son of King George III. He would become better known by his formal title, the Duke of York. Frederick had learnt his military skills in Hanover, spoke fluent German, and understood the continental military doctrines, all of which made him a good candidate for service in a coalition army. What stood against him was his extreme inexperience; he was yet to see a shot fired in anger. As an antidote to this he was given the assistance of the commander of the Brigade of Guards, the stern Major General Gerard Lake. In London, 2,000 guardsmen packed their kit, ready to fight on the continent for the first time in forty years. They were to be the lead elements of a British expeditionary force that would sit idly through a period of phony war, and then during the next year march through places such as Dunkirk, Ypres, Menin, Le Cateau, Arnhem, and Waterloo. Flanders was for centuries the crucible of the British Army.

Britain had no police force in 1792. The formation of the Metropolitan Police was still some 38 years away, and civil order was maintained by the Army. But in early 1793 Britain had an Army that was as weak in numbers and reputation as the Royal Navy was strong. Only a single brigade of infantry could be scraped together to follow the Guards, containing three regiments that some felt were 'unfit for service'.[2] 'Never was a kingdom less prepared for a stern and arduous conflict,' Lieutenant General Sir Henry Bunbury wrote years later.[3] The soldiery was weak and insufficient, and many officers had ossified or languished on half-pay since 1781. There were only 15,000 men in garrisons in the British Isles and about twice as many again deployed to the East and West Indies. Things were indeed bad after 1783, and historian Sir John Fortescue's negative views on the matter influenced later generations in many ways; but more recent re-assessments have shown that between 1787 and 1792 the army had at least reformed to some degree as regiments came back up to strength and a standard drill-system was introduced. Nonetheless, problems remained, such as rampant desertion, officers going on leave for long periods, and lack of centralised recruiting. Home recruitment was strictly catch-as-catch-can, as recruitment parties wandered the countryside with no central organising authority, regional loyalties, nor guiding policy beyond to get as many warm bodies dressed in red or blue as possible. 'Going for a soldier' was appealing only to the desperate. Most recruits came from the unemployed, often from the ranks of the drunk, who promptly deserted once sober. Bored or put-upon apprentices wishing for a more interesting life were a common source, but this was forbidden by law. Many apprentices came before the magistrates as a result and were promptly returned to their employers, to the Army's loss.

The outbreak of war was followed by an unprecedented military mobilisation in Britain, on a scale which would repeat on the resumption of hostilities in 1803, but then not be attempted again until 1914. The only civil defence force was the Militia. An Act of Parliament in 1757 ordered that every county in England and Wales was to supply and pay a quota of men between the ages of 18 and 45. A ballot system was to be used in 1793 to find 32,000 men, and these men were to be subjected to martial law whilst on active service. During peacetime, they were to be given a month's military training every year under the voluntary leadership of the gentry. The system was unpopular and inefficient. County quotas were rarely met, and no attempts were made to adjust them to the rapidly changing balance of population in the industrialised areas. Magistrates, mayors and constables had to organise transport and camps, and allocate billets in local inns. Reimbursement for innkeepers was usually insufficient. The myriad of costs was resented by parish rate-payers. Many classes were exempt from the Militia; ex-Militia officers who had served for four years, peers, university members, Anglican and dissenting clergy, articled clerks, seamen, apprentices, Thames watermen, any man under five

---

2   Hon. J. W. Fortescue, *A History of the British Army* (Uckfield: Naval and Military Press, 2004), Vol.IV, Part I, p.81.
3   Bunbury, *Narratives of some Passages*, p.vii.

foot tall. A balloted man could avoid service by paying a £10 fine or by finding a substitute, and these were usually available with the aid of agencies.

The British Army in the West Indies in 1793 existed under two commands; Barbados and Jamaica. The Barbados command oversaw the troops stationed on the Leeward Islands – Antigua, Nevis, Dominica – and the Windward Islands – Tobago, Grenada, Saint Vincent, and Barbados. The commander-in-chief at Barbados was Colonel (with the local rank of major general) Cornelius Cuyler, a 53-year-old New York-born career infantryman of Dutch descent, and he was no novice soldier. He had joined the 55th Foot at Fort Ticonderoga as an eighteen-year-old, then served at the reduction at Isle-aux-Noix and the capture of Montreal the following year. In late 1777, he became lieutenant colonel in the 55th Foot, serving at Brandywine and Germantown before sailing to the West Indies in 1778. For six years, he filled the posts of adjutant-general and quartermaster-general, went home in 1784, then returned to the West Indies in 1787 as quartermaster-general, a position he held until 1792 when he succeeded to the command of His Majesty's forces in the Windward and Leeward Islands. In 35 years of soldiering, he had been home for just eleven of them, and had served in practically every military role possible from ensign to commander-in-chief. He also knew the islands around him very well indeed. His military force was widely-dispersed, and very thinly-spread. In June 1793, he had only 2,562 rank-and-file present and fit for duty, on eight islands. The seven regiments, or parts of regiments, stationed on Barbados, 28 companies in all, could only muster 834 men, an average of less than 30 fit men per company. The strongest regiment was the 15th Foot on Dominica, at 305 men strong, about half of its establishment strength. Two regiments, the 6th and 65th Foot, were sailing down from Halifax to bolster the garrison, but even these units were also weak at 339 and 208 men respectively.[4]

The Jamaica command included Jamaica and St Domingue, and was exercised in combination with governorship by Major General Adam Williamson, a 57-year-old former artilleryman who had been sent out to Jamaica in 1790 at the expectation of war with Spain. Williamson was popular with the plantation owners on both islands for his general calmness and live-and-let-live attitude. It was symptomatic of his two major failings, a tendency of wishing to be everybody's friend, and a general lack of discipline in administration. Due to the large size of the two islands, the Jamaica command had a sizable garrison. It included eight infantry battalions – the 1/1st, 10th, 13th, 16th, 20th, 49th, 62nd, and 66th Foot; one cavalry regiment, the 20th (or Jamaica) Light Dragoons; and four companies of Royal Artillery. Of these, the 10th (North Lincolnshire) Regiment of Foot under Lieutenant Colonel Jeffrey Amherst, Junior (son of the commander-in-chief) had

---

4 GRE/A134, Number of rank and file of H.M. forces on several West Indian islands present and fit for duty according to the returns of June 1793.

seen most service, being on Jamaica since 1786. Many of the rest were recent arrivals. All were under-strength.

The Royal Navy was likewise split into two matching commands. At Barbados, Vice Admiral Sir John Laforey flew his flag from HMS *Trusty*, a 50-gun fourth-rate, accompanied by one smaller frigate and a sloop. It was pathetically small squadron with which to patrol seven hundred miles of ocean. Aged nearly 65, Laforey had seen long years of service in the West Indies, but was due to end his tenure in May 1793 with the arrival of a successor, Rear Admiral Alan Gardner. At the declaration of war, the Admiralty despatched an additional fourth-rate, two fifth-rates. and a sloop. At Jamaica, Commodore John Ford flew his flag from HMS *Europa*, another 50 gun fourth-rate, supported by a handful of small vessels. Like Laforey, his squadron was inadequate for the tasks involved.

The British Army in the West Indies at that time did not look like their fellow soldiers at home. The uniforms of the line regiments within the British Isles had much more in common with those worn in the American Revolution a generation earlier. Dull red coats (scarlet for officers), open to the waist with long tails, turn-backs and lapels in the regimental facing colour; white flannel waistcoat visible beneath; white linen trousers, close-fitting; boots (shoes) made the same for each foot, and designed to be alternated between feet each day to even out wear. But troops sent to the West Indies wore a simpler, more practical uniform. A short-tailed single-breasted red jacket without lace; white linen 'trowsers'; and a black 'round hat' – effectively a short-crowned top hat – with a plume, white for grenadiers, red and white for the battalion companies. The brim of the round hat provided minimal shade for the wearers. Officers long 'in country' could be easily identified by their use of wide-brimmed straw hats. Only the light companies differed, their men wearing Tarleton helmets, leather skull-caps with a bushy comb that rolled over the top and a visor. Men of the Royal Artillery were similarly attired, although with a single-breasted dark blue jacket rather than red. All troops were required to wear a long-sleeved flannel undershirt beneath a red woollen jacket in a theatre of war where the average daytime temperature did not vary between 25 and 27 degrees Celsius (77-81 degrees Fahrenheit) all year, and with high humidity. No wonder that men were known to fall down dead when on the march.

The infantryman's standard armament was the Land Pattern musket, usually referred to as a 'Brown Bess'. This instrument had been around since 1722, and would remain substantially unaltered at the time of Waterloo, twenty years hence. The only alteration from earlier models was a slight reduction in length, four inches, from models used prior to 1793. The piece had no sights, fired a 0.69 calibre ball, and could be fitted with a seventeen-inch-long bayonet. It could be discharged three times a minute by a well-trained soldier, or maybe once or twice by a recruit. Officers carried straight swords, or curved ones in the light companies, whilst sergeants carried nine-foot-long pikes, a practice inherited from the English Civil War. The jungle was no place for a pike, so it seems likely these were discarded as sergeants equipped themselves with muskets and short swords.

A typical British infantryman of the era in West Indies tropical service uniform. (Anne S K Brown Collection)

The sailors of the Royal Navy were far luckier than their lubber compatriots in that they were not subject to any specific uniform regulation whilst aboard ship. They typically adopted loose-fittings shirts, pants cut off just below the knee, and more often than not, bare feet. Once ashore they were expected to wear short blue jackets, scarves, socks and buckled shoes, and a wide-brimmed hat. A sailor's armament when engaged in raiding was pretty much whatever he could lay his hands on. Cutlass, musket, blunderbuss, and axe were popular. But these arrangements are not to suggest that sailors were subject to lower standards of discipline than the soldiers. They could be flogged just as readily as their land-borne redcoat brothers, and frequently were.

Some redcoats did exist aboard ships – the Marines.[5] These were musket-armed troops, allocated to ships at the rate of about one man per cannon rating, and were intended as ship-borne infantry for use in amphibious operations. They were also used for the enforcement of discipline aboard vessels. A shortage of Marines in 1793 led to the employment of some infantry battalions for this role. It was in this capacity that the 2nd (Queen's) Regiment of Foot found themselves acting in 1794, and led to the presence of Captain the Honourable George Ramsay's sole company of that unit in the West Indies, whilst the other companies of his regiment served in the Mediterranean and Atlantic theatres.

The rainy season, which at least provided some relief, was from July to November, when the trade winds subsided. The fever (or 'sickly') season was roughly the same – from July to October. Therefore, the campaigning season was, by default, December to June. Since it is imperative to this story, some description as to 'fever' is required. Yellow Fever was (and still is) caused by a virus, and is spread by the Yellow Fever Mosquito. The disease is thought to have originated in Africa and spread to the New World during the slave trade in the sixteenth century. A mild case might involve headaches, muscular pains, nausea, and fever. However most newly-arrived troops, or those yet to acclimatise, typically suffered severer forms of the disease, involving severe migraines, dangerously high fevers, crippling muscular pains, jaundice, and vomiting. A severe case of Yellow Fever usually had four stages; suffering, delirium, coma, then death. A soldier recovering from a milder case still needed three months of bed-rest, and was often of dubious physical value afterwards.

---

5   Not Royal Marines until 1802.

2

Grey

Charles Grey's background did not suggest a warrior future.[1] He entered the world in October 1729 in an upstairs room of his father's impressive tower house in Howick, Northumberland. Henry, the father, was a balding minor aristocrat aged nearly 38. The Greys had lived on this very spot since 1319, had remained industrious and influential locally, and had estates but lacked titles. His mother, Elizabeth Grey, née Wood, aged about 30, came from an estate named Fallodon about five miles to the north. Charles's older siblings included eldest son (and heir to the estate) Henry, aged seven, Hannah five, John four, Margaret three, Thomas one; but did not include the eldest child Jane who had died five years earlier aged just three. Also not included were those yet to come – Ralph in 1738 and Elizabeth in 1740. Charles had a happy childhood, tutored at home and with plentiful opportunity for outdoor pursuits. Being somewhere in the middle in a brood of eight had its advantages; young enough to be both cosseted and poked fun at, yet always with three elder brothers to bail him out of trouble. A middling student, Charles nevertheless thrived in a close and happy family atmosphere that taught him the value and importance of family connections in the pecking order of life. Such feelings were to influence his actions to the end of his days.

As the fourth son, there was little likelihood of inheritance of the estate, so Charles's options as he matured came down to three; as a gentleman farmer, service in the church, or service in the armed forces. He chose the latter. At the age of fourteen-and-a-half, his father obtained for him a commission as an ensign in the 6th Regiment of Foot, later a regiment that participated in his 1794 campaign, and he first saw action in the vicious Jacobite Rebellion of 1745 at Prestonpans and Fort William, but missed Culloden. Nonetheless, these actions were ultimately to his gain; his father was ennobled as Sir Henry Grey, 1st Baronet Howick for his

---

[1] Biographical details in this chapter are based largely upon Paul David Nelson, *Sir Charles Grey, First Earl Grey, Royal Soldier, Family Patriarch*, (Madison New Jersey: Fairleigh Dickinson University Press, 1996), principally chapters 1 to 8 covering the years 1729 to 1793. Commission dates are taken from Army Lists for the various years noted in the text.

services to the Hanoverian king in supporting the Crown against the Jacobites. The following year, at the age of sixteen, Charles went overseas for the first time, to Gibraltar for a five-year stint of unsparing tedium guarding the Rock. It was during this period (1749) that his father died, and eldest brother Henry succeeded to the title and estates as the 2nd Baron Howick. Bored and stone-broke on an ensign's income, Charles leaned on Henry to fund a step-up in rank to lieutenant just before Christmas in 1752. Further garrison service in the towns of villages of southern England followed, and in March 1755 Henry dipped into his pockets again to fund the independent 46th Company of Marines, one hundred men raised at the beat of a drum by Charles near his home to aid the Crown in the conflict which would eventually be known as the Seven Years War. As a reward, Charles was gazetted captain of the company. This new rank enabled him to transfer into the 20th Regiment of Foot on 31 May 1755 without the additional cost of purchase. This was a fortunate move. The commanding officer of the 20th was a man little older than Grey himself; James Wolfe. A flurry of departures saw Grey rise in the list of captains to the half-way mark by 1756, by which time he found himself commanding the light company, the sub-unit responsible for skirmishing and the only company permitted to operate in open order as distinct from closed ranks. The following year he accompanied Wolfe and his regiment on an ill-fated expedition to land troops at Rochefort on the French coast, with the aim of destroying docks, magazine, or shipping. In the event, it achieved none of the three, being poorly managed from the start. Nonetheless, it provided Grey with valuable experience concerning amphibious warfare; or as Arthur Wellesley was later to say about his first campaign, 'I learned what one ought not to do, and that is always something'.[2]

The 20th Foot was ordered to be part of an expeditionary force to Saxony in late 1758 as part of an Anglo-German army to combat the combined French and Saxon armies which had invaded Hanover. After months of reverses, the Battle of Minden was designed as a pre-emptive attack on the Franco-Saxon armies before reinforcements could arrive, and Charles served as an aide-de-camp to the allied commander, Prince Ferdinand of Brunswick-Lüneburg. Despite being badly outnumbered, the well-co-ordinated Anglo-Hanoverian forces advanced boldly. The 20th Foot, out near the right flank, withstood a French cavalry charge in line, an outstanding achievement on any field. The allies prevailed but the 20th ended the day a wreck, having lost 320 men, and Charles finished with a calf wound that would require three month's bed-rest. This was plenty of time to consider what he had learned on campaign – the value of audacity over numbers, the impact of shock attacks at unexpected moments, and the profound importance of coordinated actions. Another battle, at Klosterkamp in 1760, at which he commanded the light company of the 20th Foot and suffered another wound, further convinced

---

2   Elizabeth Longford, *Wellington: The Years of the Sword* (London: World Books, 1969), p.41.

him of the vitality of lighting infantry skirmishing tactics. So far the Grey of 1794 was forming nicely, but he would need more experience in command of larger units to complete his military education.

He cut an impressive figure. Tall and lean, athletic, a good rider. He had his father's thinning hair at the crown, thick black curved eyebrows over expressive blue eyes. Friends found him affable, but firm and confident in a crisis. He looked and acted every inch a commanding officer. He returned to England in late 1760 aged still only 31 and was immediately offered command, as a lieutenant colonel, of the newly-raised 98th Regiment of Foot. He therefore jumped two ranks on account of his good service in Saxony. The 98th Foot, however, soured the joy of promotion. They were a rabble of young boys and middle-aged men, all without any military experience, commanded by non-commissioned officers as inept and clueless as the other ranks. They were earmarked for overseas service but Charles contracted an illness and took to his bed for a long period, feeling so sick that he offered to resign the Army. Luckily for history his good friend and sponsor William Petty, the Earl of Shelburne, refused to deliver his resignation to the King. Perhaps some of it was love-sickness. During his recovery, on 8 June 1762, he married Elizabeth Grey of Southwick – a very distant cousin – at Bishop Wearmouth in Northumberland. He was 32, she 18. She brought money and estates to the arrangement, but she also brought love and happiness, and eight surviving children. When not with the Army, or in London, Charles was always to be found at home at Fallodon – an estate he inherited from his mother upon her death in 1764 – surrounded by his children, dogs and books.

Once recovered – and not long after his marriage – he volunteered to accompany an allied expeditionary force to Portugal to counter possible land-grabs by Spain, at the time long allied to France. His old friend, Wilhelm, Count of Schaumburg-Lippe-Bückeburg – whom he had befriended in Saxony – appointed Charles as his military secretary, with the local rank of colonel in the Portuguese Army. Charles saw this as being damned with faint praise. Of the Portuguese troops, he was revolted. 'Such wretched troops I never saw…',[3] he recorded. After spending the entire campaign at headquarters, seeing no action against the Spanish, who were ultimately repulsed back behind their borders, he returned home.

As a lieutenant colonel, it was a case of all dressed up and nowhere to go. Grey had held the rank for three years and had barely commanded a regiment in the barracks, let alone on a battlefield. The gap between martiality and reality widened the following year when his nearly-useless 98th Foot was disbanded in the aftermath of the Seven Years War. He retired to his estate at Fallodon to produce wheat, oats, and children. In this last he and his wife were particularly successful. They had Charles in 1764; Elizabeth in 1765, Henry George in 1766, George in 1767, Thomas in 1770, William in 1777, Edward in 1782, and Hannah Althea in 1785.

---

3   Nelson, *Sir Charles Grey,* p.26.

The family was comfortably secure rather than wealthy, although the situation deteriorated as the children grew older and Charles found it necessary to borrow more than £10,000 from various sources. An additional source of income from further military employment or a step-up in rank was essential. Despite being passed over for a brevet promotion to colonel, some lobbying from well-connected friends saw his name added to the list of colonels, with the added duties of an aide-de-camp to King George on 20 December 1772. One could not carry messages for the king from distant Northumberland, so Charles moved his family (at that time including four children) to a small town-house in Hertford Street, Mayfair.

By early 1777, Charles had spent nearly fifteen years in military limbo. The war in North America had so far passed him by, despite two expeditionary forces having been despatched to Boston and New York. But all that changed on 4 March with the arrival of two commissions from the king. The first appointed him regimental colonel of 28th Regiment of Foot.[4] The second appointed him a major general in North America only, giving him local rank for the duration of his service there, which was about to commence. This was a career-defining moment. He bade farewell to his family and sailed for New York City aboard HMS *Somerset* on 19 April 1777.

A full description of Grey's service in North America is outside the scope of this book, however there were two small-scale actions which monumentally influenced his later tactics in the West Indies, and indeed, earned him some notoriety in North America. The first was the Battle of Paoli on the night of 20 September 1777. Advancing on Philadelphia following victories at Brandywine and Whitehorse Tavern, Lieutenant General William Howe ordered Grey to attack Brigadier General Anthony Wayne's camp near Malvern in Pennsylvania. Commencing a little after ten o'clock at night, Grey's brigade – a composite light battalion, plus the 42nd Highlanders and 44th Foot – removed the flints from their muskets to avoid any discharges, and were ordered to go 'in a silent manner by a free and exclusive use of the bayonet'.[5] The troops charged in three waves and caught the encamped Pennsylvanian and Maryland troops completely by surprise. The panicked Continentals fled into the night; not a shot had been fired. American losses were 53 killed, 113 wounded and 71 captured. Grey's losses were just 4 killed and 7 wounded. The second action was at Old Tappan, New Jersey, on the night of 27 September 1778. Acting under orders from Lieutenant General Sir Henry Clinton, Grey led a battalion of light infantry, a battalion of grenadiers, and elements of the 33rd and 64th Foot on a surprise attack against a regiment of

---

4 Regimental colonel was (and remains) a proprietorial position usually conferred upon general officers, who at the time were in financial charge of the regiment's allowances from the government. A thrifty Colonel might therefore make a profit from his regiment; however some Colonels were known to have lavished private funds on their regiments to improve their smartness.

5 J. R. Miller, *The History of Great Britain from the Death of George II to the Coronation of George IV* (London: M'Carty & Davis, 1829), p.117.

Continental light dragoons housed in a group of farm buildings. Using cover of darkness and the bayonet only, Grey's troops went from house to house, killing fifteen and wounding or capturing 54 dragoons, including their commanding officer, Lieutenant Colonel George Baylor. About another forty escaped into the night. Again, not a shot had been fired.

Charles became, to both sides, 'No-Flint Grey'. This was a compliment within the British Army, but a form of derogation by the Americans, who saw him as a butcher. In this latter, he was probably the victim of media propagandists who sought to earn sympathy for the Patriot cause by inflating the actual losses. Notwithstanding these personal attacks, he had one of the outstanding reputations of the British officers of the war, but his health was less than good. By calling on aid from his old Lord Shelburne, Grey managed to secure a release from Clinton to go home just before Christmas 1778. America was left behind in early 1779 and he arrived home a substantive major general (having been officially promoted in late 1777), delighted to be with Elizabeth and the children at his London town-house once more, but in health that was 'in every way so precarious'.[6] Attendance at a committee before the House of Commons into the state of the American war was required from him. The hearing that came to an inconclusive end, and so, likely thinking that his campaigning days were behind him, Charles settled back into private affairs. He arranged for his third son, George, to be taken into the Royal Navy as an eleven-year-old midshipman on HMS *Roebuck*, then took the rest of the family (less Charles, at Eton) north to Fallodon to resume his days as a gentleman farmer. Another task was to purchase an ensigncy for thirteen-year-old Henry George in the 26th Regiment of Foot. But the solitude of Northumberland was not to last for long; he received a letter from commander-in-chief Lord Amherst asking him to hurry south to Plymouth to assist putting that port into a proper state of defence. Whilst this assignment was foreign to his previous experiences, it was at least on his home station, close enough to London for weekend breaks, and unlikely to play merry hell with his health. And Charles was not a man to question orders, nor to miss a chance to turn his hand to new tasks.

Plymouth was a nest of chaos. There were only 30 artillerymen to work 179 antiquated cannon. A flurry of activity was necessary, and an effort to properly man the guns came apparently just in the nick of time. The combined Franco-Spanish fleet hove in view on 17 August 1779, but did not attempt any offensive action. Charles celebrated his fiftieth birthday at Plymouth in October, living hand-to-mouth despite being a major general, parted from his children and battling bureaucracy on all sides. Over-qualified to be employed on civil duties, he must have quaked when his eldest son Charles wrote and asked permission to leave Eton and join the Army. The elder Charles nonetheless assented, and the younger was commissioned as a cornet into the 19th Light Dragoons. That plum roles were not to be his

---

6   Nelson, *Sir Charles Grey*, p.56.

was obvious in March 1782, when Sir Guy Carleton (the future Lord Dorchester) effectively offered Grey the post of second-in-command of the forces in North America. It was a war already lost. Grey was being offered another mopping-up role, managing an exodus of loyalists followed by a retirement to the Canadian frontier. Grey turned down the offer.

Charles' old friend and mentor Lord Shelburne became Whig Prime Minister in July 1782. Grey was ecstatic. He could now expect preferment, and anything to get him out of his dreary duties at Plymouth. The offers were not long in coming. In October, he was offered Sir Guy Carleton's former role as commander-in-chief, North America. Having declined the deputy position once, he thought long and hard about the offer – youngest son Edward had just been born – and finally accepted the position, but only on his own terms. Some of those terms included promotion and knighthood. With these conditions met, on 20 November 1782 Lieutenant General Sir Charles Grey started to prepare for his new assignment. He immediately met with resistance to his proposed staff appointments, contrary to his terms of employment, as well as disagreement with the navy over transport arrangements. His delay for North America was delayed for some months, possibly partly due to Grey's poor health, partly to Grey's belief that there was no use in hurrying to a withdrawal. But the delay was mainly due to the fall of Lord Shelburne's administration. The new Prime Minister, the indolent Tory Lord North, was no fan of Whigs such as Grey. North was of the view that 'he did not absolutely see the necessity of a new commander-in-chief going out'.[7] He considered Grey at best third in line of preference for such a posting, if one even existed. Sir Charles organised a meeting with the King on 23 April 1783 and pleaded his case. Despite King George receiving Charles 'in the most gracious manner',[8] Grey's commission was withdrawn.

At the age of fifty-four, and with no new conflict on the horizon, Sir Charles retired once again north to Fallodon, where youngest child Hannah was born in 1785. What followed was eight years of rural bliss interrupted only by continual financial hardship. He had put Charles through Eton and later Cambridge. He had paid the wedding costs and dowry at the marriage of eldest daughter Elizabeth to Samuel Whitbread in 1789. He arranged with John Pitt, Earl of Chatham, First Lord of the Admiralty, to have his son George promoted to captain in the Royal Navy, at the age of twenty-six. But minor military duties continued on and off. In 1785 he was appointed to a Board of Land and Sea Officers to investigate the works that would be required to make Plymouth and Portsmouth safe against a sea-borne assault. The board comprised eight army and three naval officers, one of whom was Captain Sir John Jervis, an old acquaintance of Grey's. The two settled into a warm friendship. For years Grey had lobbied the Secretary at War

---

7   Nelson, *Sir Charles Grey*, p.121.
8   Nelson, *Sir Charles Grey*, p.122.

Lieutenant General Sir Charles Grey. Defeated as much by his own superiors and failing health as by the French, he deserves to be remembered as one of Britain's best generals of the era. (National Portrait Gallery)

for a colonelcy in a dragoon regiment, which was considered far more desirable than being colonel of a regiment of foot. He got his wish on 13 July 1787 when he gained the regimental colonelcy of the 8th Regiment of Light Dragoons, which he later swapped for the 7th (Princess Royal's) Regiment of Dragoon Guards on 7 March 1789.

The outbreak of war with France in 1793 found Grey living the life of the gentleman-farmer at rural Fallodon, far from London. Now aged sixty-three, he had not seen a shot fired in anger for fifteen years. He had rejected an offer for high command in 1782 and been rebuffed from a second offer in 1783. He unquestionably thought his active campaigning days were over. But that all changed at the start of September, when a letter arrived from faraway Whitehall, sent by the Minister for War Henry Dundas. It appointed him as commander-in-chief of forces to be employed in the West Indies. And commanding the Royal Navy contingent was to be his great friend, Vice Admiral Sir John Jervis.

3

Jervis

John Jervis was six years younger than Grey, from the opposite side of the country, but cut from the same cloth.[1] He was born at Meaford in Staffordshire on 9 January 1735. His father Swynfen Jervis was a solicitor to the Admiralty, and the treasurer of Greenwich Hospital. He proved to be an extremely bright boy, and excellent scholar in Latin and Greek at grammar school at Burton-upon-Trent. At the age of twelve, young 'Master Jackey' was sent to a boarding-school at Greenwich, until the day he would be ready to go to university to study law. That all changed the day he decided to join the navy in concert with his best friend, Pat Strachan, later father of Admiral Sir Richard Strachan. The two ran away to Woolwich and hid on board a vessel for three days, after which young Jackey returned home and told his mother, as his father was absent at the time, that he wanted to be a sailor. Through some family connections the young Jervis was introduced to Commodore George Townshend, about to go out to Jamaica in HMS *Gloucester* as the new commander-in-chief. Townshend told Jervis to report to a rather uncouth first lieutenant at the docks; and so, with a twenty pound note from his father in the pocket of an over-sized jacket, the thirteen-year-old John Jervis went to sea.

Young Jackey threw himself into his new profession, living in Spartan fashion to save money. This involved washing and mending his own clothes, sometimes even making new trousers from bedclothes, but always living within his means. He was made lieutenant on HMS *Royal Anne* at the age of nineteen. He first came to prominence during General Wolfe's campaign at Quebec in 1759, where as acting commander of the sloop HMS *Porcupine*, Jervis and the frigate *Halifax* led the armed transports past Quebec to land up-river. This approach was so critical, both Wolfe and James Cook boarded the *Porcupine* to ensure the success of the mission. For his efforts, Jervis was promoted to the rank of commander and took command of the 14-gun sloop HMS *Scorpion*.

---

1 Biographical details in this chapter are based largely upon Edward Pelham Brenton, *Life and Correspondence of the Earl St Vincent*, Vol. I (London: Henry Colburn, 1838), principally chapters I to IV.

Jervis returned to England in September 1759 but almost immediately returned to North America in command of HMS *Albany*. The following year he was promoted to post captain and was attached to Admiral Sir George Rodney's Channel squadron. In 1763 Jervis's ship HMS *Gosport* was paid off and he remained unemployed for six years, until given command of frigate HMS *Alarm* in 1769, the first copper-bottomed ship in the Royal Navy. This ship was paid off late in 1772 and Jervis went on something of a sabbatical. For two-and-a-half years he toured the continent, studying shipyards and naval defences of France, Russia, Sweden, Denmark, Germany and the Netherlands. Further command followed in 1775 when he was given command of HMS *Foudroyant*, a ship with which his name came to public attention, although not all were for seafaring reasons. Serving with Admiral Augustus Keppel's fleet at the Battle of Ushant, Jervis is remembered for his defence of the beleaguered Admiral at the latter's later court-martial for neglect of duty in the face of the enemy. Jervis's passionate defence was instrumental in Keppel being acquitted.

One night in 1782 the French man-of-war *Pégase* slipped out of Brest laden with troops bound for the East Indies. Whilst serving with the Channel Fleet, the *Foudroyant* closed and fought a night-time battle which lasted 45 minutes. The French ship surrendered. Jervis only lost three men. He later attributed to his success to the build quality of the *Foudroyant,* a French ship captured in 1758, and stated he considered that 'in the art of constructing ships of war, the French were a full century ahead of us.' [2] Returning home something of a hero, Jervis was made Knight Commander of the Bath on 19 May 1782 and promoted to the rank of commodore in December of that year.

Closing in on fifty years of age, Jervis struck his pennant in January 1783 and went home to marry his cousin Martha Parker, daughter of the Lord Chief Baron of the Exchequer, Sir Thomas Parker. With her in her forties, no children came of the marriage. Although never appearing to evince much interest in politics, Jervis was returned as Member of Parliament for Launceston, Cornwall in 1783. During the elections of the following year Jervis stood for election in the independent borough of Great Yarmouth, where he was again successful, being returned as MP. It seems that politics and his new wife consumed him completely for the next decade. He stood again, this time for the Chipping Wycombe seat, and was again returned as MP in 1790. But his interest in politics was wavering. He rarely spoke in the house and when he did it was almost exclusively on naval matters, and he resigned his seat later that year. He did not stand again for political office. In 1785 Jervis was appointed to the same Board of Land and Sea Officers as was Grey. Whereas previously they only knew each other casually, the two settled into the warm friendship that would carry them through the campaign to come.

---

2   Brenton, *Life and Correspondence of the Earl St Vincent*, p.68.

Vice Admiral Sir John Jervis. A fist of iron in a velvet glove. The naval commander and Grey's best friend. (National Portrait Gallery)

But in 1785 Grey was a lieutenant general, whereas Jervis was 50 years of age and still just a commodore, equivalent to a brigadier general in the army, which was not itself a permanent rank, only an appointment. Career progress in the Royal Navy was always slow in times of peace. Elevation came in September 1787 when Jervis was promoted rear admiral of the blue,[3] and hoisted his flag in the 74-gun HMS *Carnatic*. Three years later he was promoted rear admiral of the white. Perhaps putting some of his political learnings to good use in late 1792, Jervis proposed a scheme to alleviate the financial hardship of superannuated seamen but later withdrew the proposal once Sir Henry Dundas promised that the matter would be addressed by the Admiralty Board. A few weeks later he drew attention to the hardships that newly-commissioned naval officers suffered from the delayed payments of subsistence money. Jervis could speak from his own experiences on this matter. For the remainder of his career, Jervis was ever the reformer, looking for ways to improve the service in terms of both men and machines. His disposition was like Grey's. He was generally a kind and friendly man in public, but a stern disciplinarian aboard ship.

A vice admiral's rank (of the blue) saw him appointed to command of the Leeward Islands station in November 1793, to replace Gardner. The calibre of the man who was to lead the naval portion of the expedition can be summed up by Lord Nelson, who later said of Jervis, 'they at home do not know what this fleet is capable of performing; anything and everything … of all the fleets I ever saw, I never saw one, in point of officers and men equal to Sir John Jervis's, who is a commander able to lead them to glory'.[4] The average sailors of the Royal Navy held a similar view, one summed up in the lyrics of a shipboard ditty;

> You've heard, I s'pose, the people talk,
> Of Benbow and Boscawen,
> Of Anson, Pocock, Vernon, Hawke,
> And many more then going;
> All pretty lads and brave and rum
> That seed much noble service;
> But Lord, their merit's all a hum
> Compared to Admiral Jervis.[5]

---

3 The lowest admiral rank in the Royal Navy; each rank carried three grades – blue, white and red, in ascending order.
4 From an article entitled 'The Nelson Letter and Dispatches' published in *Ainsworth's Magazine*, Volume 7, 1845, p.301.
5 Jervis's surname was pronounced to rhyme with 'service', rather than as 'Jarvis'. Song lyrics quoted in Evelyn Baring, *Political and Literary Essays* (Cambridge: Cambridge University Press, 2010), p.453.

4

Ostend and Back

Sir Charles Grey received his appointment as commander-in-chief of forces 'employed or to be employed in the West Indies' on 2 September 1793. The following day Colonel Francis Dundas wrote to his uncle Minister of War Henry Dundas saying how pleased his friend Sir Charles Grey had been with his treatment by Pitt and Henry Dundas in the matter, and drawing attention to his confidence in his ability to collaborate with his great friend Jervis. The campaign arrangements were a web of personal connections, familial, fraternal, and fiduciary, and on such bedrocks the seeds for success and failure in the campaign were sown.

Henry Dundas had decided this force should sail on or about the first day of September, to arrive in the Caribbean before November, to take advantage of the best campaigning weather. In any event, Grey did not actually receive his appointment of commander-in-chief of the expedition until after that date. But it is clear from Dundas' summaries of troops that could make up Grey's forces dated late August that such a date was totally impractical. His first published plan, dated 31 August, entailed bringing the existing regiments already in the West Indies up to full strength, then to reinforce them with troops from Gibraltar, Ireland, and England.[1] Of the seventeen infantry regiments then serving in the West Indies, eleven were in the Leeward Islands, and none were anywhere near their theoretical strength of 600 rank-and-file. Five (6th, 9th, 15th, 21st, and 65th Foot) were earmarked to be 'completed' to full strength by taking men from four regiments being drafted out – the 32nd, 45th, 48th and 67th. These regiments had completed their term of duty and were 'ordered home,' something that sounds like it ought to have occasioned great joy, except that the usual practice was to 'draft out' – in other words, transfer all the fit men to other regiments in the garrison before sending all the officers, sergeants and sick men home to recruit. 'In those days, the lot of the soldier had many disadvantages,' a regimental history later noted.

---

1   GRE/A139, Statement showing the order in which the regiments in the West Indies went abroad and the places where they were stationed with mode proposed of draughting the West India Regiments, dated 31 August 1793.

Among others there prevailed a practice destructive of all hope that he could ever return to his native country. When a soldier, in virtue of a good constitution and regularity of conduct, had survived his comrades, instead of being rewarded by removal to a better climate or being sent back to his native country, he was moved from one regiment to another while life or the ability to serve remained. The hospital or the grave was thus very often the only termination of his career of service.[2]

Dundas' plan also included drafting out men of the weak 3rd Battalion 60th Foot into the stronger 4th Battalion. This practice of drafting out was eventually discontinued after 1800, when the Duke of York became Commander-in-Chief. It had two major flaws; firstly, men arbitrarily moved from the regiment they had joined into a new regiment lost all sense of regimental identity; and secondly, the weak cadres of the drafted-out regiments sent home took a long time to recruit up to full strength, and even longer to reach a state of combat efficiency.

Assuming five regiments then in Ireland – the 39th, 43rd, 56th, 64th, and 70th – could be brought up to numbers and sent,[3] and that four regiments then serving in Jamaica could be employed,[4] as well as three regiments then in Gibraltar and nine in England,[5] Grey would have a grand total of 16,356 men, with the hope that after the campaign, he could send 10,000 of them back to England for actions on the continent against France.

Of the regiments to be drafted up to strength, the 65th (2nd Yorkshire North Riding) had served overseas since 1785, the 6th (1st Warwickshire) since 1786, and the 9th (East Norfolk) since 1788. The 15th (Yorkshire East Riding) had been in the Leeward Islands since 1790 and was considered particularly sickly. The 60th (Royal American) was a regiment destined for permanent overseas service, being composed of many non-Britons, and had been in the West Indies since 1787. The 21st (Royal North British Fusiliers) had only recently arrived in the West Indies from North America. Regimental titles were at that time a misnomer, being allocated on the requests of regimental colonels in 1782, and usually having more to do with where the colonels lived or were born than where the regiments sourced their men. Recruiting parties roamed the British Isles and took men wherever they could be found, especially in Ireland. Officers regiment-hopped as vacancies arose, equally showing little or no regional affiliation, with the exception

---

2   Archibald Forbes, *The Black Watch: The Record of an Historic Regiment* (New York: Scribener & Sons, 1910), p.151.
3   There is a note in the memo in GRE/A139 which says, 'to be draughted' next to the 39th and 64th, which suggests these two units were deemed to be less fit-for-service than the others.
4   1st Battalion 1st (Royals), 13th, 20th, and 62nd Foot.
5   From Gibraltar, 2nd Battalion 1st (Royals), 18th, and 51st Foot. The units from England were the 3rd, 19th, 27th, 28th, 42nd, 54th, 57th, 58th, and 59th Foot.

of denominated Scots Highland and Irish regiments, which tended to be more regionally homogenous.

The supposed departure date of 1 September became later September, then changed to late October. The force to be under Grey's command and confirmed to him on 2 October was to be the largest he had ever commanded.[6] He had, on paper, fourteen regiments totalling 8,400 men, plus the flank companies of fourteen regiments then serving in Ireland, another 1,960 men, plus 400 artillerymen and artificers. The whole came to something over 10,700 men with 24 cannon, somewhat down on the 16,000 originally proposed. Whilst there were no cavalrymen included, that was explainable by the mountainous and thickly-jungled terrain likely to be encountered. The West Indies was not good horse country. Henry Dundas had a second attempt at this exercise a few days later and came up with a revised total of 10,179; another attempt a week later, this time with artillerymen included, came to 10,760.[7] Tellingly, nearly 5,000 of these men were aboard ship off Spithead, at which place Vice Admiral Sir John Jervis had hoisted his flag on 3 October, and Spithead was a mere day's sailing away from Flanders.

It was Flanders that was taking pride of place in British military thinking at the time, not least because things there were going pear-shaped. The Duke of York had been driven out of Dunkirk, losing all his siege artillery, and the loss of Ostend on the Channel coast looked likely also. Eight battalions stripped from Grey's force had already been sent there, explaining the reduction in numbers discovered by Grey on 2 October. But more effort was needed. On 26 October Dundas wrote to Grey and informed him it had been decided that he should proceed to Ostend personally with four of his battalions and either defend it, or bring the garrison of eight battalions back to England as he saw fit.[8] This vital seaport was in danger of being captured by the French, and this evidently completely over-rode any planning for the West Indies expedition. No doubt disappointed by this diversion, but as dutiful as ever, Grey sailed from Deal on 28 October and arrived at Ostend with the 3rd, 28th, 54th, and 59th Foot later the same day. He immediately reported on the situation as he found it there, and despatched the 42nd Highlanders and four companies of light infantry to aid the beleaguered defenders of the 53rd Foot in the nearby town of Nieuport, five miles down the coast, which was soon relieved. Ostend was safe. The Duke of York, commanding the British forces in Flanders, wrote to Grey on 2 November giving him permission to embark his troops 'and

---

6 GRE/A142, Particulars of the force to be collected for Grey's expedition to the West Indies, dated 2 October 1793.
7 GRE/A175c/1, Return of troops allotted to Grey's expedition to the West Indies, dated 9 November 1793.
8 GRE/A143, Letter from Henry Dundas to Grey, informing him that it had been decided that he should proceed to Ostend and that he was to use his discretion whether to secure it or not, dated 26 October 1793.

proceed to his next command.'[9] Grey hung around for a few days to sort out administrative matters then returned to Deal to re-focus his attentions on the West Indian affair.

It would be hard to retain focus over the next few weeks. Grey received secret instructions dated 12 November to attack Martinique, Guadeloupe, then Saint Lucia, and once done, whether successful or not, to proceed to Saint Domingue.[10] The implication was that he should capture all the French West Indian islands, windward and leeward, in a single island-hopping campaign. It probably looked easy on a map. The local garrisons and the Jamaica command were to sacrifice some troops to bolster Grey's force. The good news was that Grey's old friend, Vice Admiral Sir John Jervis, was to command His Majesty's forces by sea. Jervis had recently done Grey an enormous favour by appointing his son George as captain of his flagship, HMS *Boyne*. The following day Grey received another letter from the Secretary of State's office providing instructions concerning the distribution of booty between land and sea forces. 'Booty' in the eighteenth century could mean many things, but he and Jervis interpreted it as any French property that might come their way. They read into the instruction official approval to apply a level of rapacity that might appal a modern observer, but was not uncommon for the time. 'We do hereby order and direct that you do settle with Sir John Jervis, or with the Commander in Chief of our ships', Dundas's letter read, 'in what manner and proportion Booty taken from the Enemy at Land during the present Expedition, shall be distributed between our Land and Sea Forces, in all cases, where the said Land and Sea Forces shall be jointly engaged in the attacking and taking of any Place, Fort or Settlement from the Enemy.'[11] Grey and Jervis discussed and agreed the division of spoils, a policy which on paper seemed to have the governmental seal of approval.

Another cooperative effort with Jervis was to be a joint appeal, issued before the start of the campaign, saying that any French colonist who wished to swear the oath of allegiance to King George could do so, there being perhaps some thought that entire islands might go over to the Crown. If this appeal failed, as seemed highly likely, Grey and Jervis could use their own discretion as to the terms of any capitulation, but any surrender must be to the King – George, not Louis. Grey also

---

9   GRE/A165, Letter from the Duke of York to Grey. Concerning the fortifications at Nieuport and other places, and giving him permission to embark his troops and proceed to his next command, dated 2 November 1793.
10 GRE/A175b, Secret instructions to Grey as Commander in Chief in the West Indies, with propositions eventually to be acceded to by Grey and Sir John Jervis, Commanders in Chief of H.M. Forces by sea and land in the West Indies, dated 12 November 1793.
11 GRE/176b, Draft of proposed separate instructions from H.M. the King to Grey as Commander in Chief of the forces in the West Indies. Concerning the distribution of booty between the land and sea forces. The same memorandum goes on to point out that the Corps of Black Dragoons, Pioneers and Artificers should receive an equal share of the Booty.

received royal permission to fill up officer commissions up to the rank of captain as he saw fit during the expedition, 'leaving the higher ranks of Major & L[ieutenant]t Col[onel] to be vacant till my approbation is given to such recommendation as he may have proposed.'[12] As always, family came first. He summoned his three sons Henry George (major in the 17th Light Dragoons), Thomas and William (both subalterns in the 7th Fusiliers) to join himself and their seagoing brother Captain George Grey RN on campaign. If he was going to benefit by the acquisition of booty, then he was making sure that his sons would also, or at the very least benefit by his own special powers of promotion.

By 17 November, Grey's sense of excitement and anticipation must have been great. All the cards looked as if they were turning in his favour. He had spent the week attending farewell events. This busy schedule included a royal levee with the King, and a dinner organised by the popular Major General Thomas Dundas for all the departing senior officers at the Freemasons' Tavern. Then, as he had done three weeks earlier, Henry Dundas found a way to queer the pitch. In a letter marked 'Secret' from Whitehall that day, he directed Grey to give away eight of his battalions for a new expedition by Lord Moira assisting the Royalists in La Vendée; in other words, half of his expeditionary force. 'I have it in commend from His Majesty to acquaint you, that unforeseen circumstances have rendered it indispensably necessary, to employ on another very pressing and important Service, such part of the Forces originally destined to be employed under your Command…' Only the 58th Foot, deemed too weak to go to La Vendée, two companies of the Royal Irish Artillery, and the Royal Military Artificers remained to Grey from the forces now bobbing in the Channel off Spithead. 'After this diminution of your force, His Majesty is sensible that you cannot be expected to carry in to full effect all the objects stated in your Instructions of the 12th Instant', Dundas added in a paragraph that must have watered Grey's eyes, 'in particular that the Force intrusted is not calculated for so difficult an Enterprise as the reduction of Fort Bourbon in Martinique, supposing the Enemy to be in a state to make any serious resistance.'[13] New instructions ensued. Grey now had to discretion as to his intended targets, with the hope they could at least include Guadeloupe and Saint Lucia, and to send any possible reinforcements to Saint Domingue afterwards. Dundas signed off with the comment, '…the island of Martinique, which is an object against which (in case of the continuation of the War) there can be little doubt that an adequate Force will be employed in the very beginning of the next Season for action in the West Indies.'[14] In plain English: do what you can with what

---

12 GRE/A182b, Memorandum from King George dated Windsor Castle 13 November 1793.
13 GRE/A183, Letter from Henry Dundas to Grey, concerning the deviation of part of his force to another enterprise and the modification of his instructions accordingly, dated 17 November 1793.
14 GRE/A183, Letter from Henry Dundas to Grey, etc.

little we have left you, but you should have a proper force available the next year. Grey was bouncing from pillar to post at the hands of Dundas.

And by this time, some of Grey's force had sailed from Ireland. Twenty-eight flank companies, fourteen of grenadiers and fourteen of light infantry, had sailed from Cork on 13 November. Organised into four ad-hoc flank battalions, they were in fact the flank companies of every British infantry regiment then serving in Ireland. These men, grenadiers and light infantry, would be extremely valuable to Grey, but their detachment would be a serious blow to their parent regiments, they being the best men from each unit. Given that the vast majority of these men would never return, the regiments involved (8th, 12th, 17th, 22nd, 23rd, 31st, 33rd, 34th, 35th, 38th, 40th, 41st, 44th, and 55th) would have to rebuild these companies from scratch, and be much weakened in the interim. Whole battalions followed. The 70th Foot sailed from Cork three days later, followed by the 43rd, 56th, 64th, and 39th on subsequent days. The window of time opportunity for Grey to accomplish his objectives was shrinking. Rather than five months, he might now have three months of the best campaigning climate, assuming that the departure could be immediate. Recognising the risks of fighting during the sickly season, he had asked Pitt's approval to apply discretion in returning home in the spring. Pitt declined, wisely requiring that circumstances of the campaign at the time must determine that decision.

Assembly of his staff had occupied the frustrating weeks of November. Finding his first choice of officers had given Grey headaches. His choice as artillery commander was willing but the Master General of the Ordnance would not release him. His nominated chief Royal Engineer was cut down by a stroke. Grey's choice of surgeon, Doctor John Hunter, refused and, in any event, would be dead of a heart attack within a few weeks. Lieutenant General Robert Prescott, currently commanding in Barbados, had written to the Undersecretary of State Evan Nepean on 24 September reminding him of his Army service dating from 1745, and seeking his patronage. Nepean responded by posting Prescott to Barbados in late 1793. Grey specifically requested Prescott's services as second-in-command for the expedition, having served with him in North America and being aware of Prescott's previous experience in the Leeward Islands. Prescott had served in Martinique before, having arrived there shortly after the capture of that island in 1762, and, after service in North America, had commanded a brigade in the British expeditionary force that left New York City to attack Saint Lucia in 1781. From August 1779 to early 1780 he was nominally in command of the British troops in the Leeward Islands, so had considerably more West Indies experience than Grey, who had none.

Another old North American colleague was Major General Thomas Dundas of Carron Hall in Stirlingshire, a 43-year-old Scot with a genius for military administration and light infantry tactics, who had commanded a composite light battalion for much of the American War. He was a man who had excelled at everything he did. He obtained his lieutenant-colonelcy in the 80th Foot, a new regiment raised by the city of Edinburgh in 1777, at the age of 27; and in 1779 sailed with them bound for South Carolina. The mother of one of his ensigns wrote to her beloved son: 'Always take Col[onel] Dundas's advice. He has seen much of the world … everybody speaks well of him and whatever character he gives of the officers of his regiment will be believed before anybody.'[15] His military service in North America was considerable. He had been present at the siege and capture of Charleston in 1780, later served with Banastre Tarleton and Lord Cornwallis in Virginia and the Carolinas, and was one of the commissioners appointed to arrange the surrender at Yorktown. In 1783 Chancellor of the Exchequer Lord John Cavendish offered Dundas a place on the board to examine the claims of the American loyalists, which Dundas accepted, although it was ultimately to stall his military career. Pausing to marry Elizabeth Eleanora Home in January 1784, he sailed for Nova Scotia in 1785 to examine the claims of loyalists settled there, despite leaving some difficult family crises, and a pregnant wife, at home. He wrote from Halifax in November 1785 telling of his 'cruel situation … forced by conviction and a sense of duty to leave my father in the state he was, and my mother and wife who both required my assistance; but my coming here was unavoidable, my future prospects and character depended upon it.' [16] Elizabeth Dundas joined he husband in 1786 and the couple spent the next two years in Nova Scotia, New Brunswick, and Canada. On returning home in 1789 his cousin Sir Thomas Dundas wrote him a secret and confidential letter, informing him that, as soon as the Regency was settled, the office of commander-in-chief would be given to the Duke of York.[17] The Duke planned to appoint 'a military man as confidential secretary' and would possibly offer the post to Colonel Dundas. But Dundas was unwilling to accept, for family reasons. Instead, Dundas, still technically a half-pay lieutenant colonel of the 80th Foot for the purposes of salary, retired to his family seat at Carron Hall, raised a family and awaited his next employment. Then Sir Charles Grey came calling.

The quartermaster-general was to be Lieutenant Colonel Richard Mitchelbourne Symes, a 46-year-old Irishman who had been Grey's aide in his North American days and had previously served as quartermaster in North America. Syme's deputy was Major Henry George Grey, Charles's 26-year-old son. The adjutant-general was yet another Dundas, 34-year-old Colonel Francis Dundas, nephew to Minister for War Henry Dundas. A son of the 4th Lord Arniston, Francis served as a Guards officer in a light infantry company in North America from 1777 until forced to surrender with Cornwallis at Yorktown in October 1781. He had commanded a battalion in Jamaica from 1787 to 1791, and therefore knew

---

15 Quoted from Thomas Dundas' biography on *The History of Parliament* website. http://www.historyofparliamentonline.org/volume/1754-1790/member/dundas-thomas-1750-94.
16 Quoted from Thomas Dundas' biography on *The History of Parliament* website.
17 Quoted from Thomas Dundas' biography on *The History of Parliament* website.

the islands well. Charles Grey's military secretary was Lieutenant Colonel Gerrit Fisher of the 60th Foot, a 47-year-old Dubliner of New York Dutch ancestry. Aides included Captain Finch Mason, Lieutenant Richard Newton Ogle (Grey's nephew), and Lieutenant John Conyngham. Thomas Dundas had a solitary aide, Captain Frederick Maitland of the 60th Foot, who had been present at the capture of Tobago in April 1793. Chief Surgeon on the staff was Dr John Wardle. Chiefs of artillery and engineers would be picked up once at Barbados. Along for the voyage was Chevalier Jean-Louis Alexandre Gédéon Ridouet de Sancé, 'a brave and ingenious French officer',[18] a former Royalist artillery captain from Anjou who had lived in République-ville for some time and was therefore well acquainted with the fortifications on Martinique.

Jervis had misgivings about the expedition. Rear Admiral Gardner had returned to England with nearly his entire squadron, leaving a skeleton force of only one ship-of-the-line, two frigates, and two sloops in the Leeward Islands. The post entitled Jervis to seven ships-of-the-line. However Jervis had been given only three ships-of-the-line, two 44-gunners, two frigates, two sloops, a store-ship, and a bomb-vessel under his command. One more frigate – HMS *Blonde* – was to join the convoy off Falmouth. Lord Chatham, the First Lord of the Admiralty, mollified him with some promises that were never kept. As Jervis later recorded:

> [W]hen the West India expedition came into discussion at the Admiralty in October 1793, Lord Chatham pledged himself to me that Rear-Admiral Gell, with one second-rate and two 74-gun ships should join me at Barbados, and that the *Leviathan*, after being new copper-sheathed … should follow. This assurance caused my taking a very strong part with Sir Charles Grey, against the unanimous opinion of all the principal land officers who maintained that our force was inadequate for the reduction of Martinique. I never received a letter from Lord Chatham, or the Secretary of the Admiralty, to inform me that these ships were countermanded.[19]

Just like Grey and his land forces, Jervis and his squadron were hamstrung from the start. The problems even extended to the ships themselves. None of the transports were big enough, or equipped with platforms large enough, to carry and disembark field artillery. Against bitter opposition Jervis managed to have two converted, their decks being strengthened and stern-ports widened.[20] Jervis also had to pull some strings to get some of his preferred officers associated with the

---

18 Cooper Wyllliams, *An Account of the Campaign in the West Indies in the Year 1794 Under the Command of their Excellencies Lieutenant General Sir Charles Grey, K.B., and Vice Admiral Sir John Jervis, K.B.* (London, T. Bensley, 1796), p.3.
19 Quoted in M.W.B. Sanderson, *English Naval Strategy and the Maritime Trade in the Caribbean, 1793-1802* (Unpublished Doctoral Thesis, London University, 1968), p.26.
20 Sanderson, *English Naval Strategy*, p.27.

expedition. One was Captain Josias Rogers of the 32-gun HMS *Quebec*, currently on service in the Channel, who found himself in a tug-of-war between Jervis and Rear Admiral John McBride, commanding the Royal Navy squadron in the Downs. Jervis prevailed. Jervis was perhaps a little more apprehensive over the choice of Commodore Charles Thompson as his second-in-command, a man whom Jervis later described as 'a gallant man, but the most timid officer' with the manners of 'a rough seaman'.[21] Nonetheless he managed to get several of his preferred specialists to join the expedition, most notably Captain John Schank, an inventive genius known throughout the Royal Navy as 'Old Purchase'. His mechanical ingenuity would be needed to solve unforeseen nautical problems during the campaign to come. Another specialist of sorts was his choice of chaplain aboard HMS *Boyne*, the Reverend Cooper Willyams. Willyams was the 32-year-old son of a former Royal Navy commander going abroad on his first expedition, a man deft with both pen and brush, who left many detailed paintings and a highly-regarded published account of the campaign to come.

The weeks leading to departure of the fleet were not without incident. On 25 October Colonel Francis Dundas wrote from Falmouth to relate an encounter between the frigate HMS *Blonde*, in which he had been travelling to Barbados, and three prowling French frigates. They had been fortunate to escape in a calm by jettisoning provisions and anchors. Captain John Markham of the *Blonde* took the opportunity while renewing stores in port to alert Earl Howe at Torbay to the dangers in the Western Approaches, especially since Jervis' convoy had been about to sail. Howe posted additional vessels to patrol the waters, and the French prowlers were not seen again.

On 21 November 1793 Sir Charles Grey said farewell to his wife and eldest son Charles in London, then was transported by carriage to Portsmouth, by which time his troops were all aboard transports. He boarded HMS *Boyne* to be greeted by his friend, Vice Admiral Sir John Jervis, and their thoughts turned entirely to the Leeward Islands.

---

21 Captain Edward Pelham Brenton, *Life and Correspondence of John, Earl of St. Vincent, etc.* (London: Henry Colburn, 1838), Vol. II , p.7.

5

The Knife-Edge

The Windward Islands are so-called because the trade winds blew out of the southeast and ships from Jamaica had to sail into the wind to reach harbour. Martinique was founded by a party of French émigrés forced out of Saint Kitts by the British on St Martin's Day, 1635, and named after that holiday. The island is some forty-three miles long by nineteen wide, with five extinct volcanoes in the mountainous northern section, swamps in the west and numerous bays and inlets on the eastern side. The whole island is encircled by coral reefs. The terrain was generally dense jungle, broken here and there by about a dozen settlements, housing some of the island's nearly 100,000 inhabitants: maybe 12,000 French planters, 6,000 mulattoes, and the rest negro slaves. The largest town and commercial hub was Saint Pierre, in the north-west, home to most of the merchant classes, whereas governmental duties resided at République-ville, changed from Fort Royal shortly after the Revolution. This was the strongest citadel on the island, located in a large and well-defended harbour about half-way down the western coast. This latter place was the seat of the Governor-General, who wielded enormous power over the French Windward Islands, but not over Guadeloupe. He was a de facto commander-in-chief, who had the capacity to declare war or settle peace treaties, but had no civil power. He was aided in this by the local soldiery, the Chasseurs de Martinique, infantrymen and artillerymen barracked mostly at the irregularly shaped Fort de la République, the ancient town fort with entrenchments and batteries. This was overlooked by Fort de la Convention (formerly Fort Bourbon), located on high ground on the southern side of Morne Garnier, some 150 metres above and behind the town of République-ville. This was generally considered the strongest French fortress in the West Indies. The Governor-General also had assorted white and mulatto militia units located in secondary forts, mainly stockades, at strategic locations. The climate was invariably hot and humid, the only distinction being between the wet and dry seasons. Snakes and swarming insects (especially mosquitoes) were plentiful.

    Britain and France had fought over these islands before. An amphibious force under Major General Peregrine Hopson tried and failed to capture Martinique in 1759, but was successful against Guadeloupe. A second attempt in 1762 under

Fort Royal, called République-ville in 1794. (Anne SK Brown Collection)

Admiral George Rodney was more successful. At that time, the island was garrisoned by more than 12,000 French soldiers and local militia. British land-forces commander, Major General the Honourable Robert Monckton, had sixteen regiments at his disposal, 8,000 troops in all including 5,000 from North America, bolstered by volunteers from Barbados, Antigua, Montserrat, St Christopher, and Nevis. It took less than three weeks for Monckton to capture Fort Royal and Morne Grenier. Monckton sent detachments to capture all the neighbouring islands – Saint Lucia, Grenada and Saint Vincent – bringing all the Leeward and Windward Islands under British control. Following the complicated negotiations which took place during the Treaty of Paris in 1763, Britain decided to keep Canada in return for giving Guadeloupe back to France. Although much more expensive to maintain, and less profitable, Canada was deemed of greater strategic value and thus control of Guadeloupe passed back to Paris. The French did not mind. They considered this sugar capital far more valuable than anything in North America. The same Treaty restored Martinique and Saint Lucia to France, and the Bourbon flag fluttered over Fort Royal for another thirty years, surrounded by numerous islands whose forts were adorned with the Union flag of Great Britain.

These numerous islands under British control had 465,000 slaves on Jamaica, the Bahamas, Barbados, Grenada, the Grenadines, Antigua, Saint Vincent, Dominica, Saint Kitts, Nevis, Montserrat, the Virgin Islands, and in the Bay of Honduras. The West Indies accounted for one-fifth of all British trade, and one-eighth of all mercantile ship tonnage. In 1793, some 2,129,750 hundredweight of sugar,

4,907,051 gallons of rum, 92,016 hundredweight of coffee, and 9,173,583 pounds of cotton were exported from the British West Indies possessions to Britain.[1] In those far-off days such exports were luxuries rather than the commodities they are today. This was worth a vast sum, and it required a sizable army and navy to defend its harvesting and transportation. Therefore, Britain had 6,000 troops in the islands, backed by a significant proportion of the Royal Navy. Militarily, as we have seen, the British West Indies was divided into two commands; Barbados and Jamaica. Trade winds blew from east to west, and therefore control of the Windward Islands was seen as a military and naval priority. The tyranny of distance lay across all strategy, as the combined commands covered a thousand miles of seaways. The Royal Navy administration mirrored that of the Army, and whilst the Leeward Islands squadron had a sound though small and hard-to-access mooring at English Harbour on Antigua, the Windward squadron lacked a good harbour. Barbados did not have a single suitable site, and relied on the open roadstead at Carlisle Bay, easy to access but prone to hurricanes. Three islands dominated the Leeward chain, Guadeloupe, Martinique and Saint Lucia, and these all belonged to the French. République-ville on Martinique was the finest fleet anchorage in the Caribbean; Admiral Jervis thought that it could 'contain the whole shipping of Great Britain'.[2] Castries in Saint Lucia was only marginally inferior to it.

On 14 July 1789 the Bastille Prison in Paris was over-run by the citizens. On 4 August, the Declaration of Human Rights was proclaimed. This momentous news took several weeks to cross the Atlantic. Martinique declared a public holiday for a celebration on 15 September. Governor Jean Joseph de Gimat on Saint Lucia declared that 14 July would be celebrated each year.[3] On such a small island, with only 18,000 slaves, news spread quickly and gave the slaves hope that they might one day be set free. A large number ran away into the interior of the island, sowing the seeds for future insurrection. When news of the Revolution arrived on Guadeloupe in late 1789, the Governor, General Marc-Antoine, Baron de Clugny, surprisingly allowed the island's Colonial Assembly to decide whether or not to support the National Assembly in Paris. The Colonial Assembly split into two camps, and for two years the Governor presided over a perilous situation on the island. The Antilles were on a knife-edge.

In January 1791 the Republican government in Paris sent four commissaries to the West Indies to spread the philosophies of the Revolution. Denied a landing on Martinique or Dominica, two of the commissaries landed on Saint Lucia where

---

1   Captain Thomas Southley, *Chronological History of the West Indies* (London: A&R Spottiswoode, 1827) Vol. III, p.72.
2   Jedediah Stevens Tucker. *Memoirs of Admiral the Right Hon[orabl]e the Earl of St. Vincent* (London: R. Bentley, 1844), p.138.
3   Robert J. Devaux, *They Called Us Brigands* (Castries: Optimum Printers, 1997), p.7.

they raised the tricolour flag and tried to work out how to handle the various factions – Royalists, Republicans, slaves, *gens de couleur* – on the island. The slaves were in a state of upheaval and many had run away to the interior. On 20 February 1791, the planters on Saint Lucia sent a message of support to the Governor of Martinique, acclaiming the Revolution but bemoaning the anarchy which had followed. Saint Lucia remained the most politically and socially fragile of the French Antilles.

News of the Declaration of War in February 1793 arrived, delayed and fragmentary, in various frigates from Europe, during the early part of the year. All inhabitants knew in their hearts that these islands had not seen the last of fighting by any means. The islands were too precious; they accounted for one-third of all French trade in 1793. Twenty percent of the French population depended on the West Indies, directly and indirectly, for their livelihoods. The vast majority of this mercantile endeavour was in the sugar trade. Sugar was a luxury item at the time, cultivated by a few colonial farmers but demanded by an increasing number across Europe. The small number of French planters on Martinique, Guadeloupe, The Saintes, Desirade, Saint Lucia, Tobago, Saint Domingue, Saint Martin, and Cayenne controlled 514,000 slaves, roughly equal to the population of Paris at the time. These planters tended to be politically conservative, Royalist in outlook, more fearful of the Revolution back at home than the British on neighbouring islands. Socially, the island population comprised three broad classes. The *grande blancs*, mainly plantation owners and aristocratic expatriates, flourished at the top of the tree. The middle classes, the *petits blancs*, were mainly merchants, artisans, farmers, fishermen, and seamen, and tended (or preferred) to be referred to as 'patriots'. Then came the *gens de couleur*, free men of colour, many of whom were half-castes, numerous but essentially poor. The very bottom of the tree was crowded by those with no say at all, perhaps 150,000 slaves on the three islands. It was the middle classes, the patriots and *gens de couleur*, who captured Guadeloupe for the French Republic in early 1793, and created conditions that were quite different to those on Martinique and Saint Lucia. At Trois Rivieres, in the night of 20 April 1793, several hundred enslaved blacks rose and killed twenty-two whites. Captured rebels later explained that their masters, Royalists to a man, had armed them as part of a larger strategy to fight the Republican threat. Fatally, the Royalists had misjudged the appeal of the Republic and its promise of future freedoms amongst the enslaved classes, and so the plan completely back-fired. Rather than betray the Republic, the slaves rose and killed their masters instead. The Republican whites and *gens de couleur* were happy to have these unexpected allies against any future Royalist threat, so pardoned the ring-leaders and called for the formation of a slave army to defend the island. And so it was that Guadeloupe benefited from a large armed force ready to fight to defend their island in the case of invasion. Sadly, this was a blind spot in British military strategy, which assumed that the three islands were much of a muchness.

The Governor-General of the French Windward Islands at this time was Lieutenant General Jean-Pierre-Antoine de Béhague, a 66-year-old died-in-the-wool Royalist. Under his administration, Martinique had effectively seceded from France 'and declared war on the Metropole'.[4] His political leanings were well known in Paris. On 4 April 1792, the French Legislative Assembly extended citizenship of the new Republic to all men of colour without bothering to consult him on the matter. To prove that nothing in French politics at that time came close to being as simple as black-and-white, one of King Louis XVI's last acts was to promote a Republican, Donatien-Marie-Joseph de Vimeur, Vicomte de Rochambeau, to the rank of lieutenant général and despatch him to Martinique restore order and bring Béhague to justice. Rochambeau was the 39-year-old son of a marshal,[5] and a future divisional commander under Napoleon.

All the while the royal standard of the Bourbons fluttered over Fort Royal on Martinique. Although one of their own, the Royalist planters hated Béhague for his heavy-handedness and wished him gone. Then the King's appointee, Rochambeau, arrived off Fort de la Convention in September 1792. The Colonial Assembly of Martinique agreed to promulgate the new race legislation, then in a sudden volte-face, refused to allow Rochambeau to disembark with his troops, firing a few cannon-shots to announce their intention of defending the town. Rochambeau sailed away. Four ships were despatched to make sure that he had made the open sea and was not coming back. The general went to Saint Domingue and Haiti instead to bide his time. In the interim, events on Martinique remained on the knife-edge. Béhague, who was declared general of the Windward Isles, and his Royalists, without the support of many planters, was in one corner, Republicans in the other. Anti-Béhague planters and free men of colour lay somewhere in between. Slaves of course did not figure in the calculations, even though they were more numerous than any other class. A small, unsuccessful slave rebellion in Saint Pierre was swiftly put down, with some executions to follow.

The Legislative Assembly in Paris was shocked to hear of the reception given Rochambeau, and naturally alarmed at the course of events. To break the deadlock, the Minister of the Navy sent Jean-Baptiste-Raymond, Baron La Crosse to Martinique in October 1792 to bring the island to heel, and install a new governor. This new expedition arrived off Saint Pierre on 1 December 1792 to find the island apparently Royalist. La Crosse sailed to Saint Lucia, an island that at the time was nick-named 'La Fidele', the loyal, because it had remained true to the Revolution. La Crosse installed himself there and wrote patriotic proclamations

---

4   Haynsworth, James Lafayette IV, 'Donatien Rochambeau and The Defence of Martinique, 1793-1794', *Consortium on Revolutionary Europe 1750-1850*, 1997, pp.180-190.
5   Our Rochambeau's father was Jean-Baptiste Donatien de Vimeur, comte de Rochambeau, 1725-1807. He was commander-in-chief of the French expeditionary force that sailed from France to help the American Continental Army in their fight against British forces. He was created Marshal by Louis XVI in 1791.

His family motto was 'To live and die valiantly'; Donatien-Marie-Joseph de Vimeur, vicomte de Rochambeau certainly lived up to his creed commanding the French defence of Martinique in February and March 1794. (Public Domain)

aimed at citizens on Martinique and Guadeloupe. This latter island softened and La Crosse was made welcome there in January 1793. Feeling distinctly unsettled by this news, and knowing that Rochambeau would almost certainly return with a strong force of troops, Governor Béhague set sail to British protection on Saint Vincent on 11 January. Many of the planters on Martinique left also, most bound for Trinidad. The Island Assembly celebrated his departure:

> Citizens, Béhague has gone! The colony is breathing. The national flag flies over our fortresses and in our harbours. The difference of opinion that had made you abandon your homes no longer exists. Citizens, La Crosse will soon be with us. We will know the forms of civil government under which we will live. Citizens, return to your homes! Your brothers invite you to do so.[6]

---

6 Henry Lémery, *La Révolution Française à la Martinique* (Paris: Larose, 1936), p.129 of the transcribed version at http://classiques.uqac.ca/classiques.

Into this power vacuum came Rochambeau, a second time. On 30 January 1793, he returned to Martinique from Haiti to become Governor-General of the French Windward Islands. Four days later he and La Crosse entered République-ville and dissolved the Island Assembly, declaring its members rebels and traitors. Rochambeau then gave his first speech to the islanders; '… you have suffered the violent slide of the perfidy and treason of your leaders; but rally around me and in concert with the civil commissioners, invested with the confidence of the nation, we will assure the happiness and prosperity of your colony.'[7]

The day after Rochambeau arrived on Martinique, Republican France declared war on Britain and Holland. News of this declaration took weeks to reach Martinique of course, but Rochambeau was a military man, and, appalled by how few regulars garrisoned the island, swiftly assembled a local defence force of all races. Four days later, on 4 February 1793, the expatriate Louis-François Du Buc, the staunchly Royalist former president of the Martinique Colonial Assembly, with family ties on the island going back a hundred years, signed an accord at Whitehall placing Martinique under British jurisdiction until the French monarchy could be re-established. The accord guaranteed the continuation of slavery. And so, the British had an excuse to intervene in what was basically French civil strife. The three advantages were plain to see; the forestalment of the spread of the Revolution to Martinique, the acquisition of lucrative sugar-rich islands, and the procurement of additional harbours for British shipping.

Rochambeau worked hard to place Martinique back on a defensible footing. On 21 June 1793 the Convention, on the understandable assumption that many good Republicans had been forced out of Martinique by Béhague and his cronies, encouraged them to return, to take oaths of loyalty and to form a local militia. Many did, but there were still Royalists on the island, mostly centred around the merchant town of Saint Pierre, and it was only a matter of time before these two groups came into conflict.

There were however more than two sides to this conflict There were four – Republicans, Royalists, slaves (or ex-slaves), and the British. In all the mental energy required to fuel this political confusion and military mobilisation, few could foresee the hardships that would ultimately be involved, nor the true cost of failure. Especially not Henry Dundas, the new Minister for War, who in February 1793, days after the declaration of war, despatched two memorandums to the British West Indian command on Barbados. The first, on 10 February, ordered the capture of Tobago; the second, on 28 February ordered the capture of Martinique, Guadeloupe, Saint Lucia, and Marie Galante. Thus from the outset the requirement for martial action in the islands was clear. But it was up the men on the ground – soldiers and sailors – to work out how to actually achieve these goals.

---

7   Haynsworth, 'Donatien Rochambeau and The Defence of Martinique, 1793-1794'.

Rear Admiral Alan Gardner arrived in Bridgetown at the end of April 1793 to take command of the Leeward and Windward Island squadrons, replacing Sir John Laforey. Gardner was a 51-year-old Englishman married to a Jamaican heiress, considered a sailor of some dash and vim. Best of all, he brought with him two 90-gun second-rates, five 74-gunners, and three frigates, completely altering the balance of naval power in the Caribbean at a stroke. This balance changed in British favour yet again a few days later, when the French Admiral Charles Joseph Mascarene de Riviere arrived at Bridgetown with his squadron, offering to surrender it to Great Britain to prevent it falling into the hands of the Republicans. He had unsuccessfully offered the same arrangement to the Spaniards on Trinidad. After some correspondence with Gardner, it was agreed that this Royalist squadron, flying the Bourbon flag, could fight along the Royal Navy squadron on the proviso that they retained their separate identity.

French Royalists arrived in Barbados in June to seek representation with the two senior British officers on the spot, namely Rear Admiral Alan Gardner and Major General the Honourable Thomas Bruce. The latter, a pudgy Scot in his mid-fifties, a son of the Earl of Kincardine, had spent much of his career on the staff in Ireland, and itched for some real action. If British troops landed on Martinique, the émigrés advised, it was highly likely the inhabitants would declare for the Bourbon monarchy. Gardner and Bruce required no further convincing that they should take advantage of this opportunity, which was in any event completely in accordance with a memorandum received from Henry Dundas two months prior, in which Dundas had instructed Gardner and Bruce to assist the Royalists on Martinique with up to two battalions plus naval support.[8] It also aligned with Bruce's earlier promises of help, which had been delayed for six weeks due to his poor health. Bruce and Gardner optimistically assembled an expeditionary force. A further fillip was the reported sighting of a French fleet sailing to the West Indies; in any event, it went to Saint Domingue and therefore posed no direct threat to the Leeward Islands. Bruce and Gardner appointed former Saint Lucia Governor Jean-Joseph, Chevalier de Gimat as commander of the Royalist forces at their disposal with the rank of colonel, and landed him on the north coast of Martinique on 27 April 1793. His task was to spread news of an impending British incursion, and to draw armed Royalists to him.

Meanwhile on Martinique, Rochambeau was swatting at Royalist incursions like annoying mosquitoes. Gimat was but one more. On 16 April the general raided a camp containing two companies of Royalists near République-ville, and scattered them into the jungle after a fire-fight lasting nearly two hours. After the action, Rochambeau's men accused his second-in-command, General Saint Cyran, of being a Royalist sympathiser after he had saved some creoles from the

---

8   Memorandum from Henry Dundas dated 28 February 1793, referenced in Hon J. W. Fortescue's *A History of the British Army*, Vol IV, Part I, p.79.

bayonets of his men. Saint Cyran was court-martialled, condemned and shot; in this hyper-charged situation, no-one was safe. Gimat and his men succeeded in establishing Royalist posts at Case Navire, Trinité, and Marin Bay. An exasperated Rochambeau wrote in his journal; 'Since my arrival in this colony, I am without soldiers, officers, engineers, artillery, silver and little to live on, and only the citizens of Saint Pierre and a few other patriots to defend the colony against the English and nearly all of the white inhabitants.'[9]

By early May, Gimat and others had established fortified in camps in six of the major regions of the island. In response to his perilous situation and in anticipation of an attack by the British, Rochambeau sent one of his aides-de-camp, la Houssayre de Cypre, home to France to explain the state of affairs and hopefully gain some succour for the island. Then on 2 May he called on all *gens de couleur* to volunteer for military service. They would be uniformed, paid and fed the same as white soldiers, with full political rights. The response was enormous. Sufficient men came forward to allow the creation of the Corps des Chasseurs de la Martinique, of two battalions. A third battalion would be added later.[10]

By 7 May, civil war on Martinique was in full swing. A Royalist warship appeared in the Bay de République-ville, supported by fourteen of Gardner's Royal Navy vessels two days later. Royalist land forces, commanded by Henri de Percin, attacked Rochambeau's position at Case Navire. The latter retreated behind the walls of Fort de la Convention and stayed put for several days, which panicked the Republican Assembly in République-ville. Finally on 11 May Rochambeau allowed a force of some 700 men under a mulatto National Guard officer, Major Louis Bellegarde, to sail across the bay and attack a Royalist post on the Levassor plantation. The fight was long and fierce, but Bellegade prevailed, and Rochambeau promoted him to the rank of lieutenant colonel in the Chasseurs. Striking while the iron was hot, he ordered Bellegarde to continue his offensive against the Royalists, using the time he had unexpectedly been granted by the non-arrival of the British invasion force. From 13 May until 18 May he continued attacks against Republican positions in the north and east of the island, to the point where Gardner ordered most of his ships back to Saint Lucia. Bruce left two officers behind, Colonel Jonathan Meyers and Captain James Fiddes, to follow up on Royalist progress.[11] They returned to Barbados at the end of May with intelligence which still suggested the Royalists were strongly placed. Gimat advised Gardner and Bruce that he thought Saint Pierre, the commercial capital, to be the Republican's weak spot. Bruce eventually

---

9 Diary entry for 2 May 1793, quoted in Haynsworth, 'Donatien Rochambeau and The Defence of Martinique, 1793-1794.'
10 Rochambeau Journal, entry of 2 May 1793, quoted in Haynsworth, *The Early Career of Lieutenant General Donatien Rochambeau and The French Campaigns in the Caribbean, 1792-1794*, p.250.
11 Fiddes was an officer of the Royal Engineers. Meyer I have been unable to find on any Army List for 1793 or 1794, so suspect him to have been a militia officer rather than a regular.

agreed to proceed with an invasion, but elected to land south of Saint Pierre, where he could capture the coastal batteries defending the town first.

The long-delayed invasion force sailed from Barbados on 10 June. It had been cobbled together from the forces available in the vicinity, and had only a single full, or nearly full-strength, regiment, Major Colin Graham's 21st (Royal North British Fusiliers) of 500 men. The flank companies of the 9th, 15th, 21st, 45th, 48th, 3/60th, 4/60th, and 67th Regiments of Foot, some 400 men, provided enough men to form two small specialist light and grenadier battalions. Of some military value was the Carolina Black Corps of 200 men, a locally-raised militia recruited from former slaves. Most dubious of all were 800 or so French Royalist militia, along for the chance to eject the troublesome Republicans from their home island despite a total lack of military training, discipline, or propriety. They were unaware that, since the end of May, Rochambeau and Bellegarde had over-run nearly all remaining Royalist strongholds on Martinique. The Royalists that they hoped would flock to their invasion force were already on the run. For all of Gardner's and Bruce's optimism for the campaign, the thing had not been thought through. Success depended upon less than a thousand regulars and a rabble of enthusiastic but unskilled 'armed farmers' with which to conquer and hold Martinique. There were no reinforcements on the horizon. Bruce had barely scraped together his flank companies from the available garrisons. As was to happen time and again in the period from 1793 to 1796, Britain placed far more trust and dependence upon the ability of the Royalists to muster support to their aid than was ever actually the case.

This force was transported aboard the second-rates HMS *Queen* and HMS *Duke* and third-rate HMS *Monarch*, as well as two French Royalist ships. The fleet arrived off Case de Navire on the west coast of Martinique, a few miles above République-ville, on 11 June. Major General Bruce went ashore with some Royalists and met Gimat. The latter urged a direct frontal assault on Saint Pierre, but Bruce refused. Gimat went off sullenly, into the jungle to gather together his Royalist army. Notably, Béhague did not show himself, and he probably took no part in the actions to follow. He had unsuccessfully challenged Gimat for the leadership before Bruce's arrival, Gimat had won and so Béhague found himself packed off to Saint Vincent. Bruce and Gimat agreed that they should attack the town of Saint Pierre, about ten miles up the cost, and that elements of the 21st Foot would land immediately to guard the disembarkation site, with the Royalists converging in the region of Saint Pierre for an attack on or about 16 June. So many had converged in fact, that Rochambeau was easily able to discern the intended target of Bruce's force.

Rochambeau left Fort de la République before dawn on 16 June with 400 mounted infantry and by using back-roads and the mountains as cover, reached Saint Pierre by lunchtime;[12] the same time as Bruce disembarked the rest of his force at Case

---

12 Rochambeau Journal, entry of 16 June 1793, quoted in Haynsworth, *The Early Career of Lieutenant General Donatien Rochambeau and The French Campaigns in the Caribbean, 1792-1794*, p.274.

Pilote, shortly to be joined by Gimat and his ragged battalion. Leaving the 21st Foot behind at Case de Navire, the Royalists advanced up the coast road on the morning of 17 June. Gimat led 200 of his men to storm a battery at a hamlet named Prêcheur, which was defended by a company of National Guardsmen under the command of Major Edouard Meunier. The Royalists beat them off, but then spent valuable time looting the village whilst Bruce's regulars cooled their heels near Case Navire. As all this was going on, Rochambeau split his force into two columns. The right column was to advance south from Saint Pierre after dark, and be in position to attack at dawn. The second was to climb into the hills and jungle, advance on the left, and be in position to hit Bruce's right flank at daylight.

Bruce landed the remainder of his force that night and they hunkered down for a serious attack in the morning. Except that Rochambeau was already one step ahead. Bruce later summed it up the best:

> The morning of the 18th was the time fixed for the attack, and we were to move forward in two columns, the one consisting of the British troops, the other of the French Royalists; and for this purpose the troops were put in motion before daybreak; but, unfortunately, some alarm having taken place amongst the Royalists, they began, in a mistake, firing on one another, and their commander being severely wounded on the occasion, the whole body, refusing to submit to any of the other officers, retired to the post from which they had marched.[13]

In fact, they had run smack-bang into Rochambeau's ambush. The head of Gimat's column blundered into Rochambeau's right-hand column, recoiled once fired upon, and then found themselves assaulted out of the jungle by the left-hand column. The whole mass, fleeing Royalists and charging Republicans, then buffeted the British regulars behind, who suffered a handful of casualties. Gimat was left on the field with a bullet in his breast and a broken skull. The regulars withdrew steadily as the Royalists dispersed hither and thither.

The following day Bruce held a conference and decided to withdraw. The Royal Navy was in no mood to stay off Martinique either. The shallow waters made manoeuvring and access to the coast difficult, and the slow-moving second- and third-rates made for easy targets. The smaller vessels had the speed and draught, but not the firepower to do any real damage to the shore batteries. Bruce ordered the troops to return to their former positions, and they re-embarked the following day. To have left the Royalists in Martinique would have been to consign them to be massacred by the Republicans, and nearly 400 were embarked over two days. The 21st Foot went on board last of all, having barely fired a shot. Bruce's force

---

13 Extract from a letter written at sea by Hon. Major General Bruce on 23 June 1793, and printed in the *London Gazette* on 13 August 1793.

returned to Barbados on 21 June having lost all confidence in their French Royalist allies. Some 12,000 people, whites and their slaves, escaped the island over the next five days, mainly aboard British vessels. The failure of the expedition led to an unfortunate fate for some 140 Royalists captured in the debacle, together with some 2,000 other Royalists or people with suspected Royalist sympathies left behind on Martinique, many of whom were imprisoned or executed by their Republican compatriots. Property to the value of 200,000,000 Francs was confiscated.

On Martinique, one invader had been repelled, but Rochambeau's troubles were far from over. Pockets of Royalists still hung on and had to be overcome bit-by-bit. Bands of slaves without masters freely roamed the countryside, looting and raping. Lieutenant Colonel Bellegarde was fractious and argumentative, and frequently acted without orders. The roads and forts needed significant works to make them battle-worthy against future British invasions, yet there were insufficient slaves to do the work, and insufficient funds to pay for the materials. Rochambeau's chief of artillery and engineers overseeing the works, Colonel le Meistre, was so fastidious that in six months only a small portion of work was complete, albeit to a very high standard. The fruits of his labour on Fort de la Convention would be seen to the Republicans' advantage in a few months' time.

News of the failed invasion reached London at the start of August. Gardner was immediately made the scapegoat, and was ordered home the same day. It was now obvious that expeditionary forces made up of scratch troops plundered from existing garrisons was not the answer, and that in future such forces would need to be carefully selected, provisioned and armed. So it was that later in the month the Admiralty appointed Vice Admiral Sir John Jervis to replace Gardner, and Henry Dundas formally received the King's permission to appoint Lieutenant General Sir Charles Grey to assemble an expeditionary force to take Martinique. Shortly after this, word arrived from Major General Bruce that the Barbados garrison had suffered so much from fever that additional troops would be needed. Unfortunately, the sub-text of this message was lost. If acclimatised troops were dropping like flies, what chance did a force of inexperienced young men fresh from the villages and farmlands of England and Ireland stand?

6

The Capture of Tobago

The island of Tobago had been a political pawn for much of the eighteenth century. Taken by Britain from France at the end of the Seven Year's War, it was handed back to France in 1783 under the auspices of the Treaty of Versailles. But in 1793 Republican France was perceived as being weak, especially in the West Indies where her naval power was believed to revolve around a single frigate and a few sloops. Henry Dundas saw the island as an easy way of striking an early psychological and political blow in the War of the First Coalition. It had been the only British West Indian island lost during the war in North America that had not been restored in 1783. It also commanded the sea-routes between Grenada and the South American mainland. The loss in 1783 still rankled at Whitehall.

So it was that in March 1793 that Major General Cornelius Cuyler on Barbados received the memorandum from Dundas to take Tobago as soon as he felt he had sufficient forces to do so. There seemed to be some idea that the residents were mainly planters and therefore Royalist, and so would welcome British intervention, although this does not seem to have been officially confirmed. Cuyler needed naval support that was not immediately available, and had to wait several weeks for Sir John Laforey's squadron, at the time off Saint Kitts, to assemble off Bridgetown. In the meantime, Cuyler assembled an expeditionary force from the forces available to him on Barbados. His largest available unit was the 4th battalion of the 60th (Royal American) Regiment of Foot, who could make available nine companies totalling 13 officers and 308 other ranks commanded by Major William Gordon. Despite their name, they were no more American than the Frenchmen they were about to encounter. The regiment had acquired that name upon its raising in 1755 in America, but the men were almost all Germans or Swiss, with a smattering of British or French Royalist officers. A composite company of light infantrymen and grenadiers of the 9th (East Norfolk) Regiment of Foot, the former the nimblest and the best shots, the latter the tallest and fiercest, was sent from Saint Kitts under the command of Captain and Brevet Major Alexander Baillie. One company of artillery, Sowerby's of the 3rd Battalion, Royal Artillery, a detachment of 3 officers and 47 men serving two six-pounders and two light howitzers, was selected to sail.[1] Because the Royal Navy had them handy, a detachment of 2 officers and 30 other ranks of His Majesty's Marines from HMS *Trusty* under Major Richard Bright was made available for service. This force spent all of 11 April boarding the Laforey's warships HMS *Trusty*, HMS *Nautilus*, and HMS *Hind* and the merchantman *Hero*, and sailed from Bridgetown the next morning.

The voyage was uneventful. The French had no inkling of what was coming, and few ships to stop them if they did. Cuyler's force arrived in Great Courland Bay on the north-western side of Tobago around one o'clock in the afternoon on Sunday 14 April 1793, and was rowed ashore by sailors. Leaving the troops to form up, and whilst the artillery was brought ashore – always a slow business – the commander and his staff of eight made their camp. Cuyler's two most senior officers present were Lieutenant Colonel Vaughan Lloyd of the Royal Artillery, and the deputy quartermaster-general in the Windward Islands, Lieutenant Colonel William Myers of the 15th Foot. Cuyler's personal assistants were his aide Captain Mungo Paumier, also of the 15th Foot, and Captain Frederick Gottschedd of the 60th Foot, his major of brigade.[2] Other officers present included chief Royal Engineer Captain James Fiddes, inspector-general of hospitals Patrick Lindsay, and deputy adjutant-general Captain Frederick Maitland of the 60th Foot. Together they drafted a summons to the French garrison at Fort Castries, about three miles south-east and across a heavily jungle-clad hill. At a quarter past four in the afternoon, Cuyler sent Captain Gottschedd off towards distant Fort Castries with the summons, which read:

> The Commander in Chief of his Britannic Majesty's force, desired me to acquaint the commanding officer of the French troops, of his having landed on the island with a considerable force, and is to be supported by a powerful fleet at an anchor in some part of the island. He summons you to surrender prisoners of war, with all the troops under your order. The officers will be allowed their parole. Their baggage shall be safe, and they will be exchanged as soon as a cartel is settled between the two nations. The British general reserves to himself the power of exchanging the officers either in this country or in Europe.[3]

Gottschedd took an hour-and-a-half to find the fort in the fading light and jungle. He was unceremoniously blind-folded by the French at the perimeter before being

---

1 From 'Disembarkation Return of His Majesty's Troops under the Command of Major General Cornelius Cuyler… the 14th of April, 1793' printed in Anon., *Anthologia Hibernica: Or Monthly Collections of Science, Belles-lettres, and History* (Dublin: R.E Mercier & Co, 1793), Vol. I, p.475.
2 The major of brigade was the chief staff officer in a brigade; perversely, usually a post filled by a captain.
3 From a report by Major Frederick Maitland, quoted in Anon., *Anthologia Hibernica*, Vol. I, p.475.

led inside. The summons was read by the staunchly Republican Lieutenant Colonel Laroque de Monteil of the 31e Régiment d'Infanterie, Military Commandant of Tobago. He penned a quick refusal:

> I am obliged to the British General for his information and kindness, and should betray the trust reposed in me to surrender without having tried the strength of the enemy. I have between four and five hundred men to depend on, and will not surrender until compelled to do so by a superior force within this fort.[4]

In fact, Monteil had barely three hundred men, but no mind. Siege warfare was all a game of bluff. Gottschedd rode back across the jungle-clad hills and delivered this refusal to Cuyler at about eight o'clock that night. Cuyler had two choices – to settle down for a siege, or to attack immediately. Having no siege equipment or heavy artillery, his choice was clear. He made his attack plans accordingly.

The expeditionary force set out at half-past one o'clock in the morning of 15 April. Needing to sacrifice firepower for speed, Cuyler left the artillery behind, as well as Lieutenant Walker and 25 men to guard the stores and beach-head. Led by a coerced local, who bolted at the first opportunity and left the British to find their own way, the infantry wound the two miles across the island, until they reached an elevated spot where all the men were ordered to strip off their knapsacks and blankets, so as to travel the last few hundred yards quickly and quietly. Silence was essential. They advanced with muskets unloaded. Somehow in the darkness the two flank companies of the 9th Foot became separated and although they approached the fort from the less well-defended north-western side, the intended direction of attack, the nine companies of the 60th Foot and the Marines found themselves at the south-eastern side, facing the big guns. So far absolute silence had been maintained, but this was ruined as shots rang out. These came not from the fort, but from French locals in a nearby house who had spotted Cuyler's troops in the darkness. As the French garrison tumbled from their bunks, Cuyler gave the order, and the Germans of the 60th Foot clambered up the barrier walls and charged into the fort with the bayonet only. The commotion caused by the shouting and sporadic musket-fire from the defenders completely denuded the landward side of the fort of French troops. Sensing the moment to perfection, Major Alexander Baillie led his flank companies of the 9th Foot directly into the heart of the fort.

It was all over in ten minutes. After a brief hand-to-hand struggle, the French garrison surrendered. There were twenty-one guns in the fort, of which eleven were 18-pounders. The French lost 15 men killed and wounded, and 196 found themselves prisoner-of-war, including some 68 of whom were regulars of the 31e Régiment d'Infanterie, eleven gunners and 80 National Guardsmen, the island

---

4 From same report by Major Frederick Maitland, quoted in Anon., *Anthologia Hibernica*, Vol. I, p.475.

militia. Another roughly 100 Frenchmen, mostly National Guards, escaped into the night, but many were captured, or gave themselves up, in the following days. Thus, seventy-three days after the declaration of war, and six weeks before British and French troops would face each other for the first time in Flanders, the first engagement of the long war between Britain and France was decided. It was a British victory, although the Germans of the 60th Foot had done most of the fighting, losing three men killed, and Lieutenant Edward Gayer and 18 other ranks wounded. The 9th Foot suffered Lieutenant Henry Stopford, one drummer, and three men wounded. Lieutenants Stopford and Gayer were thus the first British officer casualties of the war. Stopford was later killed on Grenada on 8 April 1795.[5]

By dawn on 16 April, the Union flag was fluttering above the fort, which was, as convention demanded, re-named Fort Scarborough in honour of the new owners. The men gave three cheers for King George. Tobago was once again a British possession. Thereafter followed two days of meetings with representatives from the local planter community, some French, but some British, the latter settlers who had never left the island despite the years of French occupation. Lieutenant Colonel Lloyd's artillerymen made an inventory of all the guns and ammunition in the fort, whilst Captain Fiddes of the Engineers counted the tools and weighed the lumber. Two days later Cuyler penned a dispatch and gave it to his deputy adjutant-general, Captain Maitland, to take home to England. The voyage took six weeks; Maitland arrived at Whitehall on the afternoon of Saturday 1 June, and as was common for all officers bearing good news from the front, was immediately given a brevet promotion, in this case to major. Cuyler and his force sailed back to Barbados a week later, leaving Lieutenant Colonel Myers as temporary governor of the island, with a few companies of the 4/60th as a garrison. Then fever struck. Major William Gordon, commander of the 60th Foot, died in July 1793. William's brother, Lieutenant Colonel Charles Gordon of the 41st Foot, learned of his younger brother's death when waiting for embark on Grey's expedition

The optimism that the easy capture provoked within British headquarters at Bridgetown and Kingston was unfounded. Tobago had only ever been sparsely populated by the French, many of whom were absentee landlords, and the French garrison had been tiny, with no reasonable chance of reinforcement. The next few islands might not be so easy.

---

5   Referenced in a despatch from Lieutenant General John Vaughan to Henry Dundas from Martinique dated 16 April 1795, reproduced in http://caribbeanhistoryarchives.blogspot.com.au/2017/05/circumstances-surrounding-fedon.html.

7

A Lock Step Banditti

HMS *Boyne*, a 180-foot long second-rate warship of the Royal Navy carrying 98 guns and nearly 700 sailors, sailed grandly out of Portsmouth harbour on Sunday 24 November 1793. The captain, George Grey, was a man extremely young for his post. The fact that his two most notable passengers were his father, General Sir Charles Grey, and his father's best friend Vice Admiral Sir John Jervis, had much to do with his appointment. He had seen active service since the age of fourteen, but the last twelve years had been dull and routine. Dull that was, until Britain declared war on France, some nine months earlier. Now he was going to war.

They – the *Boyne* and the other ten vessels in the fleet – had just spent three frustrating days waiting for the transport ships to form up. Now, more delays. The ships dropped anchor at Saint Helen's whilst another two days was spent waiting for the ordnance store-ships to catch up. Despite the frustrations, expedition commander General Sir Charles Grey took it all in with his usual good cheer. He was well used to delays by this time. The entire expedition was already nearly three months late.

The reinforced fleet, which finally sailed on Tuesday 26 November, contained within its stinking holds a land contingent totalling some 6,118 rank and file, including 400 artillerists and artificers, plus non-commissioned officers and officers; all in addition to the Royal Navy crews. Most were young soldiers and inexperienced, and many had never been to sea before. Practically none had been as far as the West Indies, none of the soldiers at any rate.

The passage to Cape Finisterre was pleasant enough, but strong gales hampered progress across the Atlantic. After surviving some violent storms, the fleet reached Madeira on 17 December, declining to put ashore but staying long enough to take aboard wine for the officers and ship's companies. The Queen of Portugal's birthday was celebrated on 21 December as the fleet was surrounded by gaudy-coloured local small craft; the climate was delightful. Captain Josias Rogers RN filled his days on deck, inventing a 'simple machine for moving heavy artillery where wheels cannot act'.[1]

---

1 William Gilpin, *Memoirs of Josias Rogers, Esq: Commander of His Majesty's Ship, Quebec* (London: T. Cadell & W Davies, 1808), p.34.

They crossed the Tropic of Cancer on Christmas Eve with the attendant ceremony involving King Neptune and the raising of funds to buy the ship's companies fresh vegetables on arrival at Barbados. Divine service was held on deck the following day with all the crews dressed in 'clean trowsers and jackets'.[2] Some of these jackets undoubtedly came off the following week as the temperature climbed well above eighty degrees Fahrenheit. Some of the transports and ordnance ships were so sluggish that they had to be towed by the frigates.

Sir Charles Grey and his staff aboard HMS *Boyne* arrived at Barbados on Monday 6 January 1794, to find that some vessels had already arrived, and that a laggard few were daily expected. They anchored in Carlisle Bay and were greeted with the news that Yellow Fever had carried off 58 army officers in the command in the past year, 'and privates in proportion'; the actual figure we now know as 670 dead and 785 sent home due to infirmity.[3] In other words, about ten percent of the garrison. This must have been galling news to the 1,200 men on the fleet who arrived sick; the news that the two ships transporting medical supplies had been delayed and were somewhere out at sea, date of arrival uncertain, must have caused nervous anxiety. Part of the problem, however, seems to have arisen from the laxness and inexperience of the officers, combined with the unsanitary conditions aboard ship. Major General Thomas Dundas, one of the senior officers on the expedition, observed some improvement by 20 January; 'a report will find its way home that we are unhealthy, and at one time [it] had a dismal appearance', he wrote, 'we had 1100 in hospital, but it proceeded from the shame-full neglect of the officers from Ireland, who allowed their men to get sick with filth and nastiness; the fever was smart, but not very dangerous; the men were languid and low. The best possible treatment and attention from us all has conquered the ill, and they recover; above 100 are sent to their ships daily in high health.'[4] Mister Mallet, Director-General of Hospitals on Barbados, was less optimistic. 'The Difficulties attending these Divisions in our Situation are inexpressible,' he wrote, 'and almost impractical in their Execution, and are greatly increased by the endless Demands of all Sorts of detached Corps for Medicines.'[5]

Sir Charles Grey went ashore at Bridgetown on 7 January and set up residence in Government House on Constitution Hill. The local garrison commander, Major General the Honourable Thomas Bruce, had sailed for home six weeks earlier, 'sick almost unto death',[6] following the arrival of Lieutenant General Robert Prescott.

---

2   Cooper Wylliams, *An Account of the Campaign in the West Indies in the Year 1794*, p.7.
3   Quoted in David Geggus, 'The Cost of Pitt's Caribbean Campaigns, 1793 To 1798' in *The Historical Journal*, Vol. 26, No. 3 September 1983 (Cambridge: Cambridge University Press), p.703.
4   M.I, Dundas (ed.), *Dundas of Fingask: Some Memorials of the Family* (Edinburgh: D. Douglas, 1891), p.107.
5   Anon, *Facts relative to the conduct of the war in the West Indies; collected from the speech of the Right Hon. Henry Dundas, in the House of Commons, on the 28th of April, 1796, and from documents laid before the House upon that subject* (London: J. Owen, 1796), p.109.
6   Bruce never really recovered his health and died at Exeter in December 1797.

Prescott was sixty-six years old, barely five foot four inches tall, with a small head and slender hands, shrewish of face, irascible and peppery. A blunt Lancastrian, stubborn and impatient, he had however sound judgement, integrity, and was later to show considerable bravery. One of his most trusted deputies was Colonel John Whyte of the 6th Foot, a grizzled veteran who had clocked up 33 years of service, including long periods of duty in the West Indies, and who would be a major general within a year. Whyte was Prescott's eyes and ears, and had done a tremendous job of obtaining local information from émigré French Royalist officers sheltering on Barbados. These men were more than happy to provide information that might assist in the subjugation of their detested Republican countrymen. One of them was a Monsieur de Guignod, the former chief engineer of Fort de la Convention, the main fortress on Martinique. Thus it was that Grey and his staff learnt in great detail the status of defences, which bays and forts were heavily defended and which were not. 'The defence of the Island of Martinique is established in two Citadels, one of which (Fort Royal) defends the Port, and is itself protected and covered by the other (Fort Bourbon),' read a report prepared and submitted by French Royalists:

> It consists of a number of strong Positions, which the nature of the Country presents, to defend the approach to these Citadels, and in a Redoubt formed in the interior part of the Island… this Redoubt situated upon the Morne des Olives can receive the reinforcements which may be sent from the other Islands, and even from France, and the Troops and Militia, which may unexpectedly assemble at this post, impregnable by nature, joined to those which may have been left there, would harass an Enemy without intercession, while he formed the Sieges of these Citadels… To determine the Time that these two Citadels may hold out is very difficult – it would depend on the capabilities of the Commanding Officer.[7]

By 10 January all the ships from Britain had arrived, save one containing Lieutenant Colonel Bryan Blundell and the light companies of the 44th and 55th Foot, which had lost its masts and returned to Ireland for repairs, although it seems that Blundell was able to hop ship and arrived in Bridgetown well in advance of his troops. Most of the men in the expeditionary force had never set foot outside Britain before, so Barbados must have seemed like another planet. The heat was surely the most unsettling part. Major General Thomas Dundas, an avid letter writer, wrote home after spending two days on the island; 'after a hard day's work, and dining with the admiral on turtle, I cannot possibly spend a few minutes, to my mind, so agreeably as in conversing with what I most love. Thank God, you never can see this climate as my wife, because you who dislike heat would

---

[7] GRE/A192a, Mémoire sur la defense de la Martinique [undated].

be unhappy, which I shall ever pray you never shall be; for my own part, I enjoy complete health, by means of flannel and constant perspiration.' But two weeks later he admitted, 'this climate is far from being unsupportable; the mornings and evenings are charming.'[8] Seventeen-year-old Midshipman Frederick Hoffman of the frigate HMS *Blonde* found the local food-stuffs exotic:

> This island is famed for its noyeau, guava jelly, candied fruits – particularly the pine-apple, which is put on table in glass cases – and its potted flying-fish, which I thought equal in flavour to potted pilchards… the purser purchased several tons of yams for the use of the ship's crew, some of which weighed upwards of twenty pounds each. We bought for our mess some sweet potatoes, plantains, bananas, shaddocks, forbidden fruit, and limes. There were groves of oranges, but we had not time to visit them. We saw in the market melons, guavas, sour-sops, alligator-pears, love-apples and mangoes.[9]

The expeditionary force was formally brigaded in mid-January after additional troops for his expedition derived from existing West Indian garrisons arrived. Grey created three brigades, the first (as was the custom) commanded by the senior subordinate available, Major General HRH Prince Edward, absent but presently sailing down from Canada. In his absence command went interregnum to Colonel Sir Charles Gordon of the 41st Foot, conducting a brigade with three of the strongest battalions in the force (at least on paper), the 15th, 39th, and 43rd Foot. The 15th had been in these islands since 1790 and could be considered 'seasoned' despite having an inexperienced officer corps, whereas the 39th had not seen active warfare since India in 1757, and had a weak officer corps. Sir Charles Gordon was the son of a general, a fine-looking, balding, courteous man whose correspondence shows him to have been highly ambitious, and not above pulling a few favours to gain a step or two in rank.

The second brigade went to Major General Thomas Dundas, with the 58th, 64th, and 65th Foot. Most had not seen service since Yorktown in 1781, although the 56th had last seen shots fired in anger only a few months before in Ireland, when it had quelled an anti-militia riot in Wexford. The brigade had perhaps at best a handful of men with active service experience. Well-trained they might have been, but weak in numbers and inexperienced, and in the case of the 64th Foot, particularly sickly. It is for this reason perhaps that Dundas was given a company of the 2nd (Queen's) Regiment of Foot that had been serving aboard the fleet as marines, commanded by an outstanding company officer, Captain George Ramsay. Thomas Dundas was the Laird of Carron Hall, an ascetic-looking man

---

8   Dundas (ed.), *Dundas of Fingask*, p.104 and p.107.
9   Frederick Hoffman, *A Sailor of King George* (London: John Murray, 1901), p.20.

with long sandy-brown hair, dark arched eyebrows, and a dimpled chin. He had married late, but had fathered had six children in eight years, with a seventh on the way. He had given up his regimental commission in the 80th Foot on return from North America in 1783 upon appointment to a commission to examine the nature and justice of a long list of claims for compensation to those Loyalists 'who having remained loyal to the mother-country, had suffered in their rights, properties and profession.'[10] As such, in 1794 his permanent regimental rank and pay was still only as a half-pay lieutenant colonel (unattached), despite the fact that he ranked as a local major general on the expedition. His letters home from this time are full of the longing that he would be given a colonelcy in a regiment, for dramatically better pay and prestige, and in fact he had enlisted Grey's help and patronage in the matter.[11]

Colonel John Whyte, appointed a local brigadier-general, commanded the third brigade, the 6th, 9th, and 70th Foot. The 9th had been on Barbados for five-and-a-half years and had recently participated in the capture of Tobago; they were probably the best infantry battalion Grey possessed, apart from the grenadiers and light infantry, despite nearly half the ranks being filled by new recruits. The 70th had come from Ireland with Grey, whereas the 6th had recently sailed down from Halifax, Nova Scotia, discarding their winter furs and great-coats en route. These latter two units had very experienced company officers, albeit not very many of them to go around.

In a move rooted in British military doctrine of the late eighteenth century, but also entirely characteristic of Grey, he expanded the newly-arrived flank company battalions with the addition of the flank companies of the garrison into three light and three grenadier battalions, moving some companies around to mix the experienced and acclimatised flank companies from local garrisons with the twenty-eight inexperienced companies from Ireland. This practice had been adopted by General William Howe in 1776, when he had combined all the flank and light companies of His Majesty's Army in North America into four grenadier and four light battalions. The grenadier battalions for much of the war referred to themselves as 'The British Grenadiers' suggesting that they had little difficulty in engendering their own internal *esprit de corps* whilst apart from their parent formations. No doubt this had not been lost on Sir Charles Grey after his arrival in North America in 1777. Major General Thomas Dundas, who had commanded one of the light infantry battalions in the American war, was given the job of training the light infantry to the required standard; it seems that Colonel John Campbell of Blythswood, the 38-year-old commander of the

---

10   Dundas (ed.), *Dundas of Fingask,* p.64.
11   Grey wrote to Henry Dundas on 16 March 1794 requesting the colonelcy of a regiment for Thomas Dundas. See GRE/A2243f, Concerning the attack on Fort Bourbon, the need for reinforcements and medicines, and praise of Prince Edward and Major-General Dundas.

9th Foot recently recalled from Saint Kitts, took control of the grenadiers. It is no exaggeration to say that these battalions contained some extremely talented officers. The three battalion commanders appointed to the light battalions were Lieutenant Colonels Eyre Coote, Bryan Blundell and Farnham Close. Coote was a 31-year-old Irishman and a future divisional commander in a later campaign in Egypt; his 1st Battalion included the light companies of the 6th, 8th, 9th, 12th, 17th, 22nd, 23rd, 35th, and his own 70th Foot. Bryan Blundell was a 35-year-old grandson of a former Lord Mayor of Liverpool. His 2nd Battalion contained light companies from the 15th, 31st, 33rd, 34th, 38th, 40th, and 41st Foot. The light companies of the 44th (his own regiment) and the 55th were still bound from Ireland after ship repairs and would not join the expedition until mid-March. Farnham Close was a 35-year-old Ulsterman; his 3rd Battalion contained the light infantrymen of the 21st, 39th, 43rd, 56th, 58th, 4/60th, 64th, and his own 65th Foot.

The grenadier battalion commanders under 'Blythswood' Campbell included Lieutenant Colonels Robert Stewart of the 58th Foot; an affable 34-year-old from Dublin, John Francis Cradock; and the 36-year-old Richard Henry Buckeridge from Totteridge in Hertfordshire. These battalions were not formed from the same parent units as the light infantry. The 1st Grenadiers comprised companies from the 6th, 8th, 12th, 17th, 22nd, 23rd, 31st, 41st, and 58th Foot; the 2nd Grenadiers from the 9th, 33rd, 34th, 35th, 38th, 40th, 44th, 55th, and 65th Foot; and the 3rd from the 15th, 21st, 39th, 43rd, 56th, 4/60th, 64th, and 70th Foot. Some of the company commanders were surprisingly young, assisted no doubt by a purchase system which allowed them to buy their way up the Army List as vacancies arose. John Oswald, a kinsman to Thomas Dundas commanding the grenadiers of the 35th Foot, was only 20; Devon-born Rufane Shaw Donkin commanding the grenadiers of the late-arriving 44th Foot was 21; Captain the Honourable William Stewart of the 22nd Foot grenadiers, a younger brother of Captain Lord Garlies of HMS *Winchelsea*, was only 19. Grey's second-in-command Lieutenant General Robert Prescott exercised a supervisory role over these shock troops, which were unquestionably the elite formation in Grey's force. The grenadiers were the biggest and boldest men in each regiment, the light infantry the nimblest and best shots. These brigades would provide sterling service in the campaign to come, and be destroyed by the end of it.

Providing firepower support were the men of the artillery under Lieutenant Colonel Thomas Paterson and Major Orlando Manley, detachments from six companies of the 3rd Battalion Royal Artillery and three companies of the Royal Irish Artillery, totalling 28 officers and 536 other ranks; plus, ten officers from the Royal Engineers. Unlike infantry officers and other ranks, who learnt their occupation on the drill square, these men were all trained at the Arsenal at Woolwich under the auspices of the Board of Ordnance. To act as the eyes and ears of the army, difficult given the mountainous jungle-clad nature of the islands to be invaded, 50 cavalrymen from the 7th, 10th, 11th, 15th, and 16th Light Dragoons, as well as a small detachment of West Indian light dragoons (the grandiosely-titled Carolina Corps of Black Dragoons, Pioneers and Artificers) were included.[12]

The troops slept aboard ship. They disembarked in darkness at three o'clock each morning and Grey drilled them from that time until sunrise. They drilled again from four o'clock in the afternoon until eight, when they embarked for the night. Thus, they were allowed to rest during the hottest part of the day. To the fore were the inevitable bayonet drills, pushing the troops to have the strict discipline needed to maintain absolute silence in the assault followed by a violent charge with cold steel only. Also to lessen the exertion on his men, Grey tried to round up negro servants to attend to the infantry battalions at the rate of four men per company. White slavers refused to provide men at anything less than outrageous prices, and island President William Bishop filled the gap by providing a large draft of his own slaves for army service at no cost.

Whilst the infantry forces sorted themselves into battle order on land, the naval contingent formed out in Carlisle Bay. Vice Admiral Sir John Jervis' fleet comprised his own flagship, HMS *Boyne*, 98 guns, commanded by Captain George Grey, two 74 gun third-rates, HMS *Vengeance* and HMS *Irresistible*, a 64 gunner, HMS *Veteran*, ten frigates, four sloops and a bomb-vessel – the fittingly named HMS *Vesuvius*. Sir John, as was his custom, exercised his naval command from aboard ship, and exercised his seamen on land tactics ashore, especially in the use of small arms to give his men greater utility any land-based operation. He split his fleet into squadrons, giving independent command to Charles Thompson and Josias Rogers with the local rank of commodore, to rank equal to brigadier-generals on land, and bodies of seamen and marines to serve under them. Jervis was an astute judge of men. In Rogers' case, as the captain of a small frigate, he had been promoted over the heads of older men commanding larger vessels. Somehow his genial personality massaged away any bad temper from the appointment and he soon gained a reputation for hard work and carrying the weight of command easily.

Jervis' first task after establishing at Barbados was to sail around the nearby British islands – Tobago, Grenada, and Saint Vincent – with instructions for the colonial governors to enforce an embargo against French commerce in all ports, also to advise them of the impending campaign. But what impressed upon him the most was a dreadful harbinger of things to come. Every town and port showed signs of the deadly Yellow Fever, and it was carrying men away at sea as surely as on land. HMS *Solebay* had lost every officer save the captain, and 200 out of 240 crew. Back at Barbados, other captains were using the time 'on the wing', out at sea

---

12 Order of battle assembled from GRE/A200, Return of the strength of the several corps composing the army commanded by Grey, embarked at Barbados on the expedition against Martinique, 1 February 1794; also Laws, *Battery Records of the Royal Artillery, 1716-1859* (Woolwich: Royal Artillery Institute, 1952); as well as reference to the numerous regimental histories referenced in the Bibliography.

looking for French vessels to capture; nine were taken in a very short time. Other seamen and artificers were given the task of assembling six gun-boats in dry-dock, brought to Barbados in kit-form aboard the store-ships. Each gun-boat carried a twenty-four-pounder gun in the bow, run in and out on rollers, had two masts, and a barricade on the gunwale made from bulls' hides. Oars were supplied so that the boat could be rowed in the absence of a wind, and they were intended to be commanded by a midshipman.

Militarily things were progressing well, for the present at any rate; political directions remained, as was becoming customary, always an each-way bet. Grey received a letter from Henry Dundas on 17 January, written four weeks earlier on the expectation of catching up with Grey on his arrival on Barbados, which tweaked his objectives based upon recent intelligence from Saint Domingue, advising him that events in Saint Domingue now so favoured the British that Grey could, if he wished, direct all his initial efforts against that island instead. The letter also advised him that the 22nd and 41st Foot would shortly sail as reinforcements from Cork to assist in this action; 'I should not act candidly with you, if I did not express the feeling I have, that any appropriation of your Force if necessary… would be approved of, even if it was to have the effect of postponing for the present the Object which you might otherwise aim at in the Leeward Islands.'[13]

Grey had discretionary powers in the matter; he immediately wrote to Governor Adam Williamson on Jamaica to advise him that his activities against the French Windward Islands would continue as he had planned; Williamson could send some recent reinforcements of his own to Saint Domingue, and Grey would send reinforcements down the line if he had any spare. He replied to Dundas on 20 January to re-confirm his original plan; 'an opportunity that may never return' was how he described his current plan, to take Martinique, Saint Lucia and then Guadeloupe, in that order. No doubt he realised that to go to Saint Domingue would incur losses that that might diminish his force for activities in the Windward Islands; and worse still, the time taken to go to Saint Domingue would seriously erode the time left in the year's campaign season – five months, to the end of June – before the 'sickly season' took hold. Indeed, in such circumstances, actions against Martinique might have to be deferred until the following year.[14]

Martinique had not been Grey's first choice of island to capture before he left England, but it was now. Royalist officers on Barbados who had fled Martinique were quick to point out the inadequacies of the Republican officers and troops left on the island, and the rotten state of defence of the forts, particularly Fort de la Convention. In any event, fighting and sailing his way westward from Barbados,

---

13 GRE/A187, Letter from Henry Dundas to Grey, 18 December 1793. Concerning the objectives of the West Indian Expedition and informing him that reinforcements were on the way.

14 A2243b, Letter from Grey to Henry Dundas, 20 January 1794. Giving his reasons for not sending part of his force to Saint Domingue and concerning sickness among the troops.

with the wind at his back, was more practical in the age of sail. Saint Lucia was closer, smaller, but Martinique would be the greater coup. The Royalist émigrés on Barbados pointed out that the Republicans might be content with surrendering without a fight, if they could surrender with honour. Sadly, Grey seems to have believed this. Prompted by Henry Dundas, he prepared and despatched letters to leading citizens on Martinique, no doubt known to the Royalists, asking them to submit without a fight.

Since he figures so frequently in this story, it is necessary to explain the part of Henry Dundas in events to follow. He was a fifty-one-year-old lowland Scot from Midlothian, a lawyer by training who so completely controlled Scottish politics his nick-name was 'The Uncrowned King of Scotland'. Articulate and manipulative, he became Prime Minister William Pitt's closest adviser after the declaration of war with France in 1793, despite being unencumbered by a single military bone in his body. His muddled and knee-jerk reaction management style in the early years of the war is best summarised thus: 'he was so profoundly ignorant of war that he was not even conscious of his own ignorance.'[15] However, it is equally clear that as Prime Minister, Pitt was complicit in the same decision-making process.

As the date for departure drew closer, the anxious Grey drew up detailed plans with Brigadier General John Whyte, a man with considerable experience in these islands. Grey had used the weeks on Barbados to pick the brains of émigré Frenchmen resident under British care. The Marquis de Bouillé, the former Royalist Governor of Martinique, was one such source of information; the engineer Chevalier de Sancé was another. 'To attack this island with success you must have a Body of Ten Thousand men, and a Fleet in proportion with 100 or 120 Pieces of Ordinance and Ammunition agreeable thereto,' the émigrés advised.[16] Using various plans and documents provided by these men, Grey and Jervis drew up their strategic plans for the campaign, whilst Whyte was entrusted to draw up tactical plans for the 'circumvallation of Forts Bourbon and Royal', the attack on Trinité (two plans), and for the attack on Pigeon Island (Islet de Ramieres) which guarded the southern side of République-ville Bay. Grey himself would superintend the main landing at Saint Luce, near the southern end of the island, after which troops and ships would capture the adjacent Bay of Marin, whilst a secondary force-marched north to capture French batteries lining the southern side of République-ville Bay. The first and larger of two diversions was to come at Trinité, in the north-east. Major General Thomas Dundas and his Second Brigade were to land and advance overland towards République-ville, capturing the fort at Gros Morne (named Morne des Olives in the extract above) along the way. The smaller diversion was to be a token landing at Case Navire, about three miles west of République-ville, with a reduced brigade commanded by Sir Charles Gordon.

15   Fortescue, *History of the British Army*, Vol. IV Part I, p.72.
16   GRE/A195b, Mémoire sur l'attaque de la Martinique [English translation].

On Wednesday 22 January, a few days before boarding the ships, Grey issued the first of two General Orders to the expectant troops. 'The General takes the liberty to assure them, that they are able to fight any troops upon earth,' he trumpeted, 'and he will be answerable that it would not be a contest of ten minutes between this army and the best troops of France; whether the affair was to be decided by fire or bayonet'.[17] Grey's thoughts were echoed by Captain (and Brevet Major) Robert Irving of the 70th Foot. 'We expect it will be an easy conquest as there are few white troops and the slaves they have armed will not stand above one fire, much less allow the bayonets to come near them'.[18]

Magnificent troops they might be in Grey's eyes, although as has been seen, this was questionable, they were still prone to wandering, to which Grey added this warning:

> [I]t may not be improper to explain to the soldiers the fatal consequences of straggling ever so little away from camp in quest of plunder; it is next to a certainty they will fall ignobly by the hands of the country people; or if they should escape, the may depend upon suffering the severe punishment due to disobeying military orders.[19]

In fact the entire second half of the Order was completely devoted to enforcing the rule of military law, and to inform the force that Captain Joseph Vipond had been appointed Provost-Marshal, with Sergeant Major William Allen of the 48th Foot his deputy, together with a party of two corporals and twelve privates to maintain order. Grey issued a set of 'Further Orders' on Friday 24 January which contained some last-minute advice for the troops about to embark, entirely consistent with his customary views on the value of the bayonet:

> The troops always to form two deep; the roads being so narrow in the island, it will be necessary for them to march by files.... The soldiers will bear in mind the use of the bayonet, which in possession of, they can have no excuse for retreating for want of ammunition, the bayonet being the best and most effectual weapon in the hands of a British soldier; in which mode of attack (the General assures them) no troops on earth are equal to them.[20]

---

17 Cooper Wylliams, *An Account of the Campaign in the West Indies in the Year 1794*, Appendix, pp.1-2.
18 Martin Howard, *Death Before Glory: The British Soldier in the West Indies in the French Revolutionary and Napoleonic Wars 1793 -1815* (Barnsley: Pen & Sword, 2015), p.47.
19 Cooper Wylliams, *An Account of the Campaign in the West Indies in the Year 1794*, Appendix, pp.1-2.
20 Cooper Wylliams, *An Account of the Campaign in the West Indies in the Year 1794*, Appendix, pp.6-7. Note the reference to two deep line, as opposed to the continental preference for forming three-deep. Far from being a Wellingtonian innovation, this statement indicates that its adoption perhaps had more to do with the British army's experiences in North America fighting against irregular forces in broken country.

The same order clarified the identities of ten Royal Engineer officers to accompany the invasion, under the command of Chief Engineer Colonel Elias Durnford. Next-to-last in order of seniority was a bright clergyman's son from Ipswich, 25 years-old and serving on his first overseas campaign, 1st Lieutenant Richard Fletcher, in later life Wellington's Chief Royal Engineer in the Peninsula War.

The intensive training of the fighting men was showing results. Major General Thomas Dundas wrote on 30 January; 'All are in high glee. I have worked like a horse – to good effect. I think the effects are already visible; from a lock-step banditti we shall be a regular army at our ease.'[21] The troops started to board the ships on Saturday 1 February, a slow process that involved ferrying the men out to the men of war and transports anchored in Carlisle Bay. The force that boarded the fleet that day numbered 6,085 infantry rank and file present and fit for duty, with another 224 present but sick, with another 977 sick left behind on Barbados. The flank battalions were the strongest, with musters ranging between 395 and 593 fit men, and relatively small numbers of sick men. Each flank battalion had one lieutenant colonel and one major, and a healthy complement of company-grade officers and sergeants. The Royal Artillery and Royal Irish Artillery companies were likewise reasonably healthy and well-provided with officers and non-commissioned officers. However, all was not so promising elsewhere. The inexperienced 56th Foot was so sickly that Grey expelled it from the expedition, sending part to Grenada and three companies under Captain Charles Fancourt to garrison Saint Kitts, keeping only the flank companies in hand. Gordon's 1st Brigade had the veteran 15th Foot with only 256 men present, the green and sickly 39th Foot with 217 men ill,[22] and only the 43rd Foot with above 350 men in the ranks. Thomas Dundas' 2nd Brigade was in even worse condition; the 58th and 64th Foot could only muster about 150 men each (the 64th having 274 men in hospital!) with only the 65th Foot anything like healthy at 325 men present for duty. Whyte's 3rd Brigade could only muster an average of 340 men per battalion, with the 70th Foot the strongest at 369 men. Even worse than the thinned ranks were the paucity of officers. Only two lieutenant colonels and three majors were available for service in these nine battalions; Dundas' brigade contained only eight captains, thirteen lieutenants and ten ensigns to command forty companies. Many battalions embarked without adjutants, quartermasters, or surgeons.[23]

'Our preparations close this day, and we expect to sail tomorrow,' Captain Josias Rogers of the navy wrote that afternoon. He added a pessimistic footnote: 'our force is small'.[24] Grey used his last remaining days in Barbados to write off two

---

21 Dundas (ed.), *Dundas of Fingask*, p.108.
22 The 39th Foot had only 247 other ranks present and fit for duty.
23 GRE/A200, Return of the strength of the several corps composing the army commanded by Grey, embarked at Barbados on the expedition against Martinique, 1 February 1794.
24 William Gilpin. *Memoirs of Josias Rogers, esq. commander of His Majesty's Ship Quebec* (London: T. Cadell and W. Davies, 1808), p.101.

last letters. One was to Sir George Yonge, Secretary at War, requesting promotions for his sons Thomas and William. This was an act entirely in accordance with his capacity as expedition commander, to promote officers up to the rank of captain. But it was also true to his personal character. The second was to the Commander-in-Chief of the British Army, Lord Amherst, carrying the same appeal for promotions and advising him to the imminent commencement of the campaign.[25] With his administrative duties done, late on that same afternoon, Grey gathered his sword and belongings and was rowed aboard HMS *Boyne*. Martinique and its nest of vipers waited for liberation, and his hour had come.

---

25 GRE/A2243e, Letter from Grey to Lord Amherst, 2 February 1794. Concerning promotions and the commencement of his campaign.

8

Landing and Consolidation

It was towards the exotic isle of Martinique that Grey's 6,500 barely-acclimatised redcoats and artillerymen sailed aboard nineteen men-of-war and transports from Carlisle Bay in the morning sunshine of Monday 3 February 1794, as frigate-birds wheeled overhead. 'The morning was brilliant beyond conception,' recorded Lieutenant Bartholomew James RN:

> [T]he sight grand above description. The bands of music, the sounds of trumpets drums and fifes, the high panting ardour, zeal and discipline of the soldiers and sailors, the confidence in the warmth, bravery and experience of the commanders-in-chief, and, in short, the cause we were employed in, created an emulation not to be surpassed, and a true loyal joy not to be more than equalled.[1]

Each man-of-war towed one of the gun-boats assembled at Bridgetown. Midshipman Hoffman had obviously established relationships with the locals ashore, writing:

> ...we finally bid an affecting adieu to our yellow and black legged female friends at Bridge Town, who remained on the shore waving handkerchiefs much whiter than themselves until the fleet cleared the harbour... the fleet and transports soon cleared the bay, when each ship took her station. It was a majestic sight to see so many vessels with all their canvas spread and swelling to a strong sea-breeze.[2]

Tuesday was all plain sailing, whilst in France that day the National Convention proclaimed the abolition of slavery. The fleet divided in the morning of 5 February, as the ships approached the south-eastern corner of Martinique, the

---

1   Bartholomew James, *Journal of Rear Admiral Bartholomew James, 1752-1828* (London: printed by Spottiswoode for the Navy Records Society, 1896), p.228.
2   Frederick Hoffman, *A Sailor of King George*, p.17.

three components of the force going their separate ways. The first division, under Commodore Charles Thompson, aboard HMS *Vengeance*, and Major General Thomas Dundas, sailed to land at the Baie du Galion, near the hamlet of Trinité, on the east coast. The second division, under Captain Josias Rogers and Colonel Sir Charles Gordon aboard HMS *Quebec* was to land at Case de Navire on the west coast. The third division, the main force under Vice Admiral Jervis and Grey himself, assisted by Lieutenant General Robert Prescott, was due to land at the Bay of Marin and Trois Rivieres in the south-west.

Vice Admiral John Jervis had initiated a naval blockade of Martinique immediately after arrival at Barbados. For three weeks, Royal Navy vessels had encircled the island at a distance to prevent their detection from lookouts on Martinique. As a result, the island received no communication from the outside world. Not even a single fisherman got through to warn them about the troop build-up on Barbados. Thus when the first sails were visible from Martinique in the distance at sunset on 4 February, the French assumed them to be the long-promised reinforcements from France. This notion was dispelled during the morning of 5 February, as the now much-closer vessels were seen to sport the Union Jack.

Grey's third division, sailing under a blue flag, had the least distance to travel, and consequently landed first. As Jervis's ships approached the Bay of Marin at about four o'clock, French batteries on the two headlands protecting the harbour, Pointes du Jardin and de la Borgnesse, opened fire. Grey's earlier letter asking the Martiniquais to surrender without firing a shot plainly had not worked, and the campaign was underway. Warships HMS *Boyne* and HMS *Veteran* anchored close to shore and poured salvoes into the batteries at Pointe de la Borgnesse to the point of silencing the guns. Dodging the infrequent salvos from small calibre cannon, Lieutenant Richard Bowen RN ran a small schooner along the shore to test the depth of the water, after which the fleet anchored just after dark, near the seemingly-safe Pointe de la Borgnesse. The first troops, a company of the 9th Foot under Major Alexander Baillie, started for shore aboard flat-boats and the French guns opened again, to which the far heavier guns on the fleet made a brisk reply. The French cannoneers abandoned their guns and ran off as soon as shot fell amongst them and troops formed up on shore started to advance in their direction. A mulatto National Guard captain named Compère stayed behind with eleven of his men, sworn to defend the last gun with their lives. This they did their best to do, but the fight was over and only Compère managed to escape. The infantry occupied the post and, as was customary, hoisted the Union flag to the cheers from the tars aboard the ships. They discovered and foiled a hasty booby-trap comprising a line of powder between the battery and the magazine, fired a few shots against the retreating Frenchmen, spiked the guns and re-embarked. The whole action had taken less than half-an-hour. The defenders of Pont du Jardin across the bay panicked and set fire to sugar plantations nearby, presumably since they belonged to known Royalists. The dry canes burned fiercely in the dark. To the north-west, in the hamlet of Saint Luce, two 24-pounder guns commanded by the curé of

72 BY FIRE AND BAYONET

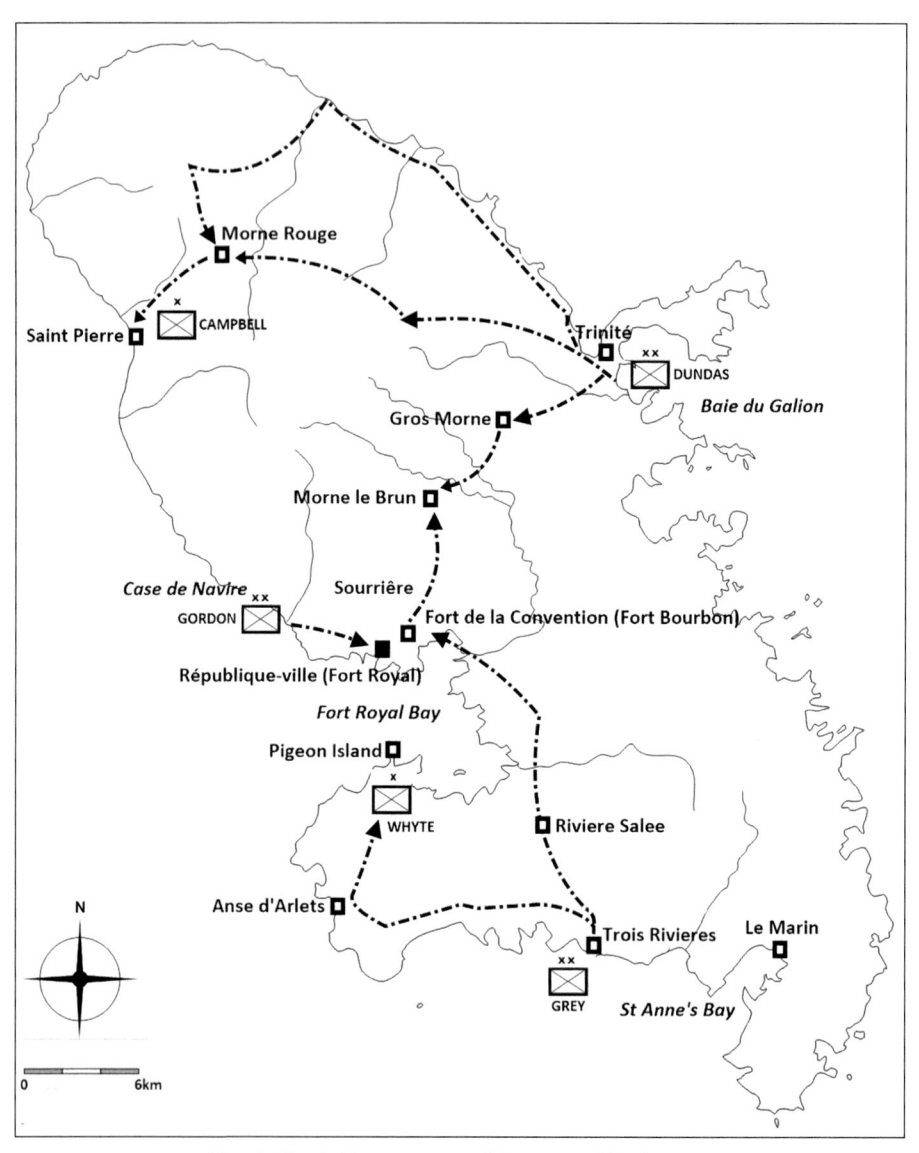

Map 2 Grey's Movements on Martinique, March 1794.

the village commenced firing at the fleet, which the 64-gun HMS *Veteran* soon silenced. Some Marines landed to spike the guns, after which another company of the 9th Foot landed to capture the battery at Pointe Dunkerque. By sunset, most of the Bay of Marin was secure, a safe landing place for Grey's troops.[3]

Lieutenant Général de Rochambeau, the Governor-General of the French Windward Islands, was a good soldier and a loyal Republican. He had been a soldier for nearly thirty years, and was certainly not afraid of the British. They were another in a long line of foes this past year. He recorded in his diary on 4 February that he believed the British would come with anywhere between 12,000 and 16,000 men, with more reinforcements due from Canada.[4] Whilst having nowhere near those numbers, Rochambeau nonetheless had a substantial force dotted around the island, composed of regulars, militia, and mulattoes. But that was the problem. With men in pennypackets everywhere, he was strong nowhere. He kept his best troops in reserve on the heights of République-ville and in the vicinity of Fort de la Convention. The backbone of his defence was a company of the regular 37e Regiment d'Infanterie (Régiment Coloniale de la Martinique, formerly Régiment Maréchal de Turenne), only sixty men all told. There were three small battalions of the Chasseurs de Martinique; a mere 300 *gens de couleur* with mostly white officers commanded by Louis Bellegarde, Edouard Meunier and l'Enclume respectively. Bellegarde's 1er Chasseurs were posted on the east coast at Trinité and Gros Morne, Meunier's 2e Chasseurs in the north. It seems that l'Enclume's 3e Chasseurs were still in the process of mobilisation. The west coast at Case Navire was defended only by gun batteries, 'abandoned to the courage of its people and the Republicans who inhabited it'. The rest were militiamen attracted to the Republican banner from all quarters, a total of about nine hundred men.[5] In terms of naval power, he had only two ships-of-war, the 28-gun frigate *Bienvenue* at République-ville and an 18-gun corvette at Saint Pierre. Artillery and Engineers maintained the fortresses and manned the guns, although a lot of ordnance on the island was either ancient, or naval armament recovered from wrecks, often manned by enthusiastic local amateurs. The coloured troops were literally fighting for their freedom, something guaranteed them by Republican France, but almost certainly lost under either the Royalists or the British. They would fight fiercely for their liberty, but with more native tenacity than any military skill.

It was upon this dispersion of enemy force and reliance on militia that Grey reckoned for success. Aware they the French were weak everywhere, he could well afford to disperse his force into the three landings. He believed that any of his brigades could knock over whatever resistance it encountered. The question was whether, on an island forty miles long, saddled by a volcano, with very few decent roads, mostly tracks, in dense jungle, could his three columns act in concert?

3   Account based mainly upon Haynsworth, *Career*, pp.393-395.
4   Rochambeau Journal, entry for 4 February 1794, in Haynsworth, *Career*, p.392.
5   Rochambeau Journal, entry for 4 February 1794, in Haynsworth, *Career*, p.392.

Timing was crucial, as was speed. The inexperience of his troops did not auger well for a long campaign, in any clime, let alone one in such torrid conditions, and with the fever season only a few months off.

Sir Thomas Dundas' division had arrived on the eastern side of the island near the Baie du Galion, but had not landed. Local commander Bellegarde sent a courier post haste to République-ville to warn Rochambeau. The latter, however, was at Saint Pierre, inspecting troops, so the message took some hours to reach him. He sent Major Edouard Meunier's 2e Chasseurs south the support Bellegarde, leaving Saint Pierre relatively undefended.[6] Political instincts then took over, and he rode south to République-ville to brief the Representative Assembly as to current events. They formed a Committee for Public Safety of twelve selected members, and issued a proclamation asking all Martiniquais to 'fight to the death rather than surrender the island'.[7] It was now well after dark, and there would be no more firing today. Day one of the campaign had ended with no British casualties and some small gains, admittedly against a gaggle of militia and civilian volunteers. Vice Admiral Jervis now had a strong, defensible mooring in Saint Anne's Bay and the Bay of Marin, although the French still held the town of Marin at the head of the bay, with secondary moorings opposite Saint Luce and a little farther west at Trois Rivieres. The only French ships in the vicinity were a frigate at République-ville and a corvette at Saint Pierre, located nowhere near any of the landings and in any event hopelessly outnumbered by Jervis's fleet.

Grey opened the ball on day two by ordering Prescott's division to land at Trois Rivieres. Close to two-and-a-half thousand men were rowed ashore in flat-bottomed boats and row-boats, completely unopposed. The 3rd Grenadiers and 2nd and 3rd Light Infantry landed first, and were sent forward towards Rivere Salée, nine miles away, at ten o'clock, followed by Whyte's brigade, the 6th, 9th, and 70th Foot, at two o'clock. The 15th Foot had been detached from Gordon's brigade and was temporarily appended to Whyte's, presumably to act as a strategic reserve. One of Grey's first acts ashore was to despatch his aides to the largest towns, République-ville and Saint Pierre, bearing flags of truce and advising them of acceptable terms should they choose to capitulate. Captain Finch Mason arrived off Saint Pierre in a small boat, to be met by the mayor, Monsieur au Cane, on horseback with an armed company and a loaded cannon at his back. Mason tried to read his summons and letter:

> We wish to spare the effusion of human blood and preserve the flourishing commercial town of Saint Pierre from the horrid consequences attending the present attack of a formidable Array of British Troops making descents

---

6   Rochambeau Journal, entry for 5 February 1794, in Haynsworth, *Career*, p.397.
7   Haynsworth, *Career*, p.398.

on different parts of this Island, at one and the same time, which cannot fail... We therefore summons the Inhabitants maturely to consider the terms offered in the Declaration and supplement herewith delivered.[8]

All the while Monsieur au Cane and his men bombarded the floating Captain Mason with threats and epithets. Mason gave up and sailed away.

Meanwhile, fifteen miles north of Grey and Jervis, Major General Thomas Dundas was superintending the disembarkation of his force, in the picturesque Baie du Galion on the eastern side of the island. Commander Robert Faulknor's sloop HMS *Zebra* had been the first ship of Commodore Thompson's squadron to make shore, firing at the French battery at Point a Chaux as he did so, driving the defenders inland. He was soon followed by the much larger frigates HMS *Beaulieu* and HMS *Woolwich*. Under the red flag of this division, Dundas landed two battalions of his brigade, as well as Coote's 1st Battalion of Light Infantry and Cradock's 2nd Battalion of Grenadiers, both under the command of his trusted deputy and best friend, Colonel John Campbell, known to friends as 'Blythswood' after his estate. The 65th Foot, too far out to sea, had to wait until morning to disembark. The advance was delayed due to the defence put up by Bellegarde's 1er Chasseurs and some militia, who were driven out of a plantation at bayonet-point. Coote's Light Infantry advanced half a mile inland to silence a battery on the heights, which they did without the loss of a man. Dundas set up headquarters on a plantation and the Royalist overseer offered to guide him up to the mountain bastion at Morne Vert-Pré. Dundas and his troops sweated up the winding path. They were attacked from above by two companies of 1er Chasseurs commanded by a Captain Octavius, and bundled back to the plantation but not before the death of an artilleryman, with two officers and three privates wounded. Finding another route up, Dundas led his force on a different road, only to be stopped again by the determined Octavius.

Morne Vert-Pré had been a diversion. The main task assigned to Dundas revolved around the capture of Trinité. About 160 French defenders were clustered atop Morne le Brun, an eminence overlooking the town, and within Fort Bellegarde on the edge of the hamlet, a fortress named after the mulatto leader who commanded there in person. Colonel Campbell and Lieutenant Colonel Coote led six companies of the 1st Light Infantry up towards le Brun into what swelled into a heavy but inaccurate fire, causing the attackers to lose two men killed and eight wounded, including two officers, Stopford and Toole, who commanded the advanced guard. The defenders, mostly National Guard, fled once threatened by the points of the light infantry bayonets. 'Campbell is too brave', Dundas wrote,

---

8 GRE/A206, Letter from Major-Gen. Thomas Dundas to Grey, 7-c.12 February 1794. Reporting on his landing and campaign in Martinique.

'his horse was wounded, but he is unhurt'.[9] Seeing that he had thirty minutes of daylight left, Dundas detached Cradock and his grenadiers, plus three companies of light infantry under the command of Major John Evatt of the 70th Foot, to attack Fort Bellegarde. The action ended inconclusively, the troops failing to dislodge the defenders, although the defenders of nearby Fort Trinité fled without much resistance once the levelled bayonets came their way. This allowed the troops to get possession of the town and all its stores. Bellegarde and his fellow defenders abandoned the fort bearing his name that night, retiring towards the mountain-top of Gros Morne, 700 metres above sea-level. As they did they set fire to the abandoned township of Trinité, causing the seamen in Dundas' force to suffer a sleepless night battling the flames under the direction of Captain John Salisbury RN. But two-thirds of the town was saved.[10]

The evening of 6 February therefore found two brigades ashore without having faced any serious opposition. In accordance with Whyte's planning, Grey had earlier despatched that officer with Close's 3rd Light Infantry, two amuzettes (light cannon), and 200 seamen along the eastern coast road to take a circuitous route around to Islet de Ramiers, or Pigeon Island in English. Grey marched the rest of his force northward towards distant République-ville. His was the movement that would secure the southern end of the island. He was relying on Dundas to secure the northern end, by approaching République-ville from the north-east. Whilst the attackers were feeling the heat from the French defenders at Trinité, Grey's men were feeling the heat from the sun. He marched them so relentlessly along the road towards République-ville that a sergeant of the 9th Foot dropped down dead in the road from heat-stroke. By sunset on the first day they had reached the southern edge of République-ville Bay near the village of Riviere Salée. Despite Grey's General Orders issued on Barbados, which warned that any man plundering the inhabitants would feel the full weight of military justice, two men plainly had not bothered to listen. Private William Milton of the 10th Light Dragoons and Private Samuel Price of the Carolina Corps were found to have robbed a merchant in Salée, adjudged guilty at a court-martial on 7 February, and hanged from a tree in front of the whole division on the morning of 8 February. Later that day Grey wrote a General Order almost apologising for having to conduct such an act. 'The Commander in Chief hopes the awful scene of this morning will have its proper effect, and not lay him again under the most feeling and painful necessity of having to repeat it, by which must certainly be the unhappy case in the persons of future offenders'.[11] 'Every exertion was made to save the white Man (a Recruit

---

9   GRE/A206, Letter from Major-Gen. Thomas Dundas to Grey. Reporting on his landing and campaign in Martinique. See also Haynsworth, *Career*, p.401-407. The town fire had been lit by Bellegarde and twelve assistants; he had earlier disobeyed orders from Rochambeau to build a battery in the town facing out to sea, and had instead built it facing inland, where it served no useful purpose whatsoever.
10 GRE/A206, Letter from Major-Gen. Thomas Dundas to Grey.
11 Cooper Wylliams, *An Account of the Campaign in the West Indies in the Year 1794*, Appendix p.12.

only 18 years old),' Captain George Nares of the 70th Foot recorded, 'but the Genl. being willing to impress on the Minds of the Blacks the strict Administration of Justice amongst the British Troops without Partiality or Distinction of Colour, was induc'd to make this sad Sacrifice at the Expense of his own Feelings.'[12]

The intrepid Brigadier General Whyte captured the hamlet of d'Arlet early on 7 February, complete with two loaded cannon, after a brief resistance from the local militia. The Mayor of Anses d'Arlet had decided to surrender following a token volley and cannon-fire in the direction of Whyte's advancing columns, after which the militia fell back to an agreed position at Morne Charles Pied, then to their homes. Whyte then used his light troops to capture the French batteries at Cap Solomon and Pointe Bourgos, taking the garrisons prisoner, losing only one man in doing so. This was an important success, since possession of these two headlands gave the British complete command of the bay of Grande Anse d'Arlet, a convenient landing place within striking distance of République-ville. Jervis duly transferred his headquarters to that place from Saint Anne's Bay, from where he opened direct communications with Grey late on 8 February. It was there that Captain Schank's platforms for unloading ordnance from ships proved highly effective. These were commonly referred to as 'sliding keel' vessels, with a centreboard that the crew could raise to permit operations in shallow waters. In addition to the unloaded guns, the nine captured heavy cannon were a bonus, and would come in useful for the reduction of the fort on Pigeon Island, whose artillery blocked the entrance to République-ville Bay. That night, Grey sent the 3rd Grenadiers forward to Trou au Chat to establish communications with Whyte.

General Rochambeau had not been idle during the days of 6 and 7 February, but what he had experienced must have almost caused him to lose heart. Everywhere he found demoralised National Guardsmen, many skulking in their homes, or urging surrender.[13] It is therefore unsurprising that the first response to the growing crisis came late, in the afternoon of 7 February, when Rochambeau sent what few regular troops he had from République-ville by sea to cut off Whyte on the southern side of the bay. They landed in the vicinity of Trois Islets and advanced to Morne Charlotte Pied, overlooking Pigeon Island. Grey discovered this movement and ordered his adjutant-general Colonel Francis Dundas to drive them off. Dundas took Lieutenant Colonel Boulter Johnstone with his 70th Foot, a division of 200 seamen armed with pikes and pistols headed by Lieutenants Thomas Ropers and William Cordon Rutherford RN, and two howitzers, to attack after midnight on the night of 8/9 February. In heavy rain, the 70th relieved the 15th, posted on a hill near Pigeon Island, and discovered that about 300 Frenchmen were occupying Morne Charlotte Pied. Captain George Nares led a patrol forward

---

12 Surrey History Centre, ESR/25/NARE/. Captain George Strange Nares, Camp Diary kept by, including a Description of Invasion and Battle of Martinique.
13 Rochambeau Journal, entry of 6 February 1794, in Haynsworth, *Career*, p.405.

to establish the French dispositions, was fired upon, and realised that a different attack route would be required. It was now about seven in the morning, and in the dawn light the 70th were now visible to the batteries on Pigeon Island, which opened a heavy fire. Taking his own and Captain Galbraith Lowry Cole's companies forward in skirmish order, with the rest of the 70th behind, Nares stayed true to Grey's favourite tactical manoeuvre – advancing in complete silence with flints removed and at bayonet point only.

The French troops dispersed into the countryside at the first shock and eventually retired to République-ville. The 70th occupied the hill, set up the two howitzers to support Whyte, and suffered over 1,000 artillery rounds fired in their direction from the guns on Pigeon Island during the course of the day and next night.[14] The same day Whyte received 200 seamen from Jervis under the command of Captain Rodney, armed with pistols, cutlasses, and pikes. He put them to work building a battery on the shore to batter the fort crowning the island – 'a steep and barren rock, inaccessible except in one place only, where the ascent is by a ladder fixed against a perpendicular wall, and the summit is ninety feet above the level of the sea'[15] – into submission.

Reinforced by artillery landed from the fleet at Anse d'Arlet, two companies of the 15th Foot, and quartermaster-general Richard Symes, the seamen and artillerymen dragged the siege artillery up the side of Mount Matherine, overlooking the island. It was not an easy task. It had rained heavily during the previous night and the path was deep in mud. Colonel Durnford and some sappers were also on hand to speed things along, and by the time the guns reached the top, the siege gun positions were completed and ready to receive the cannon. Two 5.5 inch howitzers, hauled from Riviere Salée by Boulter Johnstone's 70th Foot, were also in position to give the defenders of Pigeon Island hell.

Saint Anne's Bay to the south was not wholly secure. The French still occupied the village of Marin at the end of the bay. Grey had already made his first surrender overtures by this point. He despatched Lieutenant Milne RN and Lieutenant James Watt of the 50th Foot to deliver a package containing surrender terms to Rochambeau and the local commander at Marin. The two officers approached the town in a small boat early on 7 February with a flag of truce. The defenders opened fire on the white flag and the two officers beat a retreat, leaving their letter in the hands of a wounded defender, presumably from the action of the previous day, who they found lying on the beach with a shattered leg. Despite the arbitrariness of the delivery method, the letter was read by the French. But Rochambeau refused to surrender, and sent a company of National Guardsmen to bolster the defence

---

14 Based upon Nares, Camp Diary.
15 Jarvis Langdon, 'The French Revolution in Martinique and Guadeloupe' (Unpublished Thesis, Cornell University, 1897) p.72.

of Marin.[16] Jervis then decided to force the place by naval means. He launched all six of Schank's gunboats to bombard Fort Saint Étienne, the principal fortress in Marin, until the volume of musketry drove the boats back to the fleet. The town remained a thorn in Grey's side.

General Rochambeau re-established his headquarters at République-ville on the night of 7 February after two frustrating days touring the island's points of conflict. The Committee of Public Safety could not see that he had done anything to turn back the invaders at any point. But Rochambeau now knew the size of the task ahead of him, and claimed to even know the names of the British commanders at every landing point. He also knew that original estimates as to the size of the British forces were exaggerated. Now that he was back, the Committee of Public Safety was no longer needed, and the Representative Assembly could once again function, once they were in the safety of Fort de la Convention. But despite his soothing claims, there was one new landing force Rochambeau did not know very much about, one that he had spotted sailing north whilst travelling back to République-ville.

This force was the third and last of Grey's divisions, introduced into the fray in the morning of 8 February. Held back to allow the French to distract themselves between Grey's main force in the south and Dundas in the east, Captain Josias Rogers and his ten small ships under a white divisional flag landed Sir Charles Gordon and his 1,200-strong 2nd Brigade (1st Grenadiers, 39th, and 43rd Foot) at Case de Navire, only some five miles north of République-ville. Gordon found that the French held the north-south coast road and all the heights commanding it. The landing nearly met with disaster. The boats landing the troops found themselves under the guns of shore batteries, manned by regular artillerymen, and musketry from a company of Chasseurs under a Captain Réné. HMS *Dromedary* sailed too close to a battery on Point Negro and received two shots through her hull for her lack of care, one of which wounded her Captain, Sandford Tatham. Rochambeau, who was present, wrote in his diary how he was amazed that such a small group of defenders could fight off a large British force.[17] Hoping to prevent a bloodbath of the beach, Gordon abandoned the landing and chose a new spot in a shallow bay near Case Pilote, about two miles north. The shallow coast provided no anchorage for the ships meaning that the frigates and gun-boats could not anchor to steady themselves for a naval bombardment. It did not matter, as the French batteries at Case Pilote had virtually no ammunition. On a small beach, out of range from a French battery at Fond Capot, the Grenadiers, 39th, and 43rd came ashore in rowboats, troubled only by musketry from more of Captain Réné's Chasseurs. Eventually enough infantrymen were ashore to drive the Chasseurs back into the

---

16 Willyams, *Account*, p.20. The Republicans later declared they thought the white flag a Bourbon one, hence the shooting. Agreements were made for preventing such accidents in the future.
17 Rochambeau Journal, entry of 8 February 1794, in Haynsworth, *Career*, p.424.

jungle. Gordon's entire force was ashore by dusk, but not secure. The village was on the main north-south road between République-ville and Saint Pierre, and therefore attacks might come from either direction. Gordon needed to move his men inland.

After conferring with his deputy, Colonel William Myers, Gordon decided on a two-pronged approach. He detached five companies of grenadiers and the 43rd Foot with Myers to make a flank movement up the hills in the dark to flush out the defenders in redoubts above the village. A scrappy fight in the darkness saw Réné's Chasseurs escape, but most of the local National Guard taken prisoner. Other companies assaulted and isolated the French batteries at Navire and Pilote, at which points the crews took flight. But the inexperience of the troops and their officers was telling, as recounted by Captain William Stewart of the 1st Grenadiers;

> At sunset our detachment came in, strong out-pickets were sent out, and, no particular instructions being given to officers by Sir Charles Gordon or Colonel Noyers [Myers], the men were permitted to open blankets and the officers to lie promiscuously under the shelter of an old house. The consequence of this supineness was that, about two o'clock in the morning of the 6th [9th], a small party of the enemy, either by accident or else in reconnoitring our position, broke in among us and created a most dreadful confusion for some minutes. With the true conduct of young soldiers, the men fired upon each other, and it was with the greatest difficulty officers could stop their bayonets from being turned against friend or foe; for foe, indeed, if any ever existed, was not to be seen when the firing ceased. By this disgraceful alarm the 12th Grenadiers and my company had 2 men killed and 2 wounded desperately. Disgraceful I call it; for, whether it proceeded from an enemy, or from a false alarm given by some young sentry, the disposition of our battalion that night was such as reflected no great credit upon our commanding officers, as any enemy might have profited by the thick woody country, and cut the whole of us to pieces ere we were half awake.[18]

Despite this confusion, Gordon's troops carried the battery of La Chapelle twenty-four hours after landing, then another post at Berne the following day after an advance across difficult terrain. In the thick jungle, in unfamiliar topography comprising mostly steep hillsides, progress was slow. Myers' men were moving mostly eastwards higher up the mountainside. The approach to République-ville from the north-east was now in the hands of the British, and communication between the two main towns on Martinique was now impossible. Bellegarde and

---

18   Anon. *Cumloden Papers [letters &c. relating to the Hon. Sir W. Stewart and others, with an account of his life]* (Edinburgh: Printed for private circulation, 1871), p.4.

his 1er Chasseurs at Saint Pierre made no effort to go to the aid of the defenders at Case Pilote. A disgusted Committee ordered them to go to République-ville so as to be under Rochambeau's eye. Bellegarde ignored the order.[19]

In the north, Dundas received intelligence that the 'brigands' intended to repossess the post at Gros Morne. Left stuck staring at the smoking ruins of Trinité whilst the 65th Foot and Ramsay's company of the Queen's finally disembarked, he left a small garrison comprising 250 men of the 58th Foot and Marines under the command of Major John Skerrett at the fort and pursued Bellegarde up the steep hillsides in strict silence. He attacked Gros Morne at midnight only to find that it had been evacuated by the defenders. The prize thus fell into Dundas' lap. The road to République-ville was wide open. The fresh 64th Foot arrived at Gros Morne by ten o'clock the morning of 8 February and were left as a garrison under the command of Lieutenant Colonel James Sowerby of the Royal Artillery.

Bellegarde had been ordered to defend the place by Rochambeau, but had disregarded his orders and retreated towards Saint Pierre instead, then sat on his hands. Rochambeau was furious. 'I believe that they [Bellegarde] had received money for this treason, and [his] conduct… is most certainly an indication'.[20] Over in Saint Pierre, Bellegarde spun tales of his heroism and blamed Rochambeau for not reinforcing his Chasseurs. It was all nonsense. Then, the following day, something strange happened in République-ville. Bellegarde arrived in town with some other Chasseur officers, having left his battalion behind in Saint Pierre, contrary to his orders. Rather than clap him in irons, Rochambeau welcomed him, gave him one of his horses, then asked him to name whatever command or mission he would like to undertake. Bellegarde offered to position his 1er Chasseurs in the Sourrière Heights, north of the town, which might impede General Dundas's advance from Gros Morne. Rochambeau agreed to the proposal.[21] He must have done it through clenched teeth. As much as he distrusted Bellegarde, he knew that his battalion was one of the few options available to him in terms of semi-dependable troops.

Dundas pursued the mulatto leader towards République-ville. Heavy rain prevented Dundas from moving forward during the night of 8 February, but he marched early on 9 February with his two flank battalions, the 65th Foot, four guns, 130 seamen, and the artificers. The roads were so bad that the movement of the artillery pieces was glacial, so he ordered the flank battalions on ahead and used the 65th to guard the toiling artillerymen. The flank battalions occupied the high peak of Morne le Brun, five miles north-east of République-ville, by lunch-time on 9 February, Bellegarde and his men having again retreated without firing a shot. From this dilapidated fort on the crest of the mountain-range which ran down the centre of the island, Dundas could see the town and

---

19   Haynsworth, *Career*, p.428.
20   Rochambeau Journal, entry of 7 February 1794, in Haynsworth, *Career*, p.417.
21   Rochambeau Journal, entry of 9 February 1794, in Haynsworth, *Career*, p.434.

harbour of République-ville below him. The artillery arrived three hours later and so Dundas detached Cradock with the grenadier companies of the 9th, 38th, and 44th Foot to capture Fort Mathilde, two miles to his left, from which the French defenders flew their colours. The garrison fled without firing a shot as the grenadiers approached: 'Before dark the British Colours were hoisted on this favourite spot of the Brigands'.[22] The attackers were then also able to establish control of an inlet, the Cohé du Lamentin, immediately below them. Martinique had effectively been cut in two.

Dundas had a scare that night when, writing in his tent, a local named Barbarose stood at his tent-flap and asked to see him. The man was seized and found to be an assassin. The next afternoon he detached Campbell and five companies of light infantry to take the post of Colonne, which was taken without loss, with discretionary powers to press on to Le Maistre if possible. But Campbell found Colonne too valuable to leave undefended, and roads too bad from the recent rains.

Dundas visited Fort Mathilde as it got dark on 10 February with the grenadiers of the 33rd Foot as a reinforcement. The fort was modest at best, a colonnaded house with a wall barely two feet high on all sides, so many of the troops were engaged on picquet duty there being no room for them inside. During that night, the fort was attacked by Bellegarde with his 1er Chasseurs, under cover of the sugar canes and undergrowth. What they had not expected was for the house to be nearly empty and deserted, save for some sentries who they killed on the spot. An opportunity presented itself to loot Dundas's supply base, and so they were engaged when the grenadier companies of the 9th and 38th Foot returned from picquet duty. A bayonet assault by the grenadiers of the 9th Foot drove the Chasseurs off into the jungle, but not before the loss of Captain John Mackewan of the 38th Foot, seven privates killed and nineteen wounded. A 30-year-old lieutenant of Mackewan's company, New York-born Frederick Philipse Robinson, was promoted to fill the dead officer's position. The quantity of discarded arms and accoutrements found around the fort the next morning demonstrated the poor quality of the Republican troops facing them. Nonetheless, three companies of grenadiers and several companies of light infantry were sent to reinforce the post. 'The grenadiers from Ireland are yet young Soldiers,' Dundas wrote of the affair, 'and they have been five Days in constant Fatigue and Heat – They shewed great spirit and must soon be fine Soldiers.'[23]

Before dawn on 11 February Dundas marched the remaining four companies of Coote's light battalion to relieve Campbell at Colonne, overlooking the Heights of Sourrière, and he marched the entire battalion to occupy the post at Le Maistre, the 65th Foot taking over Colonne. By late afternoon a chain of Union flags flew

---

22 GRE/A206, Letter from Major-Gen. Thomas Dundas to Grey, 7-c.12 February 1794.
23 GRE/A206, Letter from Major-Gen. Thomas Dundas to Grey. See also Dundas (ed.), *Dundas of Fingask*, p.111.

from a chain of posts extending from above République-ville Bay to Le Maistre, fifteen miles away. Skerrett still commanded at Trinité and 200 of the 64th Foot and Queens defended Gros Morne. The 65th Foot received its baptism of fire during the night of the 11th, being attacked three times, but each time the alert picquets gave the garrison plenty of warning. The battalion's only casualty was a private killed by friendly fire whilst dashing after retreating enemies.

Dundas had secured the eastern approaches. But Gordon was struggling through the jungle in the north, and so Rochambeau decided to stop him in his tracks, if possible. He left République-ville on 10 February in the company of Commandant Jean Ducassou, 400 militia, and one cannon headed towards Gordon. Ducassou was an old soldier, well-liked by his men, but his experience could not make up for their lack thereof. Unsuited to open warfare, Rochambeau wisely instructed them to ambush Gordon on a jungle track. But then something went wrong. Rochambeau went off to scout and suddenly found himself uncomfortably near to Gordon's column. Close to capture, he escaped and made his way to a French battery at Sainte Catherine and safety. But the battery was firing at Royal Navy ships and this attracted Gordon's attention. Gordon quick-timed his men up the trail, close to Ducassou's waiting ambush. Ill-disciplined fire from the waiting militia gave the game away, and the ambush became a protracted fire-fight, after which Gordon sounded the retreat.[24] Buoyed by this seeming Republican victory, Ducassou urged his men to go to the aforementioned battery at Sainte Catherine, where artillery was involved in an unsuccessful firefight with Royal Navy ships. It was unsuccessful because the French cannon on the bluff could not depress far enough, and the ship's guns could not sufficiently elevate. Marines tried to board landing boats to come ashore and silence the battery. So Ducassou sent his men down to the beach, where they engaged in a musketry duel with both sailors and Marines. Rochambeau arrived with three cannon found in a nearby abandoned battery, sited them on the beach, had them loaded with canister and opened fire. Musket-balls could do little damage to ships, but artillery could, and so the Marines re-boarded and all sailed away.[25]

The fort at Pigeon Island had always been considered an important cornerstone for the defence of Martinique, so much so that Rochambeau had authorised the expenditure of 600,000 livres to fortify and garrison the island. Grey understood its importance also, and needed it captured. The batteries on Morne Matherine commanded by Major Orlando Manley and Captain Francis de Ruvijnes of the Royal Artillery commenced a bombardment on the fort with 22 guns in the night of 10 February. As might be expected, the French guns were trained out towards the harbour and not in the direction of the hills behind. Therefore, the ten 36-pounders, half-a-dozen 24-pounders, and smaller miscellaneous guns had

---

24   Rochambeau Journal, entry for 10 February 1794, in Haynsworth, *Career*, p.439.
25   Rochambeau Journal, entry for 10 February 1794, in Haynsworth, *Career*, p.439.

to be run around to the south side of the stone fort to reply. Captain Josias Rogers, having nothing to do at Case Navire, had brought his squadron down to a small cove near Pigeon Island where he sent a small boat with two 24-pounders ashore. The boat was pierced with shot from the French but somehow reached shore, and the big guns were able to lend their weight to the overall bombardment.

With French attention focused on Morne Matherine to the south, Jervis displayed neat sleight of hand and landed a detachment of Marines on the north side of the fort before daybreak on 11 February. The Marines could only attempt the fort by ladders tilted against the cliff face of the fort. Half the defenders became engaged against the Marines as the fire on Morne Matherine slackened. Across the water, the fighting was being followed by observers on the ramparts of Fort de la République, including Rochambeau himself.[26] The fight lasted all morning. The Marines gave up trying to scale the ladders and sniped from the beach at the base of the cliff. A round from one of the two 5.5 inch howitzers on Morne Matherine decided the affair. It rolled into the main magazine and blew the fort sky-high. The garrison lost 15 men killed and 25 wounded out of a garrison strength of 203 men, most casualties occurring in the explosion.

The garrison struck their colours. Grey's losses were five men wounded. All the heavy guns were captured, and Lieutenant Thomas Rogers RN, younger brother to Josias, was installed as governor. He ran up a silken Union flag that had been sewn by his sister-in-law Mary Rogers before leaving Spithead.[27] The capture of Pigeon Island made République-ville Bay a much safer place for ships, and in the afternoon of 11 February the Royal Navy fleet sailed into the bay, hugging the southern shore-line, and sat at anchor four miles south of and in plain view of République-ville. The French batteries at Fort de la République threw a few salvos which fell well short, then gave up. The Reverend Cooper Willyams, chaplain aboard Jervis's flagship, described the scene they now saw:

> It is impossible to conceive a more beautiful scene than presented itself on our entrance into this fine bay. On the north side we saw Fort Louis and the town of Fort Royal [République-ville]; and immediately behind it, on the top of a steep hill, was the strong fortification of Fort Bourbon, which, with the tri-coloured flag waving on its walls, formed a conspicuous object in the landscape; the parapet being built of white stone, strongly contrasted with the vivid glow of verdure on the surrounding hills. To the westward rose majestically prodigious mountains, called Les Pitons du Carbet, the hills on the side of which were cultivated, while the mountains themselves were covered with wood to their summits. Eastward the bay opens to several bays and harbours, into which some noble rivers

---

26 Rochambeau Journal, entry of 11 February 1794, in Haynsworth, *Career*, p.448.
27 Mary Rogers, née Goodhew (c.1761-1832), wife of Josias.

discharge themselves, and pleasant islands of different dimensions and forms, embellish the whole. Pigeon Island, or Islet aux Ramieres, is situated on the south side of the bay of Fort Royal, about two hundred yards from the shore, and is a steep rock, inaccessible except on one side by a ladder fixed against a perpendicular wall. The summit is about thirty yards above the level of the sea, and is three hundred paces round. It contained the following ordnance, viz. Eleven forty-two pounders, six thirty-two pounders, four thirteen-inch mortars, and one howitzer, with an immense quantity of stores and ammunition, and a large stove to heat shot; it also had good barracks. It is famous for having prevented Admiral Rodney with twelve sail of the line from entering the bay in 1782.[28]

Dismayed by the loss of Pigeon Island, Rochambeau immediately rode northwards to find out what, if anything, was happening to stop Gordon's advance. He made for Camp Décidé, high in the mountains overlooking both Case Navire and Case Pilote, a position from which troops might be able to descend on Gordon and attack his rear. Rochambeau found the post nearly unoccupied, the garrison having largely evaporated. Disgusted, he descended to the beach to find the redoubtable Ducassou and his militia defending the beach below Sainte Catherine against sailors and marines. Then bad news arrived. Gordon had just captured Camp Décidé, and was thus in their rear. Unless Rochambeau, Ducassou and his band retired to République-ville, they might find themselves cut off. They hastily did so and only just managed to avoid Gordon's troops en route.[29] By 12 February, four days after landing, Gordon and Myers were at Fort La Archet, within three miles of, and overlooking, République-ville, having occupied the now-vacant posts at Case Navire and Saint Catherine. But it had been a wearying trudge, without the dash and vim of Dundas and Whyte's efforts. Captain William Stewart, commanding the grenadiers of the 22nd Foot, later criticised Gordon for providing little guidance to his subordinates.[30]

With the capture of the Grande Anse peninsula complete, Whyte marched his force to join Grey at his headquarters, a commandeered plantation house at Riviere Salée. Prescott did likewise. Despite this success, pockets of resistance still remained to be eliminated. Late in the morning on 12 February a company of the 15th Foot under Major William Lyon and Captain Mungo Paumier surprised a strong French party on le Grande Vauclain, an eminence about five miles east of Riviere Salée, and routed them, taking many prisoners. The following day the 70th Foot repulsed a half-hearted attack at Trou au Chat.[31] The attacks were becoming

---

28 Willyams, *Account*, p.29.
29 Rochambeau Journal, entry of 11 February 1794, in Haynsworth, *Career*, p.454.
30 Howard, *Death Before Glory*, p.49.
31 Nares, Camp Diary.

more and more desultory, as morale amongst the defenders dipped. About a hundred Frenchmen and mulattoes gave themselves up to the 70th Foot on Morne le Brun on 15 February. Chief amongst them was Commandant Jean Baptiste de La Rochette, second-in-command to Bellegarde.

A week on from the landings, General Grey determined it was time to commence the final act. On 14 February, he detached a small force under Prescott, who so far had had little to do, to join Dundas at Morne le Brun. Prescott and Dundas agreed a plan of attack to capture the northern end of the island, and specifically the commercial capital, Saint Pierre. Rough country could be expected, so the freshest troops would be needed. In the evening of 15 February Prescott and Dundas conducted the 2nd Grenadiers, the 65th Foot, and the light companies of the 33rd and 40th Foot across the hilltops to Gros Morne, at the time garrisoned by the Queen's and a detachment of the 64th Foot. At this place Dundas detached Colonel John Campbell with the two light infantry companies and the 65th Foot to go overland via Bois le Buc to Mont Pelée, the towering eminence in the north of the island. In the afternoon of 16 February Prescott and Dundas arrived in Trinité, where Dundas ordered all the men's packs and blankets to be put aboard a sloop and transported around to la Basse Pointe in the far north-east of the island, to await their arrival. Leaving Lieutenant Young RN and his 75 Marines as a garrison in the town, and having picked up Captain the Honourable George Ramsay's company of the Queen's at Gros Morne and the 58th Foot at Trinité, Dundas marched his small force at four in the afternoon along the narrow coastal road towards the River Capot in the north-east. Stopping for four hours before dawn on 17 September, the force turned left at the river and ascended the arduous Calabasse Pass, five miles of which was a steep ascent. A negro boy brought Dundas intelligence that the enemy post at Morne Calabasse was evacuated. Dundas sent his aide, Captain Frederick Maitland, with four dragoons ahead to hoist the Union flag. The men had marched thirty miles across often steep, craggy countryside, on roads little more than goat-tracks, in a tropical climate. It was one of the great feats of the campaign.[32] Alas, the intelligence they had received was not correct. Elements of Major Meunier's 2e Chasseurs still held the post, but they were soon evicted and retreated to Morne Rouge.[33]

John 'Blythswood' Campbell was a tall 38-year-old bachelor from Glasgow, the holder of a landed estate who had commanded the 9th Foot for more than ten years. The column led by him had marched north-west from a fork in the road near Trinité late on 15 February. Their route had taken them across difficult mountain

---

32 And comparable with the fabled march of the Light Division to reach Talavera in 1809, which according to best reports spanned 42 miles in 26 hours. But that feat did not require climbing of mountains, nor was it conducted under tropical conditions.

33 Outline based upon details in GRE/A222, Letter from Maj.-Gen. Thomas Dundas to Grey, 17-24 February 1794. Reporting on his campaign in Martinique and the taking of St. Pierre. Also Dundas (ed.), *Dundas of* Fingask, p.110.

terrain all the following day, headed for a place called Montigne on a track that led eastwards towards Saint Pierre. At about half-past nine in the morning of 17 February his leading troops, the light company of the 40th Foot, had come under fire from irregular troops, mostly mulattoes, hidden in the jungle. Campbell formed the 40th for a bayonet charge and led them onwards, when a mulatto sniper concealed behind a bush put a musket-ball through the head of the conspicuously attired and mounted senior officer. Thus the 9th Foot lost its commanding officer, the first senior British casualty of the campaign, and the first British field officer to fall to enemy action in the long war with France. John Campbell had two brothers in the service, one of whom, a Royal Navy officer, had died on duty; another, at the time of Campbell's death, was a prisoner of war at Toulon.

The action then degenerated into a fire-fight in the jungle, an action which Dundas witnessed from distant Morne Calabasse. He sent the company of the 2nd (Queen's) under Captain the Honourable George Ramsay across to help, which they did 'in a wonderful style,'[34] and the additional fire-power hastened the retreat of their opponents. It was then that Dundas learnt of the death of his best friend. But there was no time to mourn under fire, so he sent the panting 2nd Grenadiers, exhausted after being quick-marched up a three-mile ascent after the night's long march, across in support of Ramsay. He fortified his position on Morne Calabasse, and went across just in time to see the combined forces of Ramsay and Campbell's column capture Montigne. But the French were not yet done. Just before dusk, from a strong-point known as Redoubt Coloniale, they moved against Morne Rouge. Dundas dragged troops in that direction, and managed to form up the grenadier companies of the 33rd, 34th, and 44th Foot, together with a light field-piece under the command of Captain Francis Whitworth RA. For twenty minutes, they kept up a fire-fight on a peak named Morne Bellevieu. The attackers eventually fell back to the Redoubt Coloniale, leaving behind nine dead and ten men wounded to be taken prisoners. Obviously believing another attack possible, Dundas ordered the grenadier companies of the 35th Foot and 55th Foot under Captain John Oswald to garrison Morne Bellevieu. They had 30 seamen armed with pikes in support, and, consistent with the Grey doctrine, the grenadiers advanced with flints removed, bayonets poised. But the French had fled Redoubt Coloniale, leaving two artillery pieces behind, some wounded to be taken prisoner, and scattered half-finished graves. A final counter-attack from Saint Pierre, led by militia officer Pierre Boscq, was completely ineffective and the Republicans fell back into Saint Pierre. The actions of this day had cost the brigade Colonel Campbell and four rank-and-file killed, two subalterns, two sergeants and fourteen rank-and-file wounded.[35]

---

34 Quoted in GRE/A222, Letter from Maj.-Gen. Thomas Dundas to Grey. Reporting on his campaign in Martinique and the taking of St. Pierre.
35 GRE/A207, Return of killed and wounded in the actions of Morne au Pin and Morne Rouge, 16 February 1794.

With Dundas and Prescott changing their base of operations to the north of the island, Grey moved his headquarters from Riviere Salée to Morne le Brun on 14 February to stay in contact. The Royal Navy had not been idle:

> [A] detachment of about 300 seamen, with a small party of marines, was landed, under the command of Captain Eliab Harvey, of the *Santa-Margarita*, assisted by Captains William Hancock Kelly of the *Solebay*, and Lord Garlies of the *Quebec* [sic], and by Lieutenants Isaac Wolley, Joshua Bowley Watson, Thomas Harrison, James Carthew, Alexander Wilmot Schomberg, and John W. Taylor Dixon; also Lieutenant Walter Tremenhere, of the marines. This detachment, having in charge a 24-pounder gun and two mortars, began its march from the wharf in the Cul de sac Cohée towards the heights of Sourrière, a distance of five miles, and near to which Lieutenant-general Sir Charles Grey had established his head-quarters… After cutting a road, nearly a mile in length, through a thick wood, making a passage across a river by filling it up with large stones and branches and trees, and levelling the banks of another river by the removal of immense fragments of rocks, this persevering party, before the night of the third day, to the astonishment of the whole army, got the 24-pounder on the heights of Sourrière, and the two mortars to the foot of the hill, from which the summit was about a mile distant. On the following day the howitzers and two additional 24-pounders were got to their places on the top of the hill; and this although the ascent was so steep, that a loaded mule could not walk up in a direct manner.[36]

Rochambeau had been watching these activities from an elevated spot within Fort de la Convention, but there was little he could do in the way of offensive activities. Besides, the treasury had no money. On 14 February, he met with selected captains of commerce and industry, or those who had remained, and asked for money, even going so far as to provide a personal guarantee for repayment. The lenders offered a deal which effectively imposed a fifty percent interest rate, and the Committee reluctantly agreed.[37]

The early hours of 17 February found Dundas posed to take Saint Pierre. Leaving the grenadiers of the 65th Foot to garrison Morne Bellevieu, he divided his force into two columns: the men he had marched all the way from Trinité on the right, and Campbell's men, now commanded by Major Alexander Baillie of the 9th Foot, on the left. They advanced down the mountainside at three in the morning. Mid way, Dundas received a messenger under a flag of truce bearing a letter from Commandant Molerac, the commander at Saint Pierre, asking for

---

36 James, *Journal*, p.217.
37 Rochambeau Journal, entry of 14 February 1794, in Haynsworth, *Career*, p.465.

three days' grace in which to consider terms of a capitulation. Dundas replied under a flag of truce stating that instead of three days, the French had three hours. In fact, the morale of the population of Saint Pierre was at rock-bottom; what troops there were deserted in droves.

Dundas then rested his weary troops for a short time to soak in the dawn sunlight before continuing his advance. The force pushed on to the crest overlooking the harbour, and in the picturesque sweep of Saint Pierre below, they saw seven Royal Navy ships commanded by Captain Charles Nugent anchored in the bay, engaged in silencing the seaside batteries around the town. What they could not see in detail was the advance of the force's quartermaster-general, Lieutenant Colonel Richard Symes, with Brevet-Major Frederick Maitland, three light companies, and a detachment of the 58th Foot just to the north of the town. The Royal Navy squadron had suffered bombardment by red-hot shot in the night, but been able to put sufficient weight of fire ashore to silence the batteries. Much of this was thanks to the bomb vessel HMS *Vesuvius*, effectively a floating howitzer that had rained shells down onto the town, causing it to catch fire. The teen-aged Midshipman Hoffman was a witness to the whole affair:

> As it was thought advisable to reduce some of the smaller towns before the attack on Fort Royale, we were ordered with one of the sixty-fours, two frigates, the bomb-ship and some gun-boats to assault the town of St. Pierre. We gave three cheers in the cockpit on hearing this news. At daylight we weighed, and in the evening entered the bay of St. Pierre; we were ordered to take off the hard knocks from the bomb by anchoring between her and the enemy. About 9 p.m. we all opened our fire as nearly as possible at the same time. It was a most brilliant sight; the bay was literally illuminated. The enemy's batteries began to play with some trifling effect; this added to the splendour of the scene. The night, fortunately for us, was very dark, which made it difficult for them to strike us, as they could but imperfectly discern the object they fired at; this was evident, as they fired immediately after we did. Our shot and shell could not fail every time we fired them, as we had taken the bearings of the principal places when we anchored. The cannonading ceased about 3 a.m., when all the enemy's batteries, except one, struck their colours. This was in a great measure owing to our troops investing the back of the town.[38]

The Royal Navy losses were twelve killed and twenty wounded. Those of the defenders must have been considerable. Symes and his men had landed at about four in the morning, and advanced down the coast, but had not needed to expend ammunition. Shortly afterwards the remaining French fort, seeing the town had

---

38 Hoffman, *A Sailor of King George*, p.17.

surrendered, hauled down the tricolour flag. The flat-bottomed boats so carefully assembled at Bridgetown were brought into action and landed parties of marines at about seven o'clock in the morning. The seamen and marines were

> [A]stonished at the mischief our shot and shell had done. The roof of the municipality, or town house, was nearly knocked in. At the time some of the shells fell through it, all the wise men of the town were assembled under its, as they imagined, bomb-proof roof. Two of them were killed and several wounded. The principal church had also suffered, as two sacrilegious shells had penetrated it and fallen near the altar.[39]

By daylight the Union flag was fluttering over the battered town as small boats carrying fleeing Frenchmen snuck out of the bay. Rumour had it that Major Edouard Meunier escaped wearing women's clothes as a disguise. The American ship *Lucy*, mastered by Nathaniel Treadwell, was captured unawares in the bay and added to the list of campaign booty. Dundas' officer arrived with his flag of truce and three-hour demand to find only British occupants, and returned to his chief with alacrity. The military conquest of the north of the island was almost over. One small action remained, that of pursuing a party of Frenchmen who had escaped to a five-gun battery north of Saint Pierre. Robert Faulknor's HMS *Zebra* was dispatched to guard a small flotilla of flatboats carrying Major Coote Manningham with three companies of light infantry to the battery, where they stormed ashore and dispersed the defenders.

Dundas and his weary force marched into Saint Pierre in the early evening, and Sir Thomas established his headquarters at Government House. The troops marched through in good order whilst the inhabitants watched from their doorways and windows. No man was suffered to leave the ranks to loot. As an administrator Dundas had always been a just and fair man, but Grey's orders concerning the conduct of the troops were meant to be taken seriously. Therefore, one of his first acts was a melancholy one, ordering that a drummer-boy of the 55th Foot, brought in by the provost-marshal caught in the act of plundering a house, be hanged at the gate of the Jesuit College.[40] A large and well-stocked hospital was found at the southern end of the town, meaning that the sick and wounded, many more of the former than the latter, could be better treated than on board a hospital ship. The seamen of the Royal Navy were made busy taking stock of the captured vessels in the bay, and hustling Mayor au Cane, the vicar-general, and other local notables aboard the frigate HMS *Santa Margarita* for ultimate transport to République-ville. 'I was much amused at the genuine sang-froid', Midshipman

---

39 Hoffman, *A Sailor of King George*, p.18.
40 Captain William Stewart also recorded that a private of the 58th Foot was hanged at the same time, for robbing a shop. Anon., *Cumloden Papers*, p.5.

Saint Pierre in 1794 as depicted satirically by Cooper Wylliams. Note the guillotine, and heads on spikes. (Anne S K Brown Collection)

Hoffman wrote, 'or more properly speaking, the French philosophy, of the people who kept the coffee-houses. They moved about as gay as if nothing had happened, everything was regularly paid for, and the most perfect discipline observed'.[41]

By 22 February Sir Thomas Dundas had restored order in Saint Pierre:

> However, here I am… after spending four days in the midst of confusion, order is produced; 200 sad murderers are shipped for France, their deluded followers of colour, calling themselves free, are on board to enjoy freedom there until landed in Africa… the guillotine, still bloody, was burnt by themselves the morning I took St. Pierre.[42]

---

41 Hoffman, *A Sailor of King George*, p.19.
42 Dundas (ed.), *Dundas of Fingask*, p.111.

9

Falstaff's Corps

So, with success in the south, east and north of the island, only the administrative capital of République-ville was yet to fall. This prize comprised the town itself, Fort de la République, with 64 heavy guns on a spit of land south of République-ville, Fort de la Convention on a hill to the north of the town, and the Heights of Sourriêre overlooking all three places. Fort de la République, being surrounded on three sides by water, was the more vulnerable, and had been bombarded by the Royal Navy since Jervis established his fleet on the south side of République-ville Bay on 12 February. The *Vesuvius* bomb-ship, before sailing to Saint Pierre, had proved especially useful in using its large calibre mortars to drop shells inside the fort.

With the army so dispersed around the island, the Royal Navy found all manner of ways to support their efforts. Three companies of seamen under command of Lieutenants Milne and Ogle RN, but ultimately commanded by the indefatigable Captain Josias Rogers, were landed at Point Negro, about two miles west of République-ville, to replace Gordon's men, who had moved north to Saint Pierre. Under the protection of several frigates, the transports and store-ships were sailed to the Cohé du Lamentin, an inlet in République-ville Bay about three miles east of République-ville, where a wharf was built to land stores and provisions. This location also allowed easy communication with Grey, still located at Morne le Brun, about three miles north of, and many hundred feet above, the new landing-place. The 15th Foot was detailed to defend the lines of communication. This new landing place was of great interest to the mulatto leader Bellegarde, who kept his 1er Chasseurs in hand on the Heights of Sourriêre, overlooking both République-ville and the Cohé. Ironically, the man least trusted by Rochambeau was now the commander of the only formed Republican troops in the field. On the morning of 18 February, he requested permission to attack the British landing-place at Lamentin, ostensibly to cut the army off from the fleet. Rochambeau agreed, perhaps against his better judgement.

Predictably, Bellegarde did the one thing that nobody wanted. He attacked the well-fortified British camp at Mathilde, at Morne le Brun. When Rochambeau found out, he was furious, and sent an aide to stop them. The aide arrived at

A view across the bay towards Fort Louis on the right (called Fort de la Convention in 1794) with Grey's light infantrymen in the foreground. (Anne SK Brown Collection)

Sourrière too late.[1] The Chasseurs were already at Fort Mathilde and doing badly. Prescott rushed the 9th Foot and the 70th Foot to the support of the defenders, but seemingly unaccountably then ordered them back to their camp.[2] In fact, Prescott's attack was a cover to allow Grey the opportunity to capture the undefended Heights of Sourrière. Grey picked Buckeridge's 3rd Grenadier Battalion and Coote's 1st Light Battalion to capture the heights. The sight of the grenadiers on the left and the light infantry on the right, advancing at the double, was too much for the detachment of National Guard left behind on the heights, who were immediately captured. The grenadiers and light infantry were delighted to find that meals laid out for the victorious Chasseurs were now theirs by default, and wolfed down the creole cuisine. Rochambeau tried to organise some reinforcements to defend the heights, but it was too late. Colonel Daucourt and a company of the National Guard advanced out of Fort de la Convention, but were bombarded by two small brass cannon, and lost five men killed before retiring. The Chasseurs took refuge in a redoubt; Rochambeau caught up with them and ordered them to retire to République-ville. Atypically, they obeyed this order, went down into the town, and then looted sections of it.

1   Rochambeau Journal, entry of 18 February 1794, in Haynsworth, *Career*, p.484.
2   Nares, Camp Diary.

As a penalty, Rochambeau refused to let them enter Fort de la Convention, and made them camp below its walls on the northern side, within British cannon-shot range. He later wrote in his diary, 'Bellegarde was pushed outside on his foolish expedition, while the English were taking the position that he should never have left. He lost, in addition, field artillery that I had entrusted with regret'.[3] The flankers under Coote and Buckeridge impetuously followed but were driven back to Sourrière by firing from the fort. So ended the heaviest fighting of the campaign so far; several disjointed actions that cost Grey's force ten men killed and forty-four wounded, almost all in the flank battalions. Grey had intended to assault Sourrière during the night, but Bellegarde had forced his hand, and now the only remaining pocket of resistance was République-ville, with its defended strong-posts at Fort de la République and Fort de la Convention.

The presence of so many freed *gens de couleur* to their front must have motivated conflicting feeling amongst the negroes attached to the British regiments as servants. Sir Charles Grey wrote a general order from Morne le Brun on 17 February that suggested problems had arisen that required diligence:

> The Commander in Chief hopes that every care is taken of, and humanity shewn to, the negroes attached to the regiments, and all those employed with the army; and that they are victualled, attended to, and encouraged. This the commanding officers of regiments and corps, and every officer in all departments, will attend to, and inquire into; as many have fled from the camp, which must be owing to their having been neglected, or ill used by some of the men, such treatment must be prevented in future, otherwise the army will suffer every inconvenience.[4]

Grey's essential humanity shines through yet again in these words, although he was probably only half-right. Neglect or ill-use may have occurred, but the appeal of joining the free slaves and mulattoes must have been a powerful incitement to throw off the yoke of British military servitude.

The morning of 19 February marked a full fortnight since the campaign began. With the capture of the Heights of Sourrière, Grey knew he had Rochambeau on the ropes, so sent him a summons to surrender, aided and abetted by a tip-off from a Royalist that the garrison would surrender if their commander could be convinced of the attacker's overwhelming superiority and the guarantee of honourable terms:

---

3   James Lafayette Haynsworth IV, 'Donatien Rochambeau and The Defence of Martinique, 1793-1794', *Consortium on Revolutionary Europe 1750-1850*, 1997, pp.180-190.
4   Wylliams, *Account*, Appendix p.17-18.

I have debarked fifteen thousand elite troops of the army and fleet, and the rapidity with which your exterior defences have fallen, you have proven the infallibility of my later success. Many more ships of the line are arriving at Barbados to reinforce the land and sea armies and I expect a greater advantage. Further resistance is useless.[5]

Rochambeau swiftly drafted a refusal and handed it to his aide-de-camp Colonel Rivecourt to deliver to Grey. Rivecourt and an escort rode out from République-ville to the Heights of Sourrière to deliver the letter, but returned a short time later, both men wounded and with dying horses. They had been shot at by British piquets before even reaching the enemy lines. The escort later died and Rivecourt lost an arm.[6] Since the laws of war dictated a response should be received, Rochambeau drafted another response on 20 February, and sent it with Commandant Naverres to Jervis aboard HMS *Boyne* under a flag of truce. Rochambeau's terms of capitulation stated that the island would be handed over to the British, on the condition that it would then be delivered to whomsoever took power in France – be it a new King or a Republican government.[7] Grey would not brook such terms. '[I] came expressly to take this island for his Britannic Majesty,' he replied, and that he 'hoped to take all the French islands in this quarter on the same account'.[8] He recommended that Rochambeau point out to his garrisons the weakness of their situation, and Naverres was despatched back to Rochambeau.

Now Grey reckoned upon a siege. The following day Naverres returned again advising that the garrison would defend the honour of the Republic to the last. Grey wrote again, expressing his pain at the obstinacy of the garrison. The traditional laws of war, at least as practised in Europe, dictated that a plainly surrounded force was duty-bound to surrender with honour once they had clearly made a show of resistance. But the traditional laws of war did not apply to the new French Republic. Rochambeau and the Committee were clearly aware that the guillotine awaited them at home if they capitulated. Grey had good reason to be nervous. Time was ticking away, and the fever season was getting closer. And there were still two more islands to capture.

The following day, the final act opened at eleven in the morning, when the French guns in République-ville recommenced firing. Royal Navy gunboats returned fire but were required to sheer off once the fire from the fort became too hot to bear. Grey consolidated all of his forces around the siege-works. The north of the island being secured, Dundas shipped his troops south, having left Colonel William Myers and the 58th and 65th Foot to garrison Saint Pierre. The

---

5   Quoted in Haynsworth, *Career*, p.490.
6   Rochambeau Journal, entry for 19 February 1794, in Haynsworth, *Career*, p.491.
7   Rochambeau Journal, entry for 19 February 1794, in Haynsworth, *Career*, p.491.
8   Quoted in Haynsworth, *Career*, p.492.

The Royal Navy in action against Forts Bourbon and Louis (République and Convention). (Anne SK Brown Collection)

grenadiers were encamped on the Heights of Sourrière, where Lieutenant General Prescott exercised local ground command, and the light infantry at La Coste, west of République-ville, which Dundas commanded. Grey marched the 6th and 9th Foot, his staff, and all the artillery to Sourrière, leaving only a token garrison on Morne le Brun. The 15th and 70th Foot were stationed inside Fort Mathilde to cover the landing-place at Cohé du Lamentin. The next few days were spent in the landing of heavy artillery, courtesy of Captain Schank's boats again, and the construction of batteries to invest Fort de la Convention and Fort de la République. Every artilleryman, engineer, and artificer with the force was put to work, assisted by three hundred seamen from the fleet superintended by Lieutenants Hervey, Kelly, and Carpenter. For four days, hundreds of men constructed four miles of road through dense jungle, built a bridge, and then forded a stream, all to aid in the man-handling of heavy cannon for the reduction of République-ville. It was dangerous work. The valiant Lieutenant James Milne, commanding one of the companies of seamen constructing batteries, lost both his legs to a French shell on 22 February. One was severed on impact and the other so shattered as to require amputation. He lingered in pain for several weeks and was able to briefly enjoy Jervis's reward of promotion to master and commander before dying of lock-jaw on 9 March.[9] Grey gave orders that the seamen should be 'amply supplied with

9   James, *Journal*, p.234.

provisions and rum'[10] for their services, suggesting perhaps that the land-bound commissary generally favoured the army in such matters. In any event, the spirit of co-operation between the army and the navy continued to be outstanding.

The topic of rum requires some consideration at this point, since it was a plentiful commodity on these islands. At the last British invasion of Martinique in 1762, the Earl of Albemarle had written that, 'upon my arrival here I found the troops very Sickly, and many dead, and the Sick list increasing dayly, chiefly owing to the bad rum they got on shore'.[11] The year before a battalion commander had written from Dominica; 'The Excessive heat… hath putt me under the Necessitie of giving a Gill of rum each day to each private Man… I was advised it was Necessary to the Mens healths..'.[12] It is quite possible that Grey's men spent portions of each day drunk, and very likely that they drank little water. By 1794 the medical opinion of rum had not altered since 1762, there being the belief that the drink was beneficial to Europeans in extremes of climate, hot or cold. Dehydrated men were much more susceptible to disease and exhaustion.

Everything was not well inside the French forts. The treasury had run out of money again, and the Committee ordered the town of République-ville to hand over all the money received from the sale of émigré estates. On 22 February Rochambeau refused to allow the civilians of République-ville to shelter within Fort de la République, an act which horrified the citizenry.[13] The fort was already over-crowded, and receiving most of the attention from the British artillery, so was in fact more dangerous than the town. An incident broke out on 15 February within Fort Saint-Louis that ended with the execution of a certain Elijah, one of Bellegarde's mulatto militia, a man of English origin, and the imprisonment of Pierre Millet, a coloured captain in the National Guard. Rochambeau later claimed that, egged on by Bellegarde and Pelauque, they wanted to murder the white commander and thus take command of the fort.

Relations between Rochambeau and Bellegarde had fallen to an all-time low. Thus it is no surprise that on 28 February Louis Bellegarde and his mulatto force of 240 men, locked out of Fort de la Convention, staged a sham attack on the Dillon plantation, then immediately surrendered to Grey on the condition that they would be granted safe passage to America. It is very likely that they had just received word of a decree issued by the National Convention in Paris on 4 February; 'The National Convention declares the abolition of Negro slavery in all the colonies; in consequence it decrees that all men, without distinction of colour, residing in the colonies are French citizens and will enjoy all the rights assured

---

10 Wylliams, *Account*, Appendix p.20.
11 Paul E. Kopperman, '"The Cheapest Pay": Alcohol Abuse in the Eighteenth-Century British Army', *The Journal of Military History* Vol. 60 No. 3 (1996), p.453.
12 Kopperman, '"The Cheapest Pay"', p.466.
13 Rochambeau Journal, entry of 22 February 1794, in Haynsworth, *Career*, p.497.

by the constitution'.[14] Rochambeau believed that Bellegarde had been paid to surrender. '200,000 livres have sufficed to determine this traitor,' he wrote in his journal. And later, having decided that none of the 1er Chasseurs could enter the fort, 'they can go to Hell'.[15]

Bellegarde had no friends left on the Republican side, and had been swayed to believe that he would be well-treated by the British. However only Bellegarde, his secretary Jean-Marie Pelauque and eight *gens de couleur* of Bellegarde's inner circle were granted safe passage to America on 4 March, on the condition he would never again bear arms against the Crown. The rest of his motley force had been disarmed and made prisoners of war, marched on board ship on 1 March during which 30 attempted to escape before boarding. Troops opened fire, resulting in '2 of them killed and 2 of our own Blacks by Mistake',[16] as Captain George Nares laconically recorded in his diary. It seems that Bellegarde ended up in Boston, where he had earlier sent items of wealth as a safeguard should he ever be exiled. Once in that town, some French crewmen in port recognised him and chased him as a regarded traitor. He sought safety with the French Consul and boarded an American ship bound for France later in the year, only to be captured in the mid-Atlantic by a squadron commanded by Lord Howe. His ultimate fate is unclear.

The back-breaking work of constructing the batteries must have been tedious in the extreme, especially for the seamen and artillerymen. Any diversion must have been welcome; such it was that two gunners, Alexander Ross of the Royal Artillery and Edward Brookes of the Royal Irish Artillery absented themselves from Gros Morne and were later rounded up on the suspicion of having robbed a washer-woman and a certain Madame Lamalle. They were found guilty of absenting their posts, but acquitted of robbery, and given 400 lashes each on 29 February in front of the assembled men of their regiments. Grey later commented that he felt the men were probably guilty of the robberies – in which case the punishment would have been death – but that they got off due to a lack of evidence. Another prisoner, private John Phelps of the 40th Foot, was sentenced to 800 lashes by the same court-martial, but Grey later pardoned him in consideration of the time he had been locked up, and hoped 'this instance of lenity [sic] will make a deep and lasting impression on [Phelps'] mind, and induce him to behave like a good and faithful British soldier to his king and country in future'.[17]

'I did hope before this time to have sent off this letter, with an account that Bourbon or Fort Constitution was ours,' Thomas Dundas wrote at the start of March, 'but a committee of safety from my good town of St. Pierre has got into it,

14 Edward Baines, *History of the Wars of the French Revolution: From the Breaking Out of the War in 1792 to the Restoration of a General Peace in 1815; Comprehending the Civil History of Great Britain and France During that Period* (London: H. Light, 1823), Vol.I, p.278.
15 Rochambeau Journal, entry of 28 February 1794, in Haynsworth, *Career*, p.503.
16 Nares, Camp Diary.
17 Wylliams, *Account*, Appendix pp.23-24.

and have encouraged the garrison to hold out'.[18] About the same time, Jean-Louis Sancé, the French emigrant serving as an engineer officer to Grey, wrote to the commander of Fort de la République on behalf of Grey:

> I know the person named Genty has made movements in Fort Royal to cause fires in neighbouring houses in the city. I have the honour to inform you that all the constituted authorities will be responsible on their heads for all the disorders that may occur both in the city than in the country; and you know the torment of fire is the punishment reserved for arsonists.[19]

Rochambeau's diary entries make it clear that he knew the writing was on the wall. 'Another reason I hold on to the last is because the men know it is I who can conclude a peace with the enemy that will ensure conditions (of surrender) are advantageous to them'. But he was determined never to allow Grey's men into the forts. 'I will never let those rascals in', he wrote tersely.[20]

The presence of Grey's force in a tight noose around République-ville did not preclude the presence of scattered French and mulatto 'brigands' on other parts of the island, perhaps emboldened by the National Convention's abolition of slavery. In the early morning of 4 March a party of such set fire to the village of Le Francois on the east coast, having allegedly been 'burning, plundering and murdering wherever they went' for some time.[21] Captain John Conyngham, Grey's aide, led Captain Charles, Lord Sinclair with a detachment of the 15th Foot and two companies of the 6th Foot, aided by Lieutenant James Shadwell of the 10th Light Dragoons, to a surprise attack on the plunderers, possibly laid low by liquor and therefore off their guard. In the melee some thirty-six were despatched, including their leader. Four men taken prisoner were hanged in the town square to discourage the others. The attackers suffered only two men wounded, and the remainder soon put out the fires. At least it had given the cavalry something to do in a campaign otherwise dominated by narrow trails, thick jungle, and mountainous terrain. 'This spirited action, which scarcely cost us a man,' Captain William Stewart recorded, 'gave a finishing-blow to the disturbances in the islands among the negroes and mulattoes, who hereafter conceived a dreadful idea of our activity and of our small corps of cavalry.'[22]

---

18 Dundas (ed.), *Dundas of Fingask*, p.114.
19 GRE/A218, Copy letter from Grey to Lieut.-Gen. Rochambeau, 21 February 1794. Expressing pain at the obstinacy of his garrisons.
20 Rochambeau Journal, entry of 3 March 1794, in Haynsworth, *Career*, p.508.
21 Robert John Jones, *A History of the 15th (East Yorkshire) Regiment, the Duke of York's Own, 1685 to 1914* (Beverley: East Yorkshire Regimental Association, 1964), p.245.
22 Anon, *Cumloden Papers*, pp.5-6.

His Royal Highness Prince Edward, the fourth son of King George III, a balding twenty-six-year-old major general, self-conscious and preening, arrived on Martinique on 5 March, having sailed from Halifax, Nova Scotia. He assumed command of Sir Charles Gordon's division. Grey also gave him command of all troops investing Fort de la Convention on the western side, including the camp at La Coste. 'Yesterday H.R. Highness Prince Edward arrived in this camp from Canada via Boston,' Thomas Dundas wrote the next day. 'Sir Charles has sent him to command here; and I have every reason to think that he will do very well, being disposed to do everything in his power. I find my duty easier, and Sir Charles Gordon and I carry on the laborious part of the duty'.[23] The Prince was undoubtedly earnest but his inexperience probably showed, for as Dundas observed five days later, 'the Prince is pains-taking, and now knows the sound of a cannon ball'.[24]

Although March was traditionally the driest month of the year, 1794 saw an unseasonably high rainfall on Martinique, which slowed construction work on the batteries to a crawl, particularly around the middle of the month. 'The Commander in Chief observes that soldiers do not dig a trench round their tents to carry off the wet,' Grey observed, 'the commanding officers of regiments and corps to order it to be done immediately'.[25] In the main though, the army was still healthy. Thomas Dundas put his robust state of health down to the adoption of flannel under-clothes. 'To wearing flannel I attribute the health of this army,' he wrote home on 8 March. 'I never wear linen, and some flannel shirts, and 20 yards fine flannel is the greatest present you can send me, it will soon be scarce in these parts'.[26] Flannel is a poor conductor of heat and an efficient absorber of sweat, and Dundas seems to have been adhering to the local knowledge of Europeans in hot climes. Although laughable today, medical theory at the times was that flannel kept the skin at a more or less even temperature, and prevented the chills caused by heavy perspiration on cotton or linen. Taking off the thick woollen red or blue uniform coats over the top would have been far better of course, but such actions were unthinkable for officers and soldiers generally. Only the Royal Navy seamen, who got about in whatever was comfortable, had the liberty to strip down to bare torsos and feet. Not that Royal Navy officers suffered laxness; merely that they had a far better appreciation of how to operate in tropical conditions. Captain Josias Rogers thought cleanliness in a hot climate an important consideration, and ordered his subordinates to instruct the seamen not on duty to bathe in the sea each day, but not for more than five minutes.[27]

---

23   Dundas (ed.), *Dundas of Fingask*, p.116.
24   Dundas (ed.), *Dundas of Fingask*, p.116.
25   Wyllyams, *Account,* Appendix, p.25.
26   Dundas (ed.), *Dundas of Fingask*, p.120.
27   William Gilpin, *Memoirs of Josias Rogers, Esq. commander of His Majesty's Ship Quebec* (London: T. Cadell and W. Davies, 1808), p.111.

The morning of Thursday 6 March, exactly one month since the landings, marked the readiness of Grey's batteries to commence the bombardment of Fort de la Convention. As was customary, Grey sent an officer under a flag of truce to invite Rochambeau to capitulate before the firing started. In his equally customary fashion, Rochambeau refused. Daybreak on 7 March thundered as sixteen batteries, all located less than eight hundred metres from the fort, commenced an incessant bombardment. Artillerymen and seamen in shifts laboured to keep the red-hot cannon firing by day and night. That was just on land. The gun-vessels constructed on Barbados commanded by Lieutenant Richard Bowen RN and the bomb ketch HMS *Vesuvius* maintained a fire from the bay as well. An interior wall within Fort de la Convention collapsed and fell, killing and wounding nearly fifty defenders. The Republicans carried out repairs at night, when the incoming fire was less hot. On the morning of 9 March a mortar round fired into Fort de la République ignited a powder barrel, which exploded thirty bombs, killing all the sailors manning guns nearby.[28]

Any combatant under the stress of constant cannonade usually feels the need to let off some steam by getting their own back. Thus it was on the night of 9 March that a sortie by French troops towards La Coste surprised sentries from the 3rd Light Infantry and seamen from HMS *Zebra*. A nasty little hand-to-hand fight broke out, in which the British lost thirty men killed and wounded, before the French retreated back to the fort having suffered few casualties. It was the single bloodiest event during the siege for Grey's force. The commander of the *Zebra*, Robert Faulknor, was a brave man; we met him previously as the first vessel to make enemy contact at the Baie du Galion. Faulknor was a 31-year-old from Northampton, a sailor for twenty years. He had one fault, his own freely-admitted 'unfortunate rashness and impetuosity'.[29] On 13 March, during his rounds of the shore batteries, a quartermaster of HMS *Boyne* made a contemptuous comment about Faulknor's placement of the batteries. Heated words were exchanged which resulted in Faulknor running the man through with his sword. The dead man's bloody jacket was sent on board the *Boyne* as a signal of discontent, and Faulknor's own seamen working on the battery immediately refused to serve under him. Outright mutiny was only averted by the intercession of Captain Rogers and others. Jervis immediately ordered a court-martial and placed Faulknor below decks on the *Zebra* in a state of arrest. Robert Faulknor was acquitted, stating on his honour that he had been provoked. 'For my own fate,' he wrote to a brother officer, 'than (for) that of being accessory to the death of any human being not the natural enemy of myself or my country… the hasty and sudden punishment I

---

28 Rochambeau Journal, entry for 8 March 1794, in Haynsworth, *Career*, p.512.
29 Quoted in James Ralfe, *The Naval Biography of Great Britain: Consisting of Historical Memoirs of Those Officers of the British Navy who Distinguished Themselves During the Reign of His Majesty George III* (London: Whitmore &Fenn, 1828), p.314.

unhappily inflicted on the spot will be a source of lasting affliction to my mind'.[30] He became morose and withdrawn, stayed on board ship, brooding, looking for a hazardous duty to help clear his name and reputation.

The popular and ever-cheerful Josias Rogers on the other hand spent much time ashore overseeing the construction of a battery by his seamen. He used up a few of his nine lives during the campaign, none more so when, making a round of the defences one evening in the company of his aide, Ensign Lord William Townshend, they happened upon a French patrol. One of the Frenchmen fired his musket, which misfired. Knowing that to turn and run would invite pursuit, Rogers and Townshend rushed at the firer as if they had men behind them in support, at which point the Frenchmen fled, leaving Rogers and Townshend wide-eyed and laughing. Dodging French artillery rounds during the battery-building process, Rogers nonetheless lost fourteen men to enemy fire, three in one shocking incident when a red-hot shot from the fort struck some gunpowder, blowing the men sky-high and blasting one of them into an unrecognisable mass of flesh.

Things were no less hazardous inside Fort de la Convention. Rochambeau's diary recorded the loss of his artillery commander due to a grisly event on 14 March. 'Colonel le Mestre of the artillery had his head taken off by a cannon ball. I was covered in his blood and I had a slight bruise of the heel… He was day and night on the ramparts… He leaves a wife and two children. The republic should take care of them and give them a pension because this brave man had no fortune at all except his talents, his courage and his qualities'.[31] Rochambeau had by this time just refused Grey and Jervis's offer to surrender dated 12 March, noting in his journal that 'I will defend myself in a manner to deserve the estimation of the English generals and troops'.[32] In response, Grey increased the volume of bombardment. Rochambeau's losses were high. 'I have one-sixth of my regulars out of the firing line, and another one-sixth sick with dysentery, so that the number of defenders has been reduced by a third'.[33] The garrison was also starting to starve. On 13 March Lieutenant-Colonel Saint-Frémont and a party of volunteers rowed across République-ville Bay aiming to acquire some cattle from a nearby coastal plantation. The Royal Navy was alert and soon had them rowing frantically back to Fort de la République under a rain of shot and shell.[34]

'The whole Sky is illumin'd with these Travelling Globes of Light,' Captain Nares recorded in his diary after witnessing the bombardment at night, 'and the Scene would have been considered as transcendently beautiful could the Mind have lost the Reflection that the Objects of its Admiration were invented and intended for

30 Ralfe, *Naval Biography*, p.314.
31 Rochambeau Journal, entry of 12 March 1794, in Haynsworth, *Career*, p.515.
32 Rochambeau Journal, entry of 12 March 1794, in Haynsworth, *Career*, p.513.
33 Rochambeau Journal, entry of 12 March 1794, in Haynsworth, *Career*, p.513.
34 Rochambeau Journal, entry of 13 March 1794, in Haynsworth, *Career*, p.517.

the Destruction of Mankind'.[35] The fact that the batteries worked night and day did not lessen the work-load of the seamen, who were charged with cutting saps so that guns could be advanced closer to the fort. By Monday 17 March two new batteries had been constructed at Point Carriere, on a neck of land about two hundred metres across the water from Fort Saint Louis, commanded by Captain Edward Riou of HMS *Rose*. Riou was a 31-year-old who had once sailed with Captain Cook and had survived a collision with an iceberg in the Indian Ocean five years previously. Out in the bay were the gun vessels commanded by Lieutenant Bowen. A French flûte, *Bienvenue*, was chained to the walls of Fort de la République;[36] the ship was rumoured to hold a number of captured English prisoners, whom the French would kill by blowing up the ship should the British attempt to storm the fort. Jervis ordered Bowen to prepare an assault on the flûte. Bowen led an assault force consisting of HMS *Boyne*'s barge and several small boats. The boats sailed up to the flûte at speed, and under a hail of musket-balls from infantry in the fort, where the boarding party stormed her successfully, killing and dispersing all of her crew. Only some thirteen were taken prisoner, including the captain. But there were no British prisoners aboard. They were in another vessel further up the inlet. In frustration, Bowen manned the flûte's cannons and fired a broadside into the fort. But despite a serious effort, Bowen and his men could not cut the mooring chains to manoeuvre *Bienvenue* out of the harbour. An unsuccessful attempt by a British tar to strike the flûte's tricolor was met with jeers from the fort. Bowen eventually gave up and sailed his prisoners to the *Boyne* in longboats, having lost three sailors killed and five wounded.[37]

Jervis was delighted. He mentioned Bowen in despatches, and later gave him command of HMS *Zebra*, Faulknor's old ship, with the new rank of master and commander. But most of all he, and Grey, could now see that a combined land and naval assault on Fort de la République could succeed. The French defences had been tested, and did not amount to all that much. Jervis ordered that his seamen construct scaling ladders from bamboo poles and rope, and started to assemble a fleet of gunboats and row-boats just out of French sight at Point de la Carriere under the command of Commodore Thompson. Prince Edward's infantry division at La Coste and Case Navire was put on notice to be ready for an imminent attack. Major General Thomas Dundas was still at La Coste, quietly watching the progress of HRH Prince Edward and his growing entourage. 'The Prince goes on quietly doing what he is bid, yet sometimes thinking himself the great general', he wrote to his wife, 'which he cannot yet be. My little friend Sir Charles Gordon encourages him a good deal, attending his rounds and laying it on, which is

---

35 Nares, Camp Diary.
36 Flûtes were vessels partially disarmed to serve as transports, typically rated by the Royal Navy (when captured) as sixth-rate frigates.
37 Captain William Stewart in his journal recorded Bowen as having lost '13 or 14 of his party'.

wrong. I have requested the Prince to lessen his suite on account of the men, it attracts fire and does no good'[38] The troops of his division were kept busy; on 19 March Captain Stewart's grenadiers were engaged flushing brigands out of a fort atop Morne Tartenson, a commanding spot which overlooked British batteries. The action cost three officers wounded, including Prince Edward's aide, Captain Frederick Wetherall, and 60 other ranks killed and wounded.[39]

Grey penned his first dispatch of the campaign on Sunday 16 March, summarising the campaign to date and lamenting the death of Blythswood Campbell. It arrived at Whitehall a month later, but, containing no news of victories, caused no particular stir. Pen in hand, Grey also wrote privately to Henry Dundas, asking for more troops, and in particular, more medicines, the number of sick having started to escalate.[40] There was now some urgency to complete the conquest, and perhaps capture the hospital in République-ville. Thomas Dundas had, a week earlier, suggested to Grey and Jervis a plan to take the town and hospital;

> Three hundred yards in front of the L[igh]t Infantry under a battery is their hospital, the town of Fort Royal joins it, and Bourbon is distant by a winding road about one thousand yards. When we took this post the General and Admiral did, by my suggestion, send a flag saying that now their town, their women, their children, their sick and wounded were at our mercy, they might have reasonable terms, otherwise all must be laid in ashes. They debated ten hours, and at last sent answer that they were attacked by a generous enemy, and that they should defend the fort in a manner to merit our esteem. ... [A]lthough we have it in our power, (yet) no mischief has been done to them. We can burn the town and save the hospital, and the town is full of supplies for our enemy. Our General and Admiral have too much mercy for these unmerciful rascals who sacrifice their wretched families and sick to save themselves.[41]

In fact, the curate, surgeon and apothecary of the hospital gave themselves up to the British on 12 March, letting Grey know that his batteries had killed 50 and wounded 100 of the fort's defenders since the batteries opened. Unbeknownst to Jervis and Grey, Rochambeau had received a rumour than the British intended to burn him out of the town. Leaving the hospital occupied seemed the best way of ensuring such a thing could not happen. In truth, the use of incendiary rounds against Fort de la République commenced sometime around 16 March; they were

---

38 Dundas (ed.), *Dundas of Fingask*, pp.122-123.
39 Anon. *Cumloden Papers*, p.6.
40 See dispatch in *The Gentleman's Magazine*, Vol. 75, 1794, p.372; private letter in GRE/A2243f, Grey to Henry Dundas, concerning the attack on Fort Bourbon, the need for reinforcements and medicines, and praise of Prince Edward and Major General Dundas.
41 GRE/A2243f, Grey to Henry Dundas.

used at the behest of Prince Edward in an attempt to speed up the capitulation, despite Jervis' earlier request not to set the town on fire. The Admiral had written on the topic to Josias Rogers on 17 March. 'We have a plan for taking possession of Fort Royal [République-ville] and Fort Saint Louis [Fort de la République] by the seamen in boats at night. I trust therefore it is not in the contemplation of any, on your side, to set the town on fire. If such an event should happen, the conquest will lose half its value'.[42]

Rochambeau now knew the end was near. In a bitter letter to the National Convention, he wrote, 'read to your remorse, citizens, and reflect on the enormous crime that you have committed by loosely abandoning the loyal citizens of our law'.[43] He also asked for 4,500 troops to hold the island, certainly knowing that they could never arrive in time. By 19 March, Grey had fifteen batteries ringed around République-ville. Two large batteries on Morne Tartanson to the west of the town bombarded the Ville and Fort de la République, as did a sixteen-gun battery to the north-west of town, near the hospital, all under the command of Captain de Ruvijnes of the Royal Artillery. An eight-gun battery at Vanier threatened the town from the east, and Fort de la République was also bombarded by two smaller batteries positioned on the Pointe de la Carrières, as well as by HMS *Vesuvius* out in the harbour. Nine batteries hammered Fort de la Convention from the west and north, where the ground was higher. There were three batteries on the Morne Patatte, part of the eastwards Catherine Heights, and six batteries from the heights of Sourrière, the closest of which was five 24-pounders manned by seamen barely two hundred yards from the northern bastion of the fort. Midshipman Hoffman picturesquely tells of this dangerous post:

> A party of sailors who had the management of it under a lieutenant and three midshipmen, christened it by a name that would shock ladies' ears. When the enemy's shot fired at them were not too deeply entrenched in the ground, they dug them up and returned them, the middies first writing on them in chalk the names of those quack doctors who sold pills as a remedy for all complaints.[44]

Thus it was that fifty cannons (mostly 24-pounders), 23 howitzers, and 16 mortars poured shot and shell into the town and two fortresses day and night. Captains Harvey, Kelly, Rogers, Salisbury, Incledon, Riou, Lord Garlies, Carpenter, Scott, and Bayntun of the Royal Navy had all commanded shore parties that had undertaken the bulk of the hard work. Grey believed the garrisons could not hold out much longer. 'We regret the sad necessity! But in your refusal the town and Fort

---

42   Gilpin, *Memoirs of Josias Rogers*, p.119.
43   Haynsworth, 'Donatien Rochambeau and The Defence of Martinique, 1793-1794', pp.180-190.
44   Hoffman, *Sailor of King George*, pp.20-21.

Saint Louis [République] must immediately be reduced to ashes,' Grey had written to Rochambeau on 12 March. 'It behoves you therefore to provide for the helpless sick and wounded, the women and children. For which this dreadful calamity will rest with you alone. You well know Fort Bourbon [Convention] must fall'.[45] It was time to close the game.

Fort de la République had to fall first, so that the Royal Navy could obtain an anchorage at République-ville. Therefore, the plan was primarily a naval affair, involving Commodore Thompson on the west side of Fort Saint Louis, and Captain Rogers on the eastern side, as commanders on the water. The artillerymen kept up a heavy and constant fire on Fort de la Convention all day on the 19th and into the night, to discourage any Frenchmen from reinforcing their brothers down on the docks. Then at ten o'clock in the morning of Thursday 20 March, the cannonade suddenly stopped as the man-of-war HMS *Asia* of 64 guns under Captain John Brown, supported by the HMS *Zebra* with the desperate Robert Faulknor in command, rounded the heads into the harbour, making straight for the fort. Both ships were in range of, and feeling the effects of, grape-shot from the fort when the *Asia* suddenly wore and sailed back to the squadron. Assuming that Captain Brown had been killed, Jervis despatched Captain George Grey of the *Boyne* to see what the matter was. Grey returned to say that not a man on board the *Asia* had been hurt, and that the ship was going in again: this she did, and again turned about. 'This combination succeeded in every part, except the entrance of the *Asia*', Jervis later wrote, 'which failed for want of precision in the ancient lieutenant of the port, Monsieur de Tourelles, who had undertaken to pilot the *Asia*'.[46]

Evidently M. de Tourelles got cold feet and refused to pilot the ship in, blaming an alleged dread of shoals, but more likely a real dread of what he might expect should any event place him in the hands of General Rochambeau.[47] Faulknor, thinking that he would have to wait for the *Asia* to take the credit, saw his chance. Sick and tired of being bombarded whilst bobbing in the harbour waiting for the *Asia* to do something, he took matters into his own hands. Fuelled by the courage of a desperate man, the *Zebra* sailed in hard to the fort – all his men below decks to maintain surprise – saving her fire to the last minutes, then ran aground hard up against the walls of the fort. As soon as she had, the rest of the attacking fleet 'seemed to fly towards the scene of the action'.[48] Faulknor and his crewmen spilled ashore, Faulknor at the head, yelling. He 'attempted to achieve with eighteen guns,

---

45 GRE/A230, Copy letter from Grey and Jervis (St. Vincent) to Lieut.-Gen. Rochambeau, the Mayor, President of the Municipalities, and citizens of Fort Royal, 12 March 1794. Calling for the surrender of Forts Bourbon and St. Louis and the town of Fort Royal.
46 Anon., *Bulletins and Other State Intelligence*, 1794, p.129.
47 James, *Naval History*, Vol.1, p.218.
48 Wyllyams, *Account*, p.67.

what the force of eighty was only thought equal to',[49] and described the events of that day in a letter to his mother dated 25 March;

> I had a ship's cartouch-box, which is made of thick wood, buckled round my body, with pistol cartridges in it for the pistol I carried by my side. As the *Zebra* came close to the fort, a grape-shot struck, or rather grazed, my right-hand knuckle, and shattered the cartouch in the centre of my body; had it not miraculously been there, I must have been killed on the spot – thanks to Almighty God for his kind preservation of me in the day of battle! The admiral has appointed me to the *Rose*, paying me such compliments, that it is impossible for me to relate them. The sword and colours of Fort Royal were delivered to me by the governor of the fort: and I take some credit to myself, that after the *Zebra* had stood a heavy fire, and when We had power to retaliate, for we were mounted upon the walls, I would not allow a man to be hurt, on their being panic-struck and calling for mercy. It would take a volume to relate the events which have happened to me since I left England. The *Zebra*, when she came out of action, was cheered by the admiral's ship; and the admiral himself publicly embraced me on the quarter-deck, and directed the band to play, 'See, the conquering hero comes'. Such compliments are without example in the navy – I never could have deserved them.[50]

Jervis gave the gallant Faulknor great credit in his later dispatch:

> Captain Faulknor observing that ship baffled in her attempts, and the *Zebra* having been under a shower of grapeshot for a great length of time (which he, his officers, and sloop's company stood with a firmness not to be described), he determined to undertake the service alone; and he executed it with matchless intrepidity and conduct, running the *Zebra* close to the wall of the fort, and, leaping overboard at the head of his sloop's company, assailed and took this important post before the boats could get on shore, although they rowed with all the force and animation which characterize English seamen in the face of an enemy.[51]

Midshipman Hoffman was also witness to the gallant scene:

> The gun and flat-bottomed boats were covered by the bomb-ships and frigates. A landing was soon effected; the bamboo ladders for two men

---

49 Gilpin, *Memoirs of Josias Rogers*, p.122.
50 *The Naval Chronicle,* Vol. 16, 1806, p.33.
51 Southley, *Chronological History of the West Indies,* Vol. III, p.80.

to mount abreast were placed against the outer bastion of the fort. The soldiers and sailors vied with each other who should mount first. Unfortunately, some of the ladders gave way, and the men were precipitated to the ground; and, what was still more unfortunate, some few fell on the bayonets of those below and were shockingly wounded. In about ten minutes the outer works were carried, and a marine's jacket, for want of other colours, was hoisted on the flagstaff. The enemy retreated to the inner work, but it availed them little. In less than a quarter of an hour they were compelled to give way. Several of them were cut down by the sailors, who had thrown away their pistols after discharging them. Most of them had abandoned their half-pikes before mounting, as they declared they were only in their way, and that they preferred the honest cutlass to any other weapon. The sailors and soldiers behaved well on this occasion; those who did not form the escalade covered those who did by firing incessant volleys of musketry, which brought down those of the enemy who were unwise enough to show their unlucky heads above the parapet. In about twenty minutes the British flags were floating on the flagstaffs, the French officers surrendered their swords, and were sent on board the *Boyne*.[52]

A second storming party, seamen from the camp at Pointe Negro under Captain Rogers, landed at the edge of the Ville and flooded into the town, supported by Stewart's 1st Grenadiers and Close's 3rd Light Infantry, whilst Coote's 1st Light Infantry poured musketry into the roadway and bridge which linked the town to Fort de la Convention. Coote effectively shut the back door. No Frenchman in the town was going to escape to the big fort on the hill. Captain Charles Edmund Nugent RN was the second person on the walls of the fort. The sailors hauled down the French tricolour and ran up the Union Jack as the defenders streamed northwards towards Fort de la Convention, only to find the covered road linking the two in the hands of Coote's 1st Light Infantry. Colonel Richard Symes led the assault on the western side of the town, captured the *Hôtel de Ville* and placed the National Guard commander under arrest. Rochambeau was nowhere to be found. He had escaped to Fort de la Convention. Jervis, with Grey's consent, gave Captain Nugent command of Fort de la République, but the capture had been achieved at some cost. Hoffman recorded:

> I forgot to mention that an explosion had taken place in one of the magazines of the fort before we entered it, which killed and wounded more than fifty of the enemy. About ninety of the enemy were killed and more than twenty wounded. We had forty-six killed and wounded; among the

52 Hoffman, *A Sailor of King George*, p.28.

The valiant Captain Robert Faulknor leads HMS *Zebra* to glory at Fort de la République. His death the following year robbed the Royal Navy of a fine officer. (Anne SK Brown Collection)

number were eleven officers. We found in the harbour a frigate of thirty-six guns and a corvette fitted up as a receiving ship for the wounded.[53]

What is remarkable is that there does not seem to have been any undisciplined ransacking or looting of the town, something British armies much later in the war would become notorious for. This is evidenced by Hoffman's matter-of-fact description of the aftermath. 'Several merchant ships, loading with sugar when we first entered the bay, had relanded their cargoes. The warehouses were more than half filled with sugar, rum and coffee. A party of seamen were immediately employed to load the shipping'.[54]

When later asked why he did not court-martial Captain Brown, Jervis replied, 'I thought it best to let him go home quietly'. That Brown did, only to be given command of a larger ship, HMS *Victorious*. The now-captured *Bienvenue* was

---

53 Hoffman, *A Sailor of King George*, p.28.
54 Hoffman, *A Sailor of King George*, p.28.

re-christened HMS *Undaunted*, and Robert Faulknor promoted to become her new captain. Jervis also saw that Thomas Rogers, Josias Rogers' brother, was promoted to captain before the fall of Fort de la Convention to allow him to share in the potential prize-money of that rank. Commodore Charles Thompson received no specific reward but was in fact only three weeks away from being promoted to rear-admiral of the blue on account of his seniority within the service.

With the harbour and town gone, Rochambeau had no hope of resupply. He penned a letter to Grey immediately, informing him that the troops under his command asked for an honourable capitulation, and asking Grey to name three commissioners to treat on the subject. He gave the message to Major Naverres to transmit, and wrote in his diary, 'we can only hope that we are treated favourably'.[55] He also dashed off a letter to the municipality of République-ville stating that he had 'in compliance with the repeated entreaties of the garrisons and the people of République-ville, sent a flag of truce to Grey'.[56] Grey nominated Commodore Charles Thompson, Colonel Richard Symes, and Captain John Conyngham as his commissioners. Rochambeau selected Colonel d'Aucourt, Captain Dupriret, and Lieutenant Colonel Gaschet-Dumaine junior. The articles of capitulation were discussed and agreed at Madame Dillon's house in République-ville. The garrison were to be permitted to march out of Fort de la Convention with colours flying and their arms, but were to lay the latter down at a nominated place, except the officers, who were permitted to keep their swords. They would then be granted transport by sea back to France after signing paroles by which they agreed not to take up arms against His Britannic Majesty again during the war. Local National Guardsmen not deemed dangerous would be permitted to stay. Rochambeau and his staff were to be provided with a separate frigate in which to return to France. Fearing retribution in Paris, he chose Philadelphia, a city he knew well, as his preferred destination instead. Grey and Jervis were well aware of what Rochambeau could expect if returned to France, and it was Grey who offered the American option. Rochambeau arrived in that city in the second week of April sick with scurvy, but soon recovered. With him went his mistress, a certain Madame de Tully. He despatched a detailed report to Paris in the care of Major Naverres, then established a temporary residence in Newport, Rhode Island.

Thomas Dundas was jubilant. He wrote to his wife on 22 March. 'The Prince has just received orders to take possession of the gates with the Grenadiers and L[igh]t. Infantry. He sends me a request to go with him, and Murphy is off to find a white shirt if possible, as I have not used one these 6 weeks – ragged and tough we look like Falstaff's Corps, but good stuff!'[57] HRH Prince Edward did indeed take possession of the fort at three o'clock in the afternoon of 23 March with the 1st and 3rd

---

55   Rochambeau Journal, entry for 21 March 1794, in Haynsworth, *Career*, p.535.
56   Haynsworth, 'Donatien Rochambeau and The Defence of Martinique, 1793-1794', pp.180-190.
57   Dundas (ed.), *Dundas of Fingask*, p.127.

The storming of Fort Royal on 24 March 1794. The uniform details are probably incorrect. (Anne SK Brown Collection)

battalions of the grenadiers and light infantry. The fort was re-named Fort Edward in his honour and the Union flag was hoisted and given three hearty cheers. Two days later the garrison marched out and stacked their arms, the much-reduced remnant of the 37e Regiment d'Infanterie (formerly de Turenne) leading, followed by *gens de couleur*, half-naked and half-starved. 'I must not forget to mention here that there were three ladies marched out of the fort when it surrendered,' Captain William Stewart recorded, 'who had never quitted it during the siege – Madame le Meister, the wife of the engineer who was killed; Madame de Thulie; and another lady, who belonged to Rochambeau's family.'[58] Some 600 men and their families boarded ships bound for France.

Sir Charles Grey wrote his victory dispatch on Tuesday 25 March. He declared himself 'inexpressibly happy' at the fall of Fort de la Convention. Midshipman Hoffman's frigate HMS *Blonde* was sent home with the despatches the following day: 'we were ordered to receive on board a superior officer of the Navy and Army

---

58 Anon. *Cumloden Papers*, p.8. Given 29 women are known to have been repatriated to France, Stewart presumably means European women.

with the despatches for England, also several wounded officers and the colours taken from the forts and churches. In the evening we saluted the admiral and left the bay for England'.[59] The superior army officer was Major Henry George Grey of the 18th Light Dragoons, second son of the victor, sent by his father knowing full well that any officer presented to the King bearing news of a victory received an automatic step in rank promotion. Major Grey arrived at the office of Henry Dundas in the morning of 21 April, bearing his father's hand-written despatches.

> I have the happiness to acquaint you of the complete conquest of this very valuable island, the last and most important fortress of Fort Bourbon having surrendered to his Majesty's arms at-four o'clock in the afternoon of the 23d instant; at which time his Royal Highness Prince Edward, major general of his Majesty's forces, took possession of both gates with the first and third battalions of grenadiers, and the first and third light infantry: And I have the honour to transmit to you the articles of capitulation… The navy acquitted themselves with their usual gallantry (particularly Captain Faulknor, whose conduct justly gained him the admiration of the whole army) … I send five stand of colours, laid down by the garrison, together with the two colours of Fort Bourbon, to be presented to his Majesty. The gallant defence made by General Rochambeau, and his garrison, was strongly manifested on entering Fort Bourbon, as there was scarce an inch of ground untouched by our shot and shells; and it is but justice to say, that it does them the highest honour.[60]

The superior naval officer aboard the *Blonde* was Captain the Honourable Henry Powlett, tasked with delivering Jervis's dispatch to the Admiralty. But it was Grey's dispatch that caused the greater commotion. He was understandably jubilant, and delighted to have succeeded in harmony with his great friend Jervis. 'The spirit, unanimity and perseverance of the navy and army were never more conspicuous, nor has more cordial co-operation ever been manifested between his Majesty's naval and land forces', wrote Grey in his dispatch.[61] It had indeed been a great prize. In 1790 the island had loaded 236 ships for Europe, the shipped produce being valued at £1,000,000 sterling – equivalent to about £100,000,000 today. The town of Saint Pierre contained 3,000 houses, République-ville 2,000, and Trinité 1,800. The island contained nearly 300 sugar estates, 206 cotton, and 1,465 coffee plantations. The property captured was estimated at £500,000 sterling, exclusive of public buildings. Some 125 vessels were found at Saint Pierre and République-ville,

---

59 Hoffman, *A Sailor of King George*, p.31.
60 John Grehan and Martin Mace (eds.), *British Battles of the Napoleonic Wars, 1793-1806* (Barnsley: Pen and Sword 2013), pp.43-45.
61 Grehan and Mace (eds.), *British Battles of the Napoleonic Wars*, pp.43-45.

most of which were laden with the produce of the island. 'In Fort Bourbon were found 125 pieces of cannon, and in Fort Louis 68,' historian John James McGregor wrote; 'the military stores taken, were immense; Fort de la République alone was said to have contained as much as would have been necessary in Gibraltar, during the long and vigorous siege which it sustained in the American war'.[62]

Henry Dundas immediately wrote to the King at Windsor to inform him of the news. Major Henry Grey was duly made a brevet lieutenant colonel the same day and given a bonus of £500. Faulknor was advanced to post captain, and with the King's approbation, effectively entirely exonerated. The captured colours were transported by a detachment of Life Guards and Foot Guards from Saint James' Palace to Saint Paul's Cathedral on the morning of 18 May, His Majesty having given approval for a gun salute to mark the passing of the colours. Each captured colour was carried by a sergeant of the Foot Guards regiments, then laid up inside the great cathedral. On 21 May the Houses of Parliament passed motions of thanks of the House to Sir Charles Grey, Sir John Jervis, Lieutenant General Prescott 'and others', Rear Admiral Thompson and others, non-commissioned officers and soldiers, sailors and marines serving in the West Indies. To the victors, the glory.

But not to the vanquished. The repatriated French garrison sailed first to Guernsey, then to their homeland. They comprised 773 soldiers, sailors and civilians from Martinique; included were 234 sailors and 23 soldiers, plus 29 women and 485 men classified as either 'white creoles', coloured, or expatriate Europeans. These were the lucky ones. Some 250 coloured combatants, born free or emancipated by Rochambeau – very probably the men who surrendered with Bellegarde – were sold as slaves, primarily into the Spanish West Indies colonies. On such footnotes does history too often rest.

---

62 John James McGregor, *History of the French Revolution and of the Wars Resulting from that Memorable Event* (London: G.B. Whittaker, 1828), Vol. 4, p.184.

10

Saint Lucia

Lieutenant Bartholomew James RN, a 41-year-old adventurer from Somerset who had seen much service in the West Indies and North America, was summoned to see Grey and Jervis aboard HMS *Boyne* on 28 March. He was offered the post of commissioner for confiscated produce at Saint Pierre, with clerks and a fine house. James gladly accepted. He took up residence on La Grande Rue, with a deputy, clerk, a French house-keeper, valet, cook, and two black servants. His main task was to dispose of confiscated French property, a topic we shall return to in due course. But the unceasing rains hastened something else, a taste of what awaited the expeditionary force. 'In a few days after I arrived at St. Pierre I buried every man belonging to my boat twice,' James recorded, 'and nearly all of the third boat's crew, in fevers; and shocking and serious to relate, the master, mate, and every man and boy belonging to the *Acorn* transport, that I came from England in…'.[1]

The capture of Martinique had consumed the better part of two months. Due to Rochambeau's stubbornness, this was a month longer than Grey had envisaged at the outset, meaning that there were in theory perhaps only six to eight weeks left in the campaigning season: a dangerously short time, and the inclement weather might much reduce this window. Grey decided he could spend no time enjoying the fruits of his success, and got cracking on Saint Lucia. He left his five weakest regiments behind on Martinique as a garrison – the 15th, 39th, 58th, 64th, and 70th Foot, who between them contributed a large portion of the force's 2,400 men sick – along with Lieutenant General Robert Prescott as Governor, Brigadier General John Whyte as deputy Governor, Colonel William Myers as commandant at Saint Pierre, and a small squadron under Commodore Thompson to patrol the waters. The single largest oversight of the entire campaign was now becoming obvious. Armed and equipped as a military expedition, the force contained no civil administrators, rendering it necessary for Grey to appoint military or naval men to act in such posts: appointments for which they had received little or no training or experience. Worse, these detachments eroded the already depleted

---

1 James, *Journal*, p.241.

officer corps remaining to him for further operations. A town or an island could not be administered the same as a barracks.

In the rush to press on to Saint Lucia, it became apparent that Grey's choice as Governor of Martinique, the acerbic Robert Prescott, had been left with little in the way of guidance. To make matters more difficult, Prescott was lumbered with the restored monarchical courts and laws of the island, to be retained until the King's pleasure was known, men and customs Prescott did not know nor really wish to understand. He wrote to Grey on 28 March with a list of questions that ought to have been answered at the outset.[2] Was he, as Governor, to be given an extra allowance? Was he allowed a secretary? How were taxes and customs duties to be collected? Was he allowed a barrack-master? A chaplain? Grey's dispatch of 25 March included a secret letter to Henry Dundas which contained a footnote, begging 'allowance to observe to you sir that Lieutenant General Prescott does not wish to be appointed to any permanent situation in the West Indies, at this time of his life; but to remain during the war to the end of this service; therefore, I wish his most meritorious services may be considered in a situation at home'.[3] This secret letter to Dundas also pleaded for reinforcements, clothing for the troops, 80 dismounted light dragoons for special outpost duties, and that the government consider providing his troops a free postal service to improve morale.

At best therefore Prescott was governor 'for the duration'. Prescott did indeed have military efficiency and personal integrity in spades, but as to tact and diplomacy, the cupboard was bare. Thomas Dundas wrote a lovely understatement in a letter home to his wife at about the same time. 'General Prescot [sic] remains governor pro tempore, he is not exactly what the governor of Martinico should be at this moment, but I understand that he has many good qualities'.[4] Grey added some clarity to Prescott's questions, and a whole raft of civil appointments followed. A four-man Court of the Vice-Admiralty (to which Bartholomew James reported) for the sale of captures; Captain George Grey RN as Chief Naval Officer; Major Henry George Grey as Chief Secretary and Registrar; Colonel Richard Symes as Provost-Marshal; and Benjamin Clifton, Esquire as Treasurer. Each civil post carried a healthy salary, and Charles Grey made sure his sons were well provided for. As far back as 29 March, the Collector of customs at Saint Pierre, James Bontein, had signed (or been forced to sign) an agreement to give the profits of his office to Captain Thomas Grey. The following day, Richard Symes signed a bond to pay Major Henry Grey half of the nett profits of his office as Provost-Marshal of Martinique. On 5 April Captain Thomas Grey was appointed Provost-Marshal on

---

2   GRE/A235, Queries etc. by Lieut.-Gen. Robert Prescott on various points relative to his position [at Martinique], 28 March 1794.
3   GRE/A2243g, Grey to Henry Dundas, 25 March 1794. Concerning the capture of Martinique, his plans for attempting to take the other French islands, etc.
4   Dundas (ed.), *Dundas of Figask*, p.128.

Saint Lucia. In early May William Nicolls, the Collector of Customs at République-ville, agreed to pay half of the nett profits of his post to Charles Grey's youngest son Edward (then aged just twelve) for life.[5] Two days later on Grey's urging Matthew Munro, the Secretary and Register of Guadeloupe, likewise agreed to pay half the nett revenues of his office to young master Edward Grey.[6] Sir Charles also had the power to promote men up to the rank of captain, and he used this power to boost his family members likewise. On 30 April he promoted his son and aide Lieutenant William Grey to a vacant captaincy in the 21st Foot, whilst his aide and fellow Northumbrian Lieutenant William Newton Ogle got the captaincy made vacant in the 70th Foot by the death of George Strange Nares, who had died of Yellow Fever on Martinique on 20 April 1794, aged twenty-five. It was behaviour that today we might associate with third-world dictators and single-party-state autocrats, yet at the time it raised few eyebrows.

Saint Lucia, a densely-forested volcanic speck some twenty miles to the south of Martinique, had been claimed for France by a party of settlers from that island in 1643. Despite a chequered history of possession, the island remained one of France's most important resource colonies by 1793, being a major producer and exporter of sugar. Saint Lucia is twenty-two miles in length and fifteen in breadth, and its harbour called Little Carénage was reckoned the best in the Caribbean. Thirty ships of the line could ride safely there in the most terrible of hurricanes. The population was about 30,000 people, the vast majority of them slaves. Rochambeau and La Crosse had appointed the elderly Général de Brigade Nicolas Xavier de Ricard as Governor of Saint Lucia in early 1793. It was an unwise appointment, since Ricard lacked Rochambeau's energy and will. He nonetheless had done what he could to stir up Republican sentiment on the island, and had renamed the island's capital Castries to Félicitié-ville. His garrison included one company of the 31e Régiment d'Infanterie and some National Guards, barely 400 men.

Whilst he made his plans against Saint Lucia, Grey had the benefit of a long report from a Royalist of that island, a certain Monsieur de Bexon, which, like the intelligence available before Martinique, allowed him to set his plans knowing more about the dispositions of his enemy than any of the defenders knew. Whilst suggesting an invasion force of 4,800 men, nearly twice what Grey actually had, Bexon indicated that the island had maybe 500 whites and 700 people of colour who could bear arms. 'The white inhabitants of Saint Lucia,' he reported, 'whatever be their opinion with regards to politicks, are in this moment a great deal opposed by the people of colour, and desire almost universally to be under the

---

5 GRE/A307, Bond of William Niccolls [sic] to Grey to pay him half the net profits of the office of Collector of Customs of the Port of Fort Royal, Martinique, for the use (and during the life) of his son Edward Grey.
6 GRE/A308, Agreement of Matthew Munro of Grenada, Merchant, to account for and pay to Edward Grey half the net revenues of his office of Secretary and Register of Guadeloupe to which General Sir Charles Grey had appointed him.

SAINT LUCIA 117

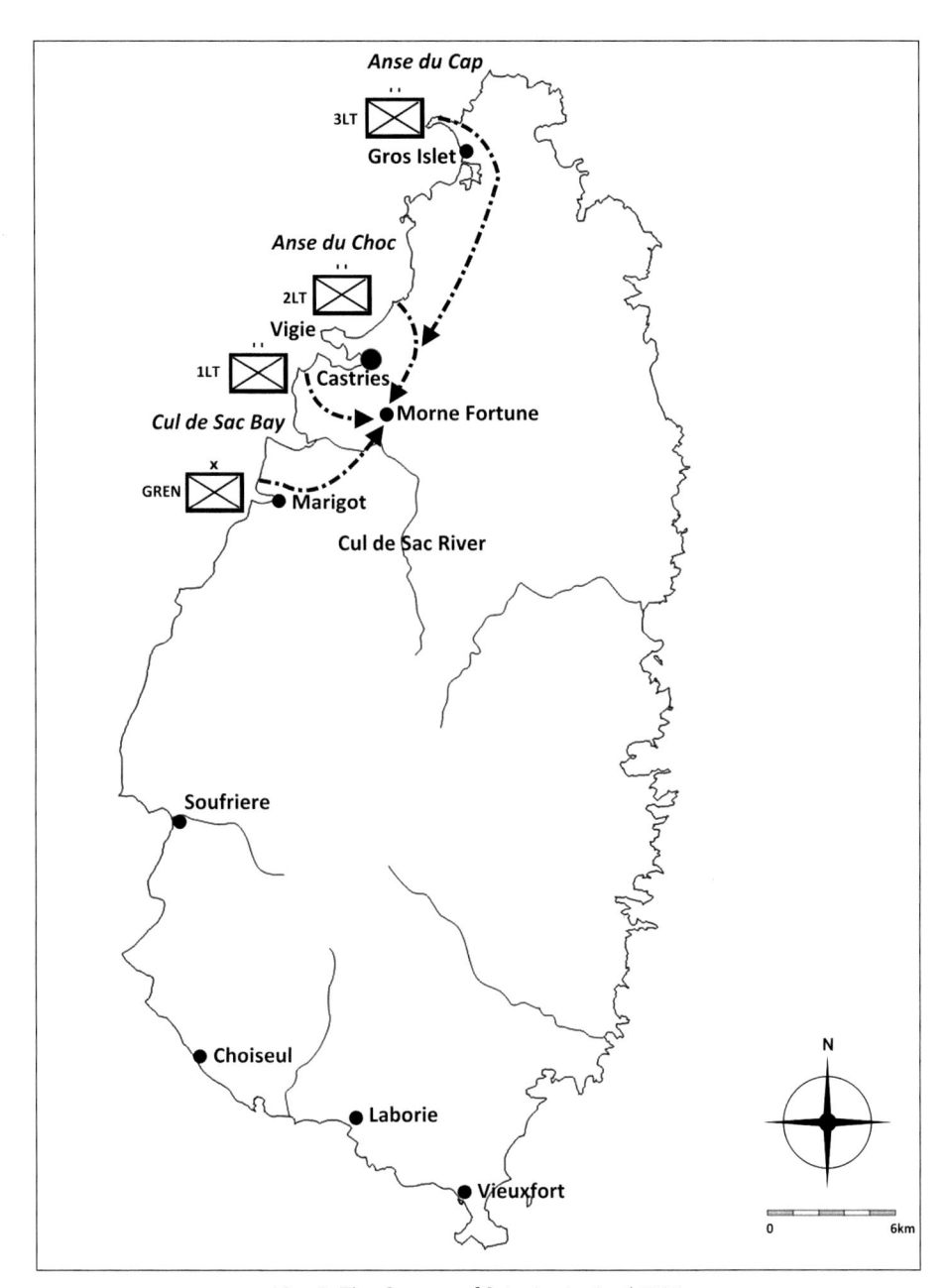

Map 3 The Capture of Saint Lucia, April 1794.

British government'.[7] Suitably buoyed, on 30 March the forces detailed for the capture of Saint Lucia boarded ships in République-ville Harbour. They represented the best of the troops available; the three grenadier battalions under Prince Edward and the three light battalions under Thomas Dundas, as well as the comparatively healthy 6th, 9th, and 43rd Foot under Sir Charles Gordon. Colonel Durnford commanded the Royal Engineers, and elements of seven companies of the Royal Artillery and Royal Irish Artillery under Lieutenant Colonel Paterson completed the task force.

The fleet sailed at eleven in the morning of Monday 31 March and anchored off the northern end of Saint Lucia by half-past nine on the morning of 1 April. Dundas' men were rowed ashore in the afternoon. Close's 3rd Light Battalion was landed at Anse du Cap by Captain Lord Garlies' squadron, HMS *Solebay*, HMS *Winchelsea* and the *London* transport, at about three o'clock. Blundell's 2nd Light Battalion was landed at Anse du Choc from HMS *Vengeance*, HMS *Irresistable*, and HMS *Rattlesnake*, commanded by Commodore Thompson, an hour later. Between them, they worked around behind the French batteries on Morne Fortuné and captured them without losing a man. In the afternoon, the rest of the fleet sailed down the west side of the island, occasionally bombarded by shore batteries to no effect, and landed Prince Edward's 1st and 3rd Grenadiers at Marigot de Roseaux from Captain Eliab Harvey's HMS *Santa Magarita*, HMS *Rose*, and HMS *Woolwich* by six o'clock. These troops advanced north to cover the Grande Cul de Sac (Barrington's Bay). After sunset, Coote's 1st Light Battalion was landed at Anse la Toc by the flagship HMS *Boyne* and HMS *Veteran*, and captured the four-gun battery at Ciceron. All day, the troops had met no resistance, and no lives had been lost. It was if the French expected to be over-run. Perhaps they did. Aware of the loss of Martinique, local Governor Ricard knew that his 400 men could not possibly halt the inexorable tide of redcoats. His men must stay at their posts to at least make a show of defiance if he ever wanted to set foot in France again.[8]

The Royal Navy fleet anchored in Grande Cul de Sac Bay on the Wednesday morning. Gordon's brigade and the 2nd Grenadiers stayed aboard the ships as a reserve. The Prince's grenadiers had spent the night camped next to a swamp. The 1st Battalion, claiming seniority, had occupied a row of huts and emerged at reveille fit and rested. The 3rd Battalion, which had bivouacked outdoors, started the day with 40 men on the sick-list. Nonetheless both units itched for action, and at dawn Prince Edward detached two companies under his brigade-major, Lieutenant George Stracey Smyth of the Prince's own regiment, the 7th Fusiliers, to capture two nearby batteries along the coast. These they found deserted, albeit

---

7 GRE/A238, Plan for the attack of St. Lucia ('translation directed by Mr. de Bexon to be made for Sir Charles Grey').
8 Wylliams, *Account*, pp.78-79.

with their tricolour flags still flying. They spiked the guns and hauled down the flags as trophies. Meanwhile the Prince moved his men out of the swamp at Grey's urging, and shifted his base of operations that night to the base of Morne Fortuné, under shot and shell the whole time but without losing a man.

There was one stronghold left to capture, that atop Morne Fortuné, and so on the pre-dawn darkness of Thursday 3 April Lieutenant Colonel Eyre Coote led four companies of 1st Light Battalion in a furious bayonet assault on a redoubt close to the main French battery. He reported killing and wounding 32, a figure probably greatly exaggerated, captured a surgeon, liberated a captive Royal Navy seaman and spiked six guns. Although claiming no losses, Coote had overlooked the assault's only British casualty, Lieutenant Richard Fletcher of the Royal Engineers, who had received a glancing musket-shot wound to the head. Another inch or two windage on the musket-ball and the future chief engineer of Wellington's Lines of Torres Vedras in 1810 would have been lost to history. Fletcher was sent to Grenada to recuperate, and did not return to the campaign.

With this last bastion gone, Grey sent Major Frederick Maitland with a flag of truce to the French commander General Ricard. Ricard responded with a burst of outrage:

> I must inform you that a most horrid act was committed at the Morne this morning, which I must suppose must have happened contrary to your orders. A black flag was hoisted to attack the hospital. The sick and wounded in their beds, an officer at the point of death and Chaplain were killed by the bayonet. The Steward and Director of the Hospital were massacred. No assistance on their part had given cause to this action.[9]

Whether this accusation was vexatious or not we will never know. Certainly, Grey took no disciplinary action. He started to plan a major assault on the morrow, carried out by grenadiers and seamen, only to be informed that Ricard would surrender, things having gone badly at his headquarters. 'Our situation is very much changed these two hours. Almost the whole of the National Guards of my garrison have deserted me,' the desperate Ricard wrote. 'One hundred men of the Battalion and myself who are of the same opinion, now ask what Conditions you will impose on them, and how far you will consult my own honour'.[10] The terms of the capitulation were formally agreed by nine o'clock in the evening. The French garrison – 155 regulars of the 31e Régiment, 9 engineers, 19 artillerymen, 89 National Guardsmen, and 19 sailors – marched out of Morne Fortuné on Friday

---

9   GRE/A240b, Letter from Major-Gen. Richard to Grey and Jervis, dated 3 April 1794. Refusing to surrender and complaining of a massacre at a French hospital.
10 GRE/A242, Letter from Major-Gen. Richard to Grey and Jervis, 3 April 1794. Accepting their conditions for the surrender of his force and the Morne Fortuné.

morning with the honours of war, piled their arms, and were put aboard transports bound for France.[11] Like Rochambeau on Martinique, Ricard chose a new life in America instead of the uncertainty of a France under Robespierre.

As he had done at République-ville, Prince Edward had the honour of occupying the fort with his grenadiers. The Union flag was run up the pole and the name of the fort was changed to Fort Charlotte, in honour of the Prince's German-born mother. Castries, or Felicitéville, was renamed Charlotteville. The hard-working Major Frederick Maitland was dispatched in a sloop with a request from Ricard that the tiny French garrison on Gros Islet (Pigeon Island), at the north end of Saint Lucia, capitulate also, which they duly obeyed. Thomas Dundas had seen enough of the island in forty-eight hours to never want to return. 'Being no admirer of this island, which, so far as I have seen, is an uncleared swamp, with high hills and fine harbours... The climate did not please any of us, and our soldiers grew sickly'.[12] Saint Lucia was at the time much less developed than Martinique. The terrain was principally thickly forested hills with every conceivable type of creepy-crawly, boa constrictors, and exotic song-birds. The island's fresh water supply was a single uncovered tank. The first signs of sickness were appearing. This was not good news for the expeditionary force.

Grey's victory dispatch from Martinique had caused much commotion in London. Now it was Jervis's turn. He penned a concise account of the four-day campaign on the Friday and handed it to Commander Christopher Parker of HMS *Blanche*, a son of Admiral Peter Parker and of a notable Royal Navy dynasty, to deliver to the Admiralty Office knowing full well that Parker would receive a step in promotion for bearing the good news, just as Henry Grey had done a few weeks earlier. Parker sailed in the sloop HMS *Rattlesnake* commanded by Lieutenant D'Arcy Preston and accompanied by Major Finch Mason of Grey's staff, and arrived at the Admiralty Office on 16 May, two days before the planned victory parade to celebrate the capture of Martinique. The celebrations were accordingly ramped up a notch.

With the capture of Saint Lucia, a second French West Indies possession had fallen, and remarkably for no loss of life on the British side. 32 guns were captured in the fort, with another 73 guns taken in outlying forts and batteries. Grey and the remainder of his force departed for Martinique early on Saturday 5 April. What had started on a Monday morning was ended by Friday afternoon, as if capturing enemy islands had become as mundane as a working week. But the results were far from mundane. Rarely before in British military history had so much been achieved for so little loss. It was an extraordinary achievement.

---

11 Return in GRE/A243, Account of the garrison of Fort Fortuné with cannon etc. and all the cannon on the battery of Pigeon Island and along the coast, 3 April 1794.
12 Dundas (ed.), *Dundas of Fingask*, p.130.

Colonel Sir Charles Gordon was appointed interim Governor of Saint Lucia on 4 April. He had been left the battalion companies of the 6th and 9th Foot plus 50 artillerymen as a garrison, 800 men in all, but only half the number he considered necessary to properly defend the island. Despite Thomas Dundas' comments, it seems that Saint Lucia was a not especially unhealthy posting, since Gordon was able to report to Grey on 18 June that he had lost no officers, and only a few men to disease. Before he left, Grey penned some advice to Gordon concerning the running of the island, perhaps conscious that Prescott had been left more or less to his own devices on Martinique a few weeks earlier, and wishing to provide more guidance this time around. He suggested that Gordon establish four military posts (Souffriere, Vieux Fort, Micoud, and Gros Islet) and that Gordon, as Governor, would have 'a full and discretionary power lodged with you,' something that would later come back to haunt both men.[13] Grey also appointed Captain Thomas Grey as Provost-Marshal, Captain William Grey as Naval Officer, Thomas Orde as Customs Collector, and Anthony Johnston as Comptroller of Customs. As on Martinique, he made sure his sons were amply rewarded in terms of civil salaries on top of their military pay. He also put together a plan for raising a regiment of Island Rangers, local troops under British officers who in their acclimatised state would be impervious to the sicknesses already laying out the redcoats. He appointed Captain Charles Maitland of the 17th Light Dragoons (cousin of his aide, Frederick Maitland) as commanding officer of the Rangers, and planned for Martinique and Guadeloupe to each contribute one infantry company and one cavalry troop each, and for smaller Saint Lucia to provide an infantry company and 20 mounted troopers.

With the cost of the expedition running so high, thoughts turned to reparations. On Martinique Prescott, politically naive, issued a proclamation on 10 April (in the names of Grey and Jervis) advising Martiniquais that;

> Sir Charles Grey and Sir John Jervis, Commanders in Chief of His Britannic Majesty's Land and Sea Forces in the Windward Islands, having resolved, that all the Provisions, and other Articles, heretofore declared to the Agents of Seizures, in the Town of St. Pierre, shall be publicly sold for the Profit of those who have seized them, all Persons, having made such Declarations, are herewith ordered, as soon as the aforesaid Agents shall desire it, to deliver up the Provisions and other Articles thus declared. All Persons, that have hitherto neglected to make similar Declarations, are also ordered, at their Risk and Peril, to make them without any further Delay.[14]

13　GRE/A245, Memorandum by Grey for Sir C. Gordon, 4 April 1794. Instructing him on measures to be taken in St. Lucia.

14　National Library of Australia, House of Commons Parliamentary Papers Online, *Proclamations, and other Papers, issued by the British Commanders in the French West India Islands*, p.7.

This led to howls of indignation from locals. Further howls came from the captains of American merchant vessels seized off Martinique by the Royal Navy, after having their ships and crews confiscated. Grey had no Admiralty court on Martinique to hear such cases of seizure, so decided to set up one of his own. He assembled a civilian 'Prize Court' to act as civil commissioners for the adjudication of prize matters – John Roberton, Joseph Beete, John Farquharson and Edward Applewhite. This court then upheld Grey's confiscations anyway. American ships were the booty of war. It was not until someone mentioned that his prize court was illegal without an actual commission from the Admiralty that he decided to tell Henry Dundas about it. In a letter dated 3 May he stated, 'It is now, however, suggested to me that some of those persons whose property has been Captured, forfeited, condemned and Confiscated, suppose me not to possess a Special Commission, under the Lords of the Admiralty, for erecting such Courts'.[15] He believed that as commander-in-chief he already had those powers.

A week later Prescott, again under the orders of Grey and Jervis, issued a proclamation to the inhabitants of Martinique telling them that they were required to choose representatives who were authorised with 'fixing, in an equitable and efficacious manner, a general contribution (the amount of which shall be made known to them), to be paid by all who possess property in the colony; the Commanders in Chief having decided that such an arrangement would be more convenient than a general confiscation'.[16] Thus it was that those islanders who had demonstrated, or at least appeared to demonstrate, loyalty to the British occupiers, were to be made to cough up to pay for the expenses of the expedition, not to mention line the pockets of the senior officers. The proclamation was roundly ignored. Fairly piqued, Prescott issued another more peremptory proclamation 10 days later, which started off by saying:

> That no attention having been paid to that of the 10th, requiring representatives to raise a sum of money adequate to the value of the conquest destined to reward the valour, to compensate the fatigue, and its consequences, sickness and mortality, and to make good the heavy expense incurred by the British officers, who, with matchless perseverance, &c. had achieved the conquest of the island, subjected it to the British government, rescued from a wretched exile the greatest number of its inhabitants, &c…[17]

---

15   GRE/A295, Copy letter from Grey to Henry Dundas, 3 May 1794. Requesting a special commission from the Lords of Admiralty for erecting and holding courts for prize causes.
16   National Library of Australia, House of Commons Parliamentary Papers Online, *Proclamations, and other Papers, issued by the British Commanders in the French West India Islands*, p.11. HCPP, National Library of Australia.
17   Prescott proclamation of 20 May 1794 quoted in Thomas Southley, *Chronological History of the West Indies*, Vol. III, p.95.

This proclamation, and others, would eventually come to haunt Grey. The Chief Justice of Grenada, the Honourable Thomas Bridgewater, suggested in a private letter to Lord Liverpool on 26 April that he thought the 'contribution' levied on Saint Lucia ought to be '£300,000 within six months'.[18] This was a truly astronomical sum. In the end the figure was adjusted to £150,000, which the citizens grudgingly accepted in lieu of confiscations, as were occurring on Martinique. But the imposition caused considerable outcry amongst those who saw the contribution as being unfairly imposed upon those who had demonstrated loyalty. '[The inhabitants] had expected to find, under an English Government, and end to the confiscation and oppression,' a French planter wrote, 'but to their great regret, they find their situation very little bettered; and a change only from one set of oppressors to another'.[19]

Prescott found himself further entangled in island politics in early May when he released a number of untried civilian prisoners from prison in Saint Pierre. The Supreme Council was appalled, considering the captives dangerous, but after providing no further detail to Prescott, they complained to Grey about Prescott's actions. Grey involved himself and asked for an explanation. 'Permit me to say,' Prescott replied, 'that I have had the same accounts of dangerous people in many parts of the Island, from many lately arrived here, and there is scarcely a day passes that I have not complaints of the actual violence and threatenings of gentlemen who have arrived and generally styled Emigrants, and who would, if they could, actually rekindle a Civil War on this Island'.[20] The sad fact was, the islanders were using the British occupation to settle old scores, leaving Prescott stuck somewhere in the middle. Grey wrote back on 12 May, enclosing a list of people to be arrested and deported. His motives were probably entirely pragmatic. He wanted to put an expedient end to the issue; to placate the leading islanders; to act decisively. But Prescott's military mind only worked in straight lines, and he could not let the order rest, writing a long-winded response on 14 May suggesting that Grey had got it wrong. He followed it up the next day with another letter listing islanders who had taken the oath of allegiance to King George, and would be liable to be executed if deported to France.[21]

Grey and Jervis called an extraordinary meeting of the Supreme Council on 15 May to discuss the matter, at which point Prescott snapped. 'The calling together

18 British Library, Liverpool Papers, Add MS 38353, Volume CLXIV.
19 Nelson, *Sir Charles Grey*, p.140.
20 GRE/A304, Letter from Lieut.-Gen. Robert Prescott to Grey, 7 May 1794. Reporting on military matters, explaining his release of 'dangerous' persons, and concerning negroes for the navy, and finance.
21 GRE/A309, Letter from Lieut.-General Robert Prescott to Grey, 14 May 1794. Concerning 'dangerous' persons in Martinique (Grey's letter of 12 May has not survived, but is quoted in this letter); also GRE/A310, Letter from Lieut.-General Robert Prescott to Grey, 15 May 1794. Concerning persons who had taken the oath of allegiance to George III and who would consequently be liable to the death penalty if deported to France.

of which body had heretofore always been the Privilege of the Governor of this Island,' he complained. 'I am sorry to say that I have been treated, I trust very undeservedly, with so little respect in other instances as Governor of this Island as to be unable.... To act in that capacity... I think it absolutely necessary to resign my Civil Employment'.[22] There is no response from Grey to be found on the public record, however a week later Prescott wrote to Grey requesting he be paid the normal salary for the Governor on an island in the West Indies, £1,200 per annum, and that a successor as Governor be speedily found, so that he could 'at my advanced time of life return to my family and to a country better suited to my age and disposition'.[23] To quieten the carping Prescott Grey appointed Du Buc as Administrator-General of Martinique on 26 May, but true to form, Prescott immediately fell out with him.[24] Du Buc wrote to Grey on 1 June and again on 9 June describing their disputes. This nonsense went on for weeks. It culminated in a proclamation Prescott issued to the citizens of Martinique on 7 July, ordering them to disregard any ordinances issued by Du Buc.[25] Four days later he wrote to the Superior Council declaring his refusal for Sir John Jervis to be allowed to meddle in the affairs of Martinique.

Things were as bad on Saint Lucia. Sir Charles Gordon's happy elevation turned sour in July. Formal complaints of extortion and bribe-taking from planters and merchants were being made against him, accusing him of taking money from disaffected persons to allow them to remain in the island; even worse, the accusations stated that he later broke faith with them and shipped them off anyway. The bribes paid to Gordon were later revealed as being in the region of £25,000. Evidently similar practices had occurred on Guadeloupe, although the officers responsible were never brought to account. A general court-martial assembled on 25 July 1794 under the presidency of Prescott, but fever had well and truly taken hold, and so the court-martial was twice interrupted by the deaths of the majority of the members. As a solution, eight members in place of the normal quorum of twelve was used, and Gordon was ultimately found guilty, sentenced to refund all the money, and to be cashiered from the Army.[26] In light of his past services he was allowed to receive the value of his commissions. It was a sad end for a long-

---

22　GRE/A316, Letter from Lieut.-General Robert Prescott to Grey, 19 May 1794. Requesting permission to resign the Governorship of Martinique on account of interference from Grey and Jervis.
23　GRE/A326, Letter from Lieut.-General Robert Prescott to Grey, 23 May 1794. Concerning his salary as Governor of Martinique and requesting Grey to try to get a successor appointed to that post.
24　GRE/A328c, Draft Commission from Grey, 24 May 1794. Provisionally appointing Du Buc Administrator General of Martinique. Although Du Buc had declined the post on 18 May, Grey appointed him anyway.
25　GRE/A361b, Proclamation by Lieut.-General Robert Prescott to the inhabitants of Martinique, 7 July 1794. Ordering them to disregard the ordinances etc. which Du Buc had issued.
26　Court martial member composition from Wylliams, *Account*, Appendix pp.47-48; also Nelson, *Sir Charles Grey*, p.158.

serving officer. Grey, in a later private letter to Judge Advocate-General Sir Charles Morgan, thought that Gordon had been let down by his advisers. 'I believe he fell into the hands of an artful and deceiving set of advisers, who led him implicitly, set by step, to do what he never could have been his intention, and what he would not only have requested, but detested the idea of, had he been aware of what he was led into'.[27]

Major Alexander Baillie of the 9th Foot, the same officer who had stormed the fort on Tobago a year earlier, and also the first man to land on Martinique, was appointed as temporary Governor of Saint Lucia until someone more senior could be found. Baillie had been in the Army for 38 years, staring his career with the 60th Foot and serving in the French-Indian Wars where had been wounded at Ticonderoga in 1758; he had then served with the 9th Foot all through the American War. He was a man well-versed in fighting in rough terrain, so it was fortunate that he was on the spot when a band of Negroes rose in revolt at the start of September. Baillie assembled two companies from each of the 6th and 9th Foot plus the island militia, and assaulted the rebels' strong-point with the bayonet, for the loss of one man killed and four wounded. A month later Baillie was promoted to lieutenant colonel and placed in command of the 58th Foot, and Grey's aide Frederick Maitland succeeded to Baillie's majority in the 9th Foot. Baillie retired shortly thereafter.

By November, the number of sick men on Saint Lucia had increased dramatically. The two battalions in garrison could only muster 340 fit men. This would be far too few to garrison the island, let alone provide reinforcements should they be needed elsewhere, as indeed they were.

---

27 GRE/A2243kk, Grey to Sir Charles Morgan, 18 January 1795. Concerning the money extracted by Sir Charles Gordon in St. Lucia and Grey's plea on Gordon's behalf.

11

High-Water Mark

Sir Charles Grey with his staff arrived back at République-ville aboard HMS *Boyne* in the evening of Saturday 5 April, two months to the day since they had first appeared off the coast of Martinique. Nine weeks were gone, and two islands captured. There were at best seven weeks left in the 'campaigning season' in which to subdue Guadeloupe, the largest of the three islands, and the best-defended. The trouble was, after leaving garrisons behind, Grey had very few troops left to crack this toughest nut. He had his three light and three grenadier battalions it was true, but these men had done the lion's share of the fighting since the start of February, and in all likelihood needed a few week's rest. Sir Thomas Dundas wrote home from République-ville with a neat summary of the campaign just ended, which indicated the toll the campaign was having on his troops; 'I landed the 1st April; the place surrendered the 3d; and on the 4th, in the evening, I sailed with my ship full of ailing light infantry men for St. Pierre, where our general hospital is; 5th, landed the sick, filled my ship with recovered men, and yesterday came here..'.[1]

The battalion companies of the 6th and 9th Foot had been left behind on Saint Lucia. The 15th, 39th, 58th, 64th, and 70th Foot had been left to garrison Martinique, and none were in fit shape to make the crossing to Guadeloupe. That left Lieutenant Colonel's James Drummond's 43rd Foot as the only line battalion fit for active service, in addition to the six battalions of flankers. Reinforcements from home had been requested, but none had arrived: nor would any arrive until mid-May. Things being what they were, the seven battalions ear-marked for the invasion of Guadeloupe made their preparations, whilst those destined to act in a garrison capacity tested their new authority in a variety of ways. Governor Robert Prescott made up for efficiency what he lacked in patience and understanding of other points of view. Thomas Dundas wrote home describing his plummeting opinion of the man on 7 April:

---

1 Dundas (ed.), *Dundas of Fingask*, p.132.

The fact is that Prescot (sic), who at present commands, is an old woman, who has not been guilty of any military act since we began our operations, and who now thinks to govern Martinico like a justice of the peace, giving liberty and our laws to a rascally banditti, who have for years past been employed in acts of murder, robbery, etc.[2]

He also wrote about his fellow major general, Prince Edward, whom he was now seeing as a purely parade-ground soldier. 'The Prince talks of Nova Scotia. Indeed, he could do no good here; for although he pays every attention to his duty, yet the head seems of little use, it is parade, it is form and fashion which occupies his attention'.[3]

Guadeloupe, located eighty miles north of Martinique, towards the lower end of the Leeward Islands chain, had been discovered by Christopher Columbus on his second expedition in 1493. He named the island Santa María de Guadalupe de Extremadura, after the image of the Virgin Mary venerated at a Spanish monastery in Guadalupe in Spain. The original natives, the Awawaks, had always called the island Karukera, or island of beautiful waters, before the Caribs arrived in the eighth century and killed them all. Columbus left no settlers, his only lasting legacy being to name a fruit he thought looked like a pine-cone as 'the pine of the Indies' or the pineapple. Like Martinique, Guadeloupe had been claimed by the French in 1635, and, also like the other two islands, had suffered a chequered history of possession. The French waged a brutal war against the Carib natives from 1636 to 1639, eventually winning following the arrival of reinforcements from Saint Christopher in 1640. By 1654 roughly one-third of the population of Guadeloupe was of European origin, with the remaining two-thirds being indentured servants. By 1671 the European population had dropped to 13 per cent due to the influx of African slaves. Guadeloupe was formally annexed into the Kingdom of France in 1674. In 1714, the French general government of the West Indies islands divided in two, and Guadeloupe was placed under the control of the governor on Martinique. The island was another major source of sugar, an industry then worth £6 million a year. Guadeloupe comprised two irregularly-shaped islands, Grande-Terre in the east and Guadeloupe proper, also called Basse-Terre, in the west. They were joined by a narrow swampy girdle of land known locally as La Rivière Salée, adjacent to which sat the capital, Pointe-à-Pitre. Basse-Terre was dominated by a mountain range running north to south like a spine from which sprang many fine watercourses. Grande-Terre was altogether flatter and used primarily for agriculture.

As he had done in preparation for the invasions of Martinique and Saint Lucia, Grey had interrogated French émigrés to gain a thorough understanding of the geography and defences of Guadeloupe. This manifested itself in two memoranda

2   Dundas (ed.), *Dundas of Fingask*, p.134.
3   Dundas (ed.), *Dundas of Fingask*, p.134.

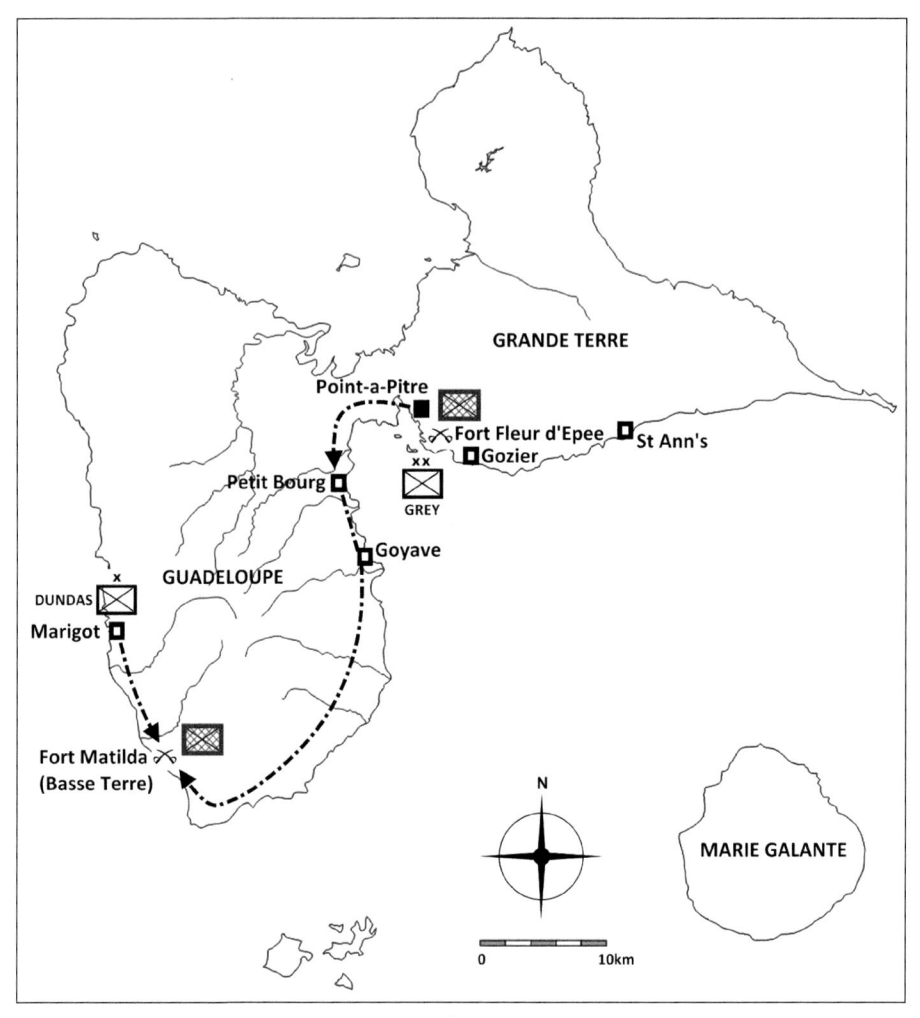

Map 4 The Capture of Guadeloupe, April 1794.

dated April 1794, which Grey had translated into English and circulated to senior officers, containing both terrestrial and nautical observations. 'It has been calculated that for the defence of Guadeloupe it was necessary to have a body of troops of at least 4 or 5,000 men,' one of them stated, 'which would require 8 to 10,000 men attack it'.[4] Grey had only a fraction of this number of attackers; though he did not know it yet, the French garrison numbered close to 5,000, perhaps even more.

4   GRE/A251b, Mémoire sur l'attaque de la Guadeloupe [English translation].

The defences of Guadeloupe included a considerable array of artillery batteries and redoubts, albeit manned by a mixture of regulars and locals. Twenty batteries in all, including five at Palmiste and four above Fort Saint Charles, seemed likely to give any attackers a hot time.[5]

The capital of Guadeloupe was, and still is, Pointe-à-Pitre, situated on low-lying land bordered in 1794 by swampland to the north and a good harbour called the Carénage to the south. A small hill with a strong battery called Morne Gouvernement overlooked the town from the north-east. The seaward approaches to Pointe-à-Pitre were controlled by two forts, Saint Louis and Fleur d'Epée, located on headlands overlooking a very picturesque harbour named Grande Baie. A road ran from Pointe-à-Pitre past Fort Fleur d'Epée and onwards to Gozier, a seaside hamlet with a good landing beach, then onward eastward to Saint Ann's. There were few other habitations on Grande-Terre. From Pointe-à-Pitre a road also ran westward, across Riviere Salée and some low-lying swamp west of it, then forked. It ran northward to Lamentin, southward to Petit Bourg, another fine landing place, then Goyave and Trou de Chien, finally curving around the southern tip of the main island before reaching the town of Basse-Terre. This latter place was one of the main towns of Guadeloupe and surmounted by Fort Saint Charles. Basse-Terre was overlooked, as was anywhere near the coast on the main island, by the mountain range which ran down the centre of the island.

Not being able to waste any more time, Lieutenant General Sir Charles Grey departed Martinique in the morning of 8 April. In addition to his seven battalions, Grey had a company of the Carolina Corps, his Royal Engineer officers, and 358 artillerymen from eight companies: all the best men left excluding the sick and infirm left behind on Martinique. The resources of the Royal Navy had however taken a different tack, being bolstered by the arrival of fifteen frigates and sloops since the start of the campaign, notwithstanding that four ships had been despatched on a sideshow. The hard-working Captain Josias Rogers, with the 32-gun frigates HMS *Quebec* and HMS *Ceres*, 28-gun frigate HMS *Rose*, and a sloop of war, had been sent to capture the Saintes, a small cluster of islands near Guadeloupe. These were carried on the morning of 10 April without the slightest loss by a party of seamen and marines.

The expeditionary force arrived off Pointe-à-Pitre at noon on Thursday 10 April, and, seeing the batteries on shore, Grey thought it best to delay any landing until dark. Grey and 1,000 men landed at Grande Baie at one o'clock in the morning of 11 April, all the while under a badly aimed fire from Fort Fleur d'Epée, which Captain Lord Garlies silenced by sailing HMS *Winchelsea* close under the fort, during which he was badly wounded in the face. Due to delays, only a few

---

5   Based upon a return of the defences of Guadeloupe in GRE/A250a, A List of the Batteries from Trois Rivières to Palmist, and from Palmist down to Fort St. Charles [English translation]. The return is undated but chronological order in Grey Papers suggests early April 1794.

companies of the 1st and 2nd Grenadiers, one company of the 43rd Foot, and 500 seamen and marines under the command of Captain George Grey RN were actually present to be landed. After making some observations, Sir Charles brought the rest of the force, badly delayed by winds and current, ashore later that day.

Grey divided his force into two divisions. The first, under Prince Edward, comprised the grenadiers and 100 seamen. The second under Dundas containing the two light battalions, some marines and another 100 seamen. The attacks were, as always, to be conducted in darkness, in silence, and at bayonet point. He split the attacking force into three columns. Prince Edward was to take a smaller fort of Morne Mascotte, located on a hill to the north and therefore commanding the main fort. Dundas was to take Fort Fleur d'Epée itself. Lastly, his Chief of Staff Colonel Richard Symes was to lead a reserve force, the 43rd Foot and more seamen, to command the coast road that linked to Pointe-à-Pitre road in support of Dundas.

Grey attacked the fort just before dawn on 12 April. A shot from HMS *Boyne* announced the start. 'At 2 o'clock I left the waterside with about 900 men, light infantry and sailors, to attack the stronghold of the enemy on the part of this island called Grand Terre,' Thomas Dundas later recorded. 'The Prince followed at half past 3 with Grenadiers, Colonel Symes at 4 with a mixed corps. We were to meet at 5, and, by a signal, attack. I fell in with two parties of the enemy on the march, but by the steady gallantry of my light infantry we did the business quietly, losing, however, some men... At 5 Symes and I attacked Fleur d'Epée and carried it by storm, putting most of the garrison – 150 – to the bayonet. Some more escaped. Our loss is considerable – of officers and men 58, some sailors killed and wounded'.[6] In fact the entire affair was over very quickly. The lithe and lightly-armed sailors climbed and entered by the embrasures whilst Close's 3rd Light Battalion led the way, burst through the gates and laid about the defenders with the bayonet. After a brief resistance, the defenders bolted. A British seaman from the *Boyne*, dressed in a blue Royal Navy jacket, wrapped the Union flag around himself and was in the act of pulling down the tricolour from a flagstaff in the fort in order to raise a flag of victory when a group of redcoats ran around the corner. Seeing the blue-clad figure, who they immediately assumed to be French, they shot him down. Luckily the seaman survived, thanks to the care of the surgeon-general of the fleet, but it was a bad omen.[7] The only bright side was that the colours of the 2e Regiment de Guadeloupe were captured by Midshipman Herbert of HMS *Veteran* and handed to Sir Charles Grey.

Captain Robert Faulknor, who attracted incident to his person like no other in this campaign, found himself in a tricky situation, which once again must have caused his mother's heart to skip a beat on reading his letter home:

---

6   Dundas (ed.), *Dundas of Fingask*, p.136.
7   Willyams, *Account*, pp.89-90.

In a former letter I related to you my receiving a shot in a cartouch-box that was buckled round the centre of my body; since which I commanded a detachment of seamen at the storming the strong fort of Fleur d'Epée at Guadeloupe, and which was thought impracticable to be taken by assault. The grenadiers, light infantry, and seamen, were sent on this service. The side of the mountain which the seamen had to get up was almost perpendicular, and defended by nature and art. All difficulties were overcome: but by the time we got upon the ramparts, we were so blown, and our strength so exhausted, that the strongest amongst us were unmanned. l was attacked by two Frenchmen, one of whom made a thrust at me with his bayonet, which went through the arm of my coat without wounding me, and the other made a blow at me, which I parried, and he eluded mine in return, but immediately sprung upon me, clasping his arms round my neck, and, fixing his teeth in the breast of my shirt, wrenched the sword out of my hand, and tripped me up; falling with great violence upon the ground, with this French officer upon me. In this situation two of my own seamen flew to my relief, and saved my life, and at a moment when the man upon me had his hand lifted up to stab me. An escape so providential, and an event so critical, calls for my warmest thanks to the Almighty. The conquest of this fort determined the fate of Guadeloupe: the troops, who had intended before to make a vigorous opposition, now ran before us, and we had little to do afterwards but to march through the island – a march indeed of great severity in a climate so unhealthy. Thus ended the conquest of the French West Indies before the rainy season had set in, which alone might have frustrated all our hopes.[8]

The fort was captured for 15 killed, 45 wounded as well as two men missing. French losses were 67 killed and 55 wounded, plus 110 taken prisoner. The 3rd Lights had suffered most, losing 12 killed and 24 wounded. The town of Pointe-à-Pitre quickly fell as the routed local troops fled westward – many of the inhabitants escaped in boats to Basse-Terre – and at a stroke, Grey had control of Grande-Terre, the entire eastern half of Guadeloupe. This meant Fort Saint-Louis, the town of Pointe-à-Pitre, and the new battery upon Islot-à-Cochon. He commandeered a house in the town and penned a short dispatch home, to be sent home by Lieutenant William Pierrepoint aboard the cutter HMS *Seaflower*. The same despatch contained a secret letter to Henry Dundas, jointly signed by Grey and Jervis, begging leave for both to be recalled to England, since 'no active Service can arise to call for our

---

8   Southley, *Chronological History of the West Indies*, Vol. III, p.90.

joint Exertions during the Hurricane Months,' promising to 'return to these Seas at the Expiration of the unhealthy Season'.[9]

Leaving the 43rd Foot to garrison Pointe-à-Pitre and Grande-Terre, two days later Grey boarded HMS *Quebec* under Captain Rogers and took Prince Edward's 1st and 2nd Grenadiers, Coote's 1st Light Infantry, and the artillery ten kilometres across the water to Petit Bourg, on Basse-Terre. According to Grey, their arrival was met with 'great Demonstrations of Joy by the French People on Marquis de Bouille's Estate'.[10] He then initiated an unopposed march south along the coast road towards the town of Basse-Terre, 25 kilometres to the south-west, shaded by Royal Navy ships following the march offshore. It was half of a pincer movement; the other half was Thomas Dundas with the 3rd Grenadiers and 1st and 2nd Light Infantry, who landed in a small bay near Marigot, at the village of Vieux Habitants, ten kilometres north-west of Basse-Terre on the evening of 17 April. His men destroyed two batteries on Morne Magdalene, after which Blundell's 2nd Light Battalion carried several enemy posts during the night. The two forces reunited outside the once-pretty town of Basse-Terre the following day, or such of it as remained; for the defenders had burned the western part of it the night of 17 April.

With Grey's column fatigued from the long march, they rested as Grey sent the Governor, Georges Henri Victor Collot, an ultimatum. All day on 19 April Grey waited for a reply. When none came, he ordered a dual-pronged night-time bayonet attack. The fact that the flank battalions had become seasoned veterans is borne out by the journal of Captain William Stewart of the 1st Grenadiers;

> To such a pitch of steadiness had our battalions attained by long practice in those night proceedings, that not a whisper could be heard nor a man be found misplaced from his file during the course of a march which, from the severity of the weather and the desperate magnitude of the undertaking, would have staggered and rendered impatient the very same troops but four months before.[11]

Dundas' light infantrymen stormed the French defences from the north, Grey's grenadiers from the south. The French outer defences at Fort Saint Charles fell with barely a fight.

---

9   Anon. *Facts relative to the conduct of the war in the West Indies; collected from the speech of the Right Hon. Henry Dundas, in the House of Commons, on the 28th of April, 1796, and from documents laid before the House upon that subject* (London: J. Owen, 1796), p.114.
10 GRE/A2243j, Grey to Henry Dundas, 22 April 1794. Concerning the capture of Guadeloupe and requesting to return to England to recruit his health.
11 Anon, *Cumloden Papers*, pp.9-10.

The town of Basse-Terre in Guadeloupe in 1794. (Anne SK Brown Collection)

About half an hour before daylight, our infantry and seamen, having advanced by different directions round the hill, set up a general cheer, and dashed in upon the enemy, who were supposed to be on the battery. From the darkness of the morning and the woody nature of the hill, the greater part of them instantly fled without a possibility of taking them; but about 20 of them who stood their ground and offered what little resistance lay in their power were put to the bayonet on the spot.[12]

Collot offered to surrender on 20 April, provided he could have the same terms afforded to his counterparts on Martinique and Saint Lucia. Grey agreed, and so Collot capitulated, surrendering 900 men of the 14e and 50e Régiments d'Infanterie and 800 National Guardsmen at Fort Saint Charles, plus 187 pieces of ordinance of various calibres, from one-pounders up to 36-pounders. As was now customary, Prince Edward marched into the fort with his grenadiers and some light infantry, ran the Union flag up the staff, and re-named the place Fort Matilda as the troops gave three cheers.

Whereas Rochambeau on Martinique had been valiantly stubborn, and Ricard on Saint Lucia hopelessly outnumbered, Collot had been timid and inept. His 5,900-man garrison had been overrun in ten days by an invading force less than half its strength. Grey's men had never seriously been troubled, and had all of Guadeloupe in the bag for the loss of only 86 men. Perhaps civil strife explains Collot's timidity, as evidenced in this message from Jervis to Grey dated at seven in the evening of 20 April. 'The flag of truce is on board the *Boyne*, and I enclose

12 Anon, *Cumloden Papers*, p.10.

the proposal. Collot has escaped from the post of Palmiste into Fort Saint Charles, the people of colour in desperation had determined to put him to death, they even talked of killing their wives and children and have continually fired upon each other'.[13]

Grey and Jervis were jubilant. 'I have now the greatest satisfaction in informing you of the entire reduction of the French in these seas,' Jervis wrote to the Admiralty on 21 April.[14] It was another extraordinary success, the high-water mark of all British military efforts in the West Indies between the declaration of war and the Peace of Amiens. Thus it was time for another victory dispatch, this one to be carried by Sir Charles Grey's aide, his fourth son Thomas. This one arrived at Whitehall on 21 May, two days after his 12 April memorandum, and caused further rejoicing in the capital. Thomas was promoted to major in an independent company the following day at the age of 23. For Collot, there was no option of returning to France. He wrote to Grey on 26 April asking for his family and himself to be removed to North America, to which Grey assented the following day after Collot signed his parole. 'For General Collot, the honours of war, and a frigate to go to America' read the conditions of his surrender,[15] and so a few days later he, his wife, son, daughter, secretary and aide boarded a ship for Boston.

But the knife-edge on which the success or failures of campaigns balance had been crossed. Events were now on the downward curve. Problems started to emerge. Seven battalions were much too small a force to garrison Guadeloupe. The men were exhausted from nearly three months of constant campaigning. Prince Edward and his suite had duly returned to Nova Scotia on 26 April aboard Captain Faulknor's frigate HMS *Blanche*, no doubt wishing to escape the torrid climate and the sickly season, leaving his brigade in the care of Dundas. The few Royal Engineer officers on hand had been dispersed across the islands – Captain Chilcott to Saint Kitts, Captain Douglas to Saint Lucia, Captain Johnstone and Lieutenant Fletcher on Martinique – meaning that new works or repairs on Guadeloupe had insufficient superintendence to speed their construction. The flank companies of the regiments serving on other islands were sent back to make those battalions whole again, thus dissolving the marvellous grenadier and light battalions and reducing the garrison on Guadeloupe to a bare minimum. Seven of the nine Royal Artillery companies also sailed away, six to Martinique and one to Saint Kitts. And always present, but starting to show its cursed hand in a truly substantial manner, came Yellow Fever.

---

13 GRE/A270a, Letter from Vice-Admiral Sir John Jervis to Grey, 20 April 1794. Concerning Major-Gen. Collot and the 'people of colour' in Guadeloupe.
14 *Bulletins and Other State Intelligence*, 1794, p.184.
15 GRE/A270c, Présomption (?) de Capitulation, 20 April 1794. Stating the terms on which it was believed Gen. Callot would surrender Fort St. Charles [English translation].

'After all, I confess it was hard work, now it is over,' wrote Thomas Dundas on 11 May, 'and this climate distresses me. Our fine soldiers, full of spirit and strong constitution, sink under fever, and I cannot save them'.[16] So many officers had fallen that the senior officers started a subscription for officers' widows. Grey donated £100, Sir John Jervis £100, Prince Edward £50, and Thomas Dundas the same. A surgeon of the Royal Navy has left us one of the most graphic accounts of the effect of the terrible affliction;

> The Epidemic Yellow Fever, or, as it is perhaps more properly styled, the Caucus, Ardent, or Burning Fever, had fully established itself on board. We lost nine men by it out of about twenty, who had been attacked ever since the winter solstice, when it first made its appearance. In many of the cases the fatal nature of disease declared itself from the beginning, by attacking with a rigor, vomiting of aeroginous bile; which, about the fourth day, changed to a pitchy blackness, tenesmus, diarrhoea, haemorrhage from the nose; on the second day intense thirst, ardent heat of skin, inflamed praecordia, as indicated by pain and resistance at the pit of the stomach, jaundice on or before the fourth day, and many other dangerous symptoms… Bleeding, though apparently indicated by the strength, rapidity and fullness of the pulse, was not attended with good effects; several men were bled, and all of them died; drinks of tamarinds, saline mixture, orangeat, lemonade, cooling emolient glysters, having the head shaved, and embrocating it and the whole body with the juice of limes, formed the treatment which appeared to answer best.[17]

Captain Josias Rogers was exposed to the worst effects of the fever. At the start of May, he heard that his nephew, a teen-aged lieutenant aboard the Boyne, had the fever; Rogers sent for him and installed him in his own cabin aboard HMS *Quebec*. On 8 May the young man died. A few days later, Lieutenant James Rogers, younger brother to the captain, was seized by fits and died of the same ailment in the same room. Captain Rogers refused to re-enter his pestilent cabin and slept on the quarter-deck; this, together with a voyage northward into American waters and a healthier climate, probably saved him. For the time being. On 2 July he wrote; 'I hear the *Boyne* has buried two hundred men since the capture of Guadeloupe'.[18]

Grey himself was also sick. 'I am sorry to say seriously say to Your Lordship,' he wrote to Lord Shelburne on 23 April, 'which I dare not say to my dearest Wife,

---

16   Dundas (ed.), *Dundas of Fingask*, p.147.
17   Leonard Gillespie, *Observations on the diseases which prevailed on board a part of His Majesty's Squadron on the Leeward Island Station between Nov. 1794 and April 1796* (London: G. Auld for J. Cuthell, 1800), pp.11-12.
18   Gilpin, *Memoirs of Josias Rogers*, p.142.

that I feel myself very much exhausted by my exertion both of Body and Mind, and am at this instant very far from well'.[19] He wrote home on 6 May to advise Whitehall that as far as he was concerned, the campaign was over. He had only enough troops to garrison his conquests, they were worn out by three months campaigning in difficult country, and in any event the sickly season was almost upon them.[20]

Ironically the day before, after a long delay due to foul winds, the four regiments from Ireland – the 22nd (Cheshire), 23rd (Royal Welsh Fuzileers), 35th (Dorsetshire), and the 41st Foot, 2,300 men in all – had landed on Martinique. With a warning from the British consul at Virginia in his pocket to the effect that a French fleet was in Hampton Roads, suggesting somewhat spuriously that the Americans might declare war against England, Grey detained the 35th and the flank companies but sent the rest forward at once to Jamaica, together with Brigadier General Whyte, and the whole ended up on Saint Domingue. In order to compensate for the loss of these four fresh regiments, Grey ordered the flank companies of the sickly regiments garrisoning Martinique, the 15th, 58th, 64th, 65th, and 70th, to cross to Guadeloupe.[21] Grey in particular was sorry to see Whyte go. 'You will find him an active, experienced and zealous officer, possessed of considerable abilities,' he wrote to Adam Williamson, 'and I am much indebted to him for the great stake he had in contributing to our conquests here'.[22] It seems that at this time Grey and Jervis were concocting the idea of a short expedition to Cayenne, a French colonial town on the coast of South America, 'so as not to leave the French a Port or resting Place to assemble in this Part of the World, should we succeed'.[23] The naval command for this proposed expedition was to have been by invested in Josias Rogers with nine frigates, three brigs and four gun-boats; the military command divided between Colonel Myers and Colonel Charles Lennox.

This impractical plan soon faded from their thoughts after hearing Cayenne had been reinforced, so Grey despatched the eight flank companies of the four recently-arrived regiments off to Jamaica to re-join their parent battalions, further weakening his prized flank battalions in so doing. But the passage was horrendous for some, as the following account graphically reveals:

---

19 Nelson, *Sir Charles Grey*, p.135.
20 GRE/A2243o, Grey to Henry Dundas, 6 May 1794. Concerning reinforcements for Major-General Williamson and an expedition against Cayenne.
21 GRE/A302, General Orders, 6 May 1794. Stating that Brigadier-General Whyte was to command troops for Jamaica, and concerning procedure in case of vacancies or promotions in Regiments in the West Indies.
22 GRE/A301, Extract of letter from Grey to Major General Williamson, 5 May 1794. Informing him of the surrender of Guadeloupe and its dependencies, etc.
23 Anon, *Facts relative to the conduct of the war in the West Indies*, p.115.

On the 8th of June, eight flank companies… arrived at Port au Prince, under the command of Lieutenant Colonel Lennox. They consisted, on their embarkation, of about seventy men each, but the aggregate number, when landed, was not quite three hundred. The four grenadier companies, in particular, were nearly annihilated. The frigate in which they were conveyed became a house of pestilence. Upwards of one hundred of their number were buried in the deep, in the short passage between Guadeloupe and Jamaica, and one hundred and fifty more were left in a dying state at Port Royal. The wretched remains of the whole detachment discovered, on their landing at Port au Prince, that they came not to participate in the glories of conquest, but to perish themselves within the walls of an hospital! So rapid was the mortality of the British army, after their arrival, that no less than forty officers, and upwards of six hundred rank and file, met an untimely death, without a contest with any other enemy than sickness, in the short space of two months after the surrender of the town.[24]

As to further reinforcements, a letter from Henry Dundas dated 28 April made it clear that there would be no more before the first week of November. The letter arrived aboard the man-of-war HMS *Intrepid*, which also carried the 80 fresh light dragoons requested by Grey at the end of March, dismounted, but with saddles and bridles. It warned that any reinforcements sent would 'necessarily consist of recruits,' inferring what Grey well knew, that they might be useless initially and sickly not long after. Instead, Henry Dundas proposed to detain in the West Indies eight regiments currently proposed to be drafted out and ordered home. These were the 10th, 16th, 32nd, 45th, 48th, 49th, 3/60th, and 67th Foot: the fact that they reportedly needed 3,433 recruits to complete them to 600 men each shows that they were weak indeed. The proposal now was to beef them up over a period of time with recruits sent from home until the regiments regained their official strength of 600 rank-and-file each. '[They] will besides have the advantage, on their arrival in the West Indies, of being immediately incorporated with experienced and seasoned Non-commissioned officers and Privates, and will, by their means, become efficient Corps in a very short time,' Henry Dundas wrote hopefully.[25] Dundas was also hopelessly inaccurate, for five of the eight proposed regiments (the 32nd, 45th, 48th, 3/60th and 67th) had already been drafted out and the cadres sent home to England from Barbados on 18 April, ten days before Dundas even wrote his letter. The cadres of these five regiments totalled 58 officers, 10 staff, 112 serjeants, 60 drummers and 379 other ranks. All other men had been drafted

---

24 Bryan Edwards, *An Historical Survey of the French Colony in the Island of St. Domingo* (Cambridge: Cambridge University Press, 2010, facsimile of 1797 edition), chap. xi. p.174.
25 GRE/A288, Letter from Henry Dundas to Grey, 28 April 1794. Concerning reinforcements.

out to other regiments in the West Indies, mainly those on Saint Domingue. So there it was: Dundas' plan was worthless. Indeed, Grey should have known better; in January, Dundas had ordered Lieutenant General Sir Robert Boyd to send the 1st and 18th Foot from Gibraltar as reinforcements for Grey. Both regiments were already en route to Corsica, so they were never despatched. No reinforcements could be expected for at least six months.[26]

The loss of the commanding officer was unlikely to benefit the expedition either. Grey was not well and suggested in letters home, even as early as 22 April, that he should be recalled. He appointed Thomas Dundas Governor of Guadeloupe, hoping that he, Prescott, and Gordon could look affairs in these islands in his absence, given that they now appeared secure. Over on Guadeloupe, Major General Thomas Dundas composed a long letter home on 20 May:

> I shall write… to assure you that in staying here I feel myself doing my duty to my country, and, I trust, to my family, that my hours would be soured if I felt that you was unhappy, that it would be unlike yourself to be so at any time, but when we retire to within ourselves then I feel it is impossible to stem a torrent of tears, which rush upon me from some trouble, some vexation, much gratitude to the Almighty for His care and protection, and the most confident hope and belief that I shall be restored to my dear wife, my lovely infants, and dear friends.[27]

Sadly, it was to be his last letter. Thomas Dundas had dinner with Sir Charles Grey and Admiral Jervis at Basse-Terre at the end of May, felt ill, and asked to be excused. Three days later, he was dead of Yellow Fever at Basse-Terre at the age of 43. It was a mortal blow to the expedition; there was no brigadier the men liked better, or that Grey trusted more. He was the first British general officer to die on campaign in the war with France. His wife, Lady Eleanor, probably received the news of his death at the end of June, just before she was due to give birth to their youngest child, Elizabeth. Her re-telling of a dream she had the night before is a mix of heart-rending sadness and military bumbling:

> I dreamt that I was walking in a large green field. The sky was cloudy, and its dark hue was reflected in a river which flowed below the field, and farther on fell into the Firth of Forth. As I walked on by the side of the river I observed a vessel in full sail coming from the sea. It came rapidly along and passed me. It also looked dark and black from the sombre tint of

---

26   Strength details based upon 1 April 1794 returns from GRE/A534, Abstract of monthly returns of H.M. Forces in the Caribbee islands, January- November 1794, also Abstract of the monthly returns of the Royal Artillery in the Caribbee islands, January – December 1794.
27   Dundas (ed.), *Dundas of Fingask*, p.156.

the sky. But just after it had passed a faint, sickly ray of sunshine glanced upon the stern, and I read these words, 'From St. Vincent'. I instantly felt heart-struck, and exclaimed, 'That vessel brings me fatal tidings!' I then awoke. I had not recovered from the unpleasant shock of this dream when the letter-bag was brought to me, being seven in the morning. I tore open the paper and the leading article was an extract from St. Vincent, which stated the death of Sir Charles Grey (who commanded the expedition). I was greatly shocked, knowing the intimacy between him and my husband, but felt great thankfulness that my worst fears had proved unfounded. Alas! it was himself! Through some unaccountable error the mistake was made in the names.[28]

Thomas Dundas was buried in the main bastion at Fort Matilda, at least for the time being. Grey was devastated at the loss of his old friend. 'In him His Majesty and country lost one of their best and bravest officers and a most worthy man,' he wrote in a letter to Horse Guards a few days later, 'I feel too severely the loss of so able an assistant on this arduous service, and a valuable friend ever to be lamented'.[29] Well might he have lamented his loss. With Gordon under a cloud on Saint Lucia, and Whyte despatched to Saint Domingue, the subordinate Grey depended most upon for the successful conduct of the land campaign was gone. All that Grey had left was the obnoxious Prescott and a clutch of valiant but limited field officers. Accordingly, he re-shuffled his command structure. Lieutenant Colonel Eyre Coote took over command of the remaining flankers, whilst Lieutenant-Colonel Bryan Blundell took over command at Basse-Terre. To fill the yawning gap in the ranks of available general officers Grey appointed his old friend Richard Symes a brigadier general – a temporary appointment in a given theatre of war, not a rank – back-dated to 25 May, and also Governor of Guadeloupe in place of Dundas. Four days later Grey likewise promoted Colonel Francis Dundas to the same appointment. These men were solid, efficient officers, but they were staff men, neither field commanders nor civil administrators.

By this time Grey and Jervis had left Guadeloupe, having sailed to other islands in the region to inspect the strong-posts and fortifications, there being no other pressing military or naval matters to require their attention. Jervis ordered his second-in-command, Rear Admiral Charles Thompson, to safeguard the station with the rest of the fleet during their absence. As a precaution against the coming hurricane season, Thompson was ordered to establish his headquarters and keep the 23 ships of his squadron in safe anchorage in Trois Islets off Martinique. Given the Royal Navy's other duties, thirteen out of the squadron's smaller warships were allowed to proceed beyond the boundaries of the station. Guadeloupe, Saint

---

28 Dundas (ed.), *Dundas of Fingask*, p.164.
29 Quoted in *The Gentleman's Magazine, and Historical Chronicle*, 1794, Volume 64, Part 2, p.795.

Vincent, Grenada, and Tobago were entirely devoid of naval protection. Jervis had been concerned for some weeks that his limited squadron had been so preoccupied with military activities that it had neglected it's maritime duties, but then unaccountably acted as if all danger had passed. Thinking their successes had built a stronger foundation than was actually the case, Grey and Jervis had grown entirely complacent. Imagine their surprise, given these conditions, upon being told they had a serious problem on their hands. French reinforcements had arrived.

12

Enter Hugues

On 23 April 1794, three days after the fall of Guadeloupe, a small French naval squadron under the command of Capitaine de Vaisseau Corentin Urbain de Leissègues left Rochefort bound for the French Antilles. On board were the Bataillon Sans Culottes, which was in fact a two-battalion, 1,300-man colonial unit formed from the 1er Chasseurs des Pyrénées Occidentales under the command of Chef de Bataillon Jean Boudet, as well as two companies of artillery under the command of Capitaine Mathieu Pélardy. They were sailing in response to Rochambeau's calls for assistance dated early March, and most intriguingly, they did not yet know that Martinique, Saint Lucia and Guadeloupe had fallen. Aboard were two généraux de brigade, Aubert and Rouyer, and Adjutant-General Cartier. Safely stowed in the hold was a brand-new guillotine. But the most important passenger was a French civil commissioner, a darling of the Republicans, a 32-year-old hard-nut sent to extend Jacobin terror to the Caribbean. His name was Victor Hugues.

Hugues was not a rough jumped-up Revolutionary thug. His parents had been silk traders, bourgeoisie. He had been born in Marseilles in 1762, and educated well. As a teenager his father had relocated the family to Saint Domingue to further their fortunes. Young Victor travelled the Atlantic on merchantmen, and spent much time navigating the Caribbean islands, so knew the region well. The family prospered, but Victor lost it all in the Haitian Revolution of 1791. According to one account he escaped the terror by hiding in the basement of a burnt-out building, then had to wade out to a waiting schooner to flee whilst being shot at by brigands. Behind him in ruins lay his old life, a butchered brother, and all possessions lost. He sailed to Marseilles with only the clothes on his back, made his way to Paris and joined an extreme Jacobin group known as 'Mountain', so-called as they always occupied the highest rear rows in the Convention chamber. He channelled his hatred towards the Royalists, the clergy, and the nobles. So ardent was his Jacobin fervour that the Convention named him Procureur of the *Comité de Salut Public* (Committee of Public Safety) in Rochefort. Allegedly, he set up a guillotine in the courtroom to more swiftly expedite justice. In September 1793, he ordered the execution of nine senior naval officers thought to be guilty of complicity with the British invasion force at Toulon. Having a Caribbean background, he was appointed one of two Civil Commissioners to the Windward Islands in 1794. Pierre Chrétien was the other. He was dispatched with the public mandate of abolishing slavery. His private mandate was to kill all those of the classes he hated.[1]

The French squadron, bearing the national colours of France, was seen off the town of Saint François early on Tuesday 3 June. It sailed along the coast towards Pointe-à-Pitre, oblivious to the presence of Grey and his men. That an enemy squadron had arrived unchallenged by the Royal Navy was the fruit of the Admiralty's earlier deception and under-manning of Jervis' squadron. Jervis had been forced to spread his ships over a wide area to support the activities of Grey's garrisons as well as chase privateers, with eleven warships off station. Therefore, only a single frigate, HMS *Winchelsea*, was careening at English Harbour off Guadeloupe that fateful day in order to halt the men who were about to turn Grey's campaign on its head. At four o'clock in the afternoon the French squadron, two frigates, *Thétis* and *Pique*, one corvette, two large ships armed en flûte, and five transports carrying 1,100 troops, arrived off Pointe-à-Pitre.[2] No doubt the British presence became obvious to the French as they neared the shore, and spied from afar the Union flag flying from transports in the Outer Harbour.

Two days later the civil commissioners Victor Hugues and Pierre Chrétien waded ashore to add spine to the French defence of these islands. Hugues got straight down to the work with the intensity for which he later became notorious. The military commander Général de Brigade Claude Aubert and his adjutant-general Charles Etienne Rouyer disembarked their troops at Pointe de Salines and Hugues ordered them to immediately burn and plunder all the nearby Royalist homes and farms. Chillingly, he soon after penned a letter to the Committee of Public Safety advising them that he had formed a military commission to judge 'aristocrats' captured under arms, and had in fact already guillotined some.[3]

The nearest British garrison was that at Fort Fleur d'Epée, a fortress on a hill overlooking the picturesque and aquamarine Grande Baie, about three miles south-east of Pointe-à-Pitre, and the defences of that place at this time comprised the 43rd Foot, with only 13 officers and 174 men fit for duty, 180 Royalists, and an officer and six men of the Royal Artillery. The Royalists were dead-keen to come to grips with the French regulars, and we can only assume that Drummond reluctantly gave them their head that evening. As on previous occasions, they proved completely useless as soldiers. At eight o'clock that night 180 Royalists, with Captain John Alexander M'Dowall of the 43rd Foot at their head, marched

---

1   William S Cormack, 'Victor Hugues and the Reign of Terror on Guadeloupe 1794-1798', in *Essays in French Colonial History*, pp.31-41; also Richard Ballard, *The Unseen Terror: The French Revolution in the Provinces* (London: I. B. Taurus, 2010), Chapter 5.
2   James, *Naval History*, Vol. 1, p.222.
3   Cormack, 'Victor Hugues and the Reign of Terror', p.34.

from the fort. 'While proceeding along the road leading to Gosier, a few shots were fired, probably from a piquet of the enemy,' it was reported, 'instantly the most shameful panic prevailed throughout the Royalist party. A general discharge of musketry took place. Many of the men threw away their arms and deserted; and about 30 returned to the fort with Captain M'Dowall. Three of the Royalists were killed, and four wounded on this unfortunate occasion'.[4]

Hugues and Chrétien decided to strike while the iron was hot and resolved to attack as soon as they could feed their troops. The attack came in the wee hours of 6 June. Commanded by 25-year-old Jean Boudet and led by Pierre Chrétien, the French assaulted Fort Fleur d'Epée in overwhelming force, some 1,200 men advancing noisily in the darkness. Lieutenant Colonel James Drummond ordered a 24-pounder gun and some field pieces to fire grape, which cut the leading Frenchmen to ribbons, and caused them to halt for several minutes whilst their officers harangued them. Then all hell was let loose. Boudet's two battalions of colonial chasseurs marched to the foot of the hill then stormed the fort. The disease-ridden defenders of the 43rd Foot repulsed them for about 15 minutes, after which the French retired to the base of the hill. But some Royalist militia in the fort panicked and rushed the gates to escape. About half the Royalists fled, leaving Drummond and the exasperated defenders of the 43rd to hold the place with one side of the fort completely abandoned. As Frenchmen swarmed over the walls, Drummond unleashed a platoon of the 43rd he had kept in reserve to defend the gate, but it was too late. He pulled all his men back into a tight formation and drove the French off with musketry volleys for a time, until the attackers overwhelmed them. The 43rd broke and dispersed.

Drummond and most of his men escaped but 45 men were missing, presumably taken prisoner. Drummond found that he could muster only 40 men on his arrival at the next post, Fort Saint-Louis. He collected another 33 men at Morne Gouvernement, and embarked at Petit-Canal in two boats for Grande-Terre, arriving in safety in the morning of 10 June. Behind him were left sick at Pointe-à-Pitre one captain, one ensign, seven sergeants, and 94 rank and file, now in French hands. The only upside was that some of the missing at Fort Fleur-d'Epée later escaped and joined their colonel. An unconfirmed later report stated that some of the British captives had been slaughtered in vengeance for supposed depredations at Fort Fleur d'Epée the previous April. Drummond had effectively given up the eastern island of Grande-Terre to the French. One of those taken prisoner was Grey's commanding Royal Engineer, Colonel Elias Durnford, along with his 20-year-old son Elias Walker Durnford, a subaltern. Elias Durnford senior died of Yellow Fever after being exchanged at Tobago on 21 June. He had been a serving Royal Engineers for 35 years. The uncharitable and insensitive Prescott thought he knew who was to blame, and it was easy to criticise a man who had died three days

4 James, *Naval History*, Vol. 1, p.223.

The beginning of the end. The capitulation of the defenders of Fort Fleur d'Epée on 7 June 1794. Much worse was to follow at Berville and Fort Matilda. (Public Domain)

earlier. 'If (the) report says true the blame of all this business must fall on the late General Dundas, as his neglect of a post on which the security of Grande-Terre depended and on some sort his own, was unpardonable'.[5]

The local commander, Lieutenant Colonel Blundell, had already dispatched a fast schooner to Saint Christopher's to raise the alarm. Grey received the news of the French landing early in the morning of 5 June, when he and Jervis were aboard HMS *Boyne* taking on water in contemplation of a return to Britain as soon as possible. This gruel had no sooner been digested than a second message followed, reporting the death of Thomas Dundas.[6] The very same afternoon Jervis and Grey sailed aboard HMS *Boyne*, with HMS *Veteran* in support, for Guadeloupe, Jervis having previously despatched HMS *Winchelsea* to Antigua and HMS *Nautilus* to Martinique to collect any spare troops. Grey and his staff landed at Basse-Terre on 7 June, whilst Jervis, with four men-of-war, sailed directly to Pointe-à-Pitre. He arrived at noon on 8 June and anchored off the harbour, and no doubt discovered things much to his displeasure. A French squadron moored within the Carénage,

---

5 GRE/A354a, Letter from Lieut.-General Robert Prescott to Grey, 30 June 1794. Expressing pleasure at Grey's military success, criticizing the late General Dundas' neglect, and making observations on Grey's attitude towards him (Prescott).
6 Captain William Stewart heard this news whilst aboard his brother's ship (Lord Garlies' HMS *Winchelsea*) at Barbados, headed home on leave. 'With him [Dundas] perished our best hopes of opposition to this new enemy… and it may rarely be the lot of any one officer to be so universally lamented, with so just a cause for every portion of regret,' he recorded in his journal. William Stewart then sailed back to Guadeloupe.

for one, and Pointe-à-Pitre and the surrounding defences in French hands for another. Sensing weakness in their opponent, Victor Hugues and Pierre Chrétien issued a proclamation on 7 June, that all Republicans were required to rally to drive the British out, or be considered a traitor, and that all blacks on Guadeloupe were free and equal.

Grey made Basse-Terre his headquarters and appointed Colonel Francis Dundas commander at Petit Bourg, but it would be some time before he could assemble enough troops to conceive of trying to recapture Grande-Terre. On 10 June, his wishes were granted, at least in part. The 35th and 39th Foot plus Lieutenant O'Brien's company of Royal Artillery arrived from Martinique, and the flank companies of the 21st Regiment of Foot (Royal North British Fuzileers) and Lieutenant Young's company of Royal Artillery arrived from Antigua aboard HMS *Winchelsea* as reinforcements. On 13 June Grey wrote to Evan Nepean that it was only a matter of being 'more alert, vigilant, and striking harder' to bring Hugues to heel.[7] The following morning boat-loads of Hugues' men were seen crossing from Pointe-à-Pitre to Petit Bourg, ostensibly to attack a British sloop and transport anchored there. HMS *Winchelsea* sailed in close and dispersed the rowers with cannon-fire. The French were finally moving west, and had reclaimed the low-lying land west of Riviere Salée, a handsome plantation owned by a Monsieur de Berville, by this time probably dead. They burned his house down, along with his sugar-mills and store-houses, then set up an encampment at Pointe Saint Jean (also known as Gabarre), a spit of land a ferry-ride away from Pointe-à-Pitre.

Alarmed by this development, Grey ordered Francis Dundas with the 1st Light Infantry and the 39th Foot on a ten-kilometre march through swampy country at night. They attacked the Republican position defending the river crossing at Pointe Saint Jean in Grey's preferred mode, in silence and at bayonet point. For the loss of seven killed and nine wounded, they reportedly killed 200, although this seems wildly exaggerated, and put the rest to flight, many of whom drowned trying to swim to Pointe-à-Pitre. The camp fell into British hands and Captain John Pratt of the Royal Irish Artillery constructed a battery of four heavy guns at the point. They were too far away to bombard Pointe-à-Pitre, but were at least within reach of French ships in the Carénage and Inner Harbour.[8]

More British reinforcements started to arrive offshore. Firstly, from Saint Kitts came the battalion companies of the 65th (2nd Yorkshire, North Riding) Regiment of Foot. On 15 June Grey reconstituted a new Grenadier Battalion from the grenadier companies of the 6th, 9th, 15th, 21st, 22nd, 23rd, 35th, 56th, 58th, 4/60th, 64th, and 66th Foot under his military secretary, Lieutenant Colonel Gerrit Fisher of the 60th Foot, and a new Light Battalion from the light companies of the same regiments under Lieutenant Colonel William Gomm. Then HMS *Veteran* arrived

---

7   Nelson, *Sir Charles Grey*, p.144.
8   Wylliams, *Account*, p.115.

on 17 June with two flank companies from Saint Vincent, and four from Saint Lucia. The navy provided two battalions of seamen under the command of Captain Lewis Robertson of HMS *Veteran* and Captain Charles Sawyer of HMS *Vanguard*, which were attached to the army. These two ships, along with HMS *Solebay* and HMS *Winchelsea*, were ordered up to l'Ance a Canot under the command of Rear Admiral Thompson. That particular bay had been judged a safer place to disembark than the Bay of Gozier, due to the milder surf, and the height of the country surrounding it. Lieutenant Colonels Coote and Cradock, who had some weeks earlier departed for England on leaves of absence, but then been detained on Saint Christopher's after contracting Yellow Fever, arrived back on Guadeloupe aboard HMS *Redbridge* on 18 June, accompanied by the flank companies of the 22nd Foot. On 26 June a schooner from Martinique arrived with two companies of grenadiers from Marin Bay, and was followed the next day by a third company in a small sloop. These men ultimately allowed Grey to reconstitute the 2nd Battalions of grenadiers and light infantry.

The re-capture of Guadeloupe commenced on 19 June. Troops climbed aboard flat-boats at three o'clock in the morning, each man carrying three day's provisions, one day's grog, and rum in kegs sufficient for one more day. The seamen battalions were armed with hatchets and tomahawks. The light infantry battalion was to land with two amuzettes, and the grenadiers with two three-pounders. These troops, commanded by Brigadier General Symes, rowed ashore first and landed without opposition, then pushed on to the heights. They were followed by the 65th Foot and two six-pounders commanded by Captain de Ruvijnes. By that evening the whole had taken post at Gozier. HMS *Solebay*, HMS *Winchelsea*, and HMS *Assurance* were employed in landing artillery and stores, supplying the troops with provisions and water during the day, and rowing guard at night. The water in the neighbourhood of the landing-place was found to be undrinkable, and Grey was forced to admonish his men in General Orders, forbidding them from going wandering in search of fresh water. He ordered the rolls to be called every two hours.[9] The situation plainly did not improve, for the following day he threatened that 'the first man caught in the act of plundering [is] to be hung on the spot'.[10]

The French, who Grey had assessed as having 2,900 men, only 500 being regulars, once again fled westward to Pointe-à-Pitre. In order to boost morale, Grey ordered that his troops assemble at six o'clock in the evening of 21 June 'to be marched to a conspicuous situation, in view of the enemy', and fire a *feu de joie* in celebration of the Duke of York's victory at Beaumont-en-Cambresis in France on 26 April, a victory that only masked the fact that the Duke's campaign was not going well.[11] The following day the 9th Company of Grenadiers (mostly of the

9   Wylliams, *Account*, Appendix p.36.
10 Wylliams, *Account*, Appendix p.39.
11 Wylliams, *Account*, Appendix, pp.37-38.

22nd Foot), commanded by the newly-returned Captain the Honourable William Stewart, and a party of seamen commanded by Lieutenant Isaac Wolley RN, marched along bad roads to Saint Ann's Fort, about twelve miles to the east, to dislodge some local defenders.

> We had received information that a large body of the enemy were in possession of the town and battery of St Anne's, at which place they had first effected their landing about three weeks before, and that the revolted slaves were spreading terror and rapine throughout that neighbourhood. My instructions were to take under my command my own company, a party of 60 seamen under Lieutenant Woolley [sic], and about 100 Royalists under M. de -------'s orders, to whose instructions I was also in some measure to conform. I was to gain the battery by surprise, if possible, before sunrise, and, having succeeded in the defeat of the enemy, destroy the guns, and scour the town and country of the plundering hordes.[12]

They did this in the usual Grey style. The grenadiers stormed the front, while the seamen and Royalists attacked the flanks.

> Although, from the nature of a deep ditch which ran through a sugar-cane patch immediately under the hill, I was unable to collect above 20 men over it for fear of being heard by the enemy's sentinel, who now stood within ten yards of us, yet, what from the darkness of the night, and from the peculiar steadiness and silence of the men, we rushed upon the fellow with a loud cheer, and pushing him into the further end of the battery, came up time enough with the rear of the enemy (who instantly ran out at the other end, firing a number of random shots and every gun that was loaded, except the only useful one, which pointed up the road that we rushed in by) to put 10 or 12 of them to the bayonet. A few of the blacks who were in the guard-house met the same fate; nor was any life spared except one poor negro boy who fortunately ran to me for protection.[13]

Unfortunately, some French Royalists who had attached themselves to the column ran amok, going into the nearby town 'where they began the most brutal excesses' until Captain Stewart reined them in.[14] News of large French reinforcements approaching forced Stewart and Wolley to give up the fort the next day.

Despite having freed all the slaves as ordered by the Committee of Public Safety on 7 June, Victor Hugues was starting to modify his views on the matter. In a

---

12 Anon. *Cumloden Papers*, p.12.
13 Anon. *Cumloden Papers*, p.12.
14 Wyllliams, *Account*, p.117.

proclamation of 18 June, he clarified that all black citizens were still expected to work. 'The Republic, in recognising the rights you hold according to nature, had not intended to remove your obligation to earn your living by work,' Hugues advised them.[15] Black men who were not in the army should return to the plantations. Those who did not would be considered traitors and given the full rigour of the law. The effect, as Hugues had probably always intended, was to ensure great numbers of them joined the army. A few weeks later Hugues advised the Committee of Public Safety that although he had always doubted the island's Negroes could be given liberty, he had to admit they had conducted themselves well since emancipation. However, Hugues constantly shifted his views on the matter, and a few months later stated that he believed the colony would be destroyed if the blacks were granted full equality.[16]

Back on Martinique, Robert Prescott busied himself inventing new ways to fall out with Grey and Jervis. Believing that Grey was getting bad advice from Jervis, on 16 June he issued an order that any orders given on shore by Vice Admiral Sir John Jervis were to be disregarded. Grey's response to this does not exist, but Prescott's letter in return of 17 June provides a few clues. 'Sir John Jervis's signature can be of no consequence to me,' he replied. 'I make myself contemptible in submitting to a Code of Laws issuing from the Quarter Deck of the *Boyne*'.[17] Grey tried to conciliate Prescott, who blew his top in a letter dated 27 June, taking, firstly, aim at the numbers of men available for the force, which at this stage of the campaign sound somewhat like back-pedalling; 'I have, of late, so often cursed the day and hour that I agreed to serve here with you,' Prescott wrote. 'Before your arrival at Barbados I wrote to England, that if the Eight Regiments were countermanded, as was reported, the attack on this Island must be given up. When you arrived, and told me you meant to attack it, notwithstanding this diminution of our force, and that as it appeared to me, in so positive a manner, as to preclude representation on my part, I said nothing, but my sentiments notwithstanding were not in the least altered'.[18] And then he brusquely defended derogatory comments about Jervis made by himself in a private letter to Grey; 'You tell me, "so many parts of your letter reflect upon the Admiral, unjustly. I will at once say that I must certainly show it to him". Do you mean this as a threat, Sir Charles? I never meant that he should be a stranger to my opinion of him, and when you shall so acquaint him therewith, you shall find that, if necessary, I will defend what I have said to you,

---

15 Cormack, 'Victor Hugues and the Reign of Terror', p.37.
16 Cormack, 'Victor Hugues and the Reign of Terror', p.37.
17 GRE/A346, Letter from Lieut.-General Robert Prescott to Grey, 17 June 1794. This same letter also contained eight pages of criticism against Du Buc and a wide variety of other grievances.
18 GRE/A353, Letter from Lieut.-General Robert Prescott to Grey, 27 June 1794. Concerning his dissatisfaction, his opinion about the attack on Martinique and remarks he had made in a letter to Grey about Jervis.

respecting him, with equal glory and honour to myself'.[19] On 9 July Grey got his military secretary, Gerrit Fisher, to write a summary of all Prescott's and Du Buc's letters since 17 June, to which Grey added some annotations. 'Most extraordinary language,' he wrote next to the summary of Prescott's 17 June letter.[20] From this point onwards, Grey was careful to keep duplicate copies of all correspondence with Prescott.

Prescott's letters might have been unwelcome, but vainglorious letters from the enemy were probably not welcome either. Hugues wrote to Grey and Jervis on 22 June, using official Republican letterhead, under which he crossed out 'Nous Commissaires' and corrected it to 'Le Commissaire'. 'The army of the Republic has conquered by valour the forts of Fleur d'Epée and Pointe-à-Pitre,' it trumpeted. 'French generosity makes no victim of his enemies misfortune; they are treated in accordance with the rights of war, besides which we have sick English soldiers, after we captured the town, from which we have proper confessions'. Then, in a theme that was to become predictable, Hugues proceeded to accuse Grey's men of barbarity. 'But I have just learned indirectly that the English have butchered the patriots of la Desirade, and that they butchered everyone regardless of sex. I demand a positive response. We have 411 prisoners of both sexes, and it would pain us to have to use retaliation. We do not ask quarter for ourselves; our motto is glory or death; we depend on our courage, and our bayonets. Hondschoote, Dunkirk, Mauberge, Toulon and Fort Fleur d'Epee; we are alive and in Europe, as in America, Republicans are triumphant'.[21] The fact that Hugues held 411 prisoners was probably true, but the allegations of butchery were most likely a provocation or repetition of an unsubstantiated rumour. Grey and Jervis replied the following day, emphatically denying the charges.

In a bizarre turn of events, the American Royalist Benedict Arnold just happened to be on Guadeloupe when Hugues invaded, with five thousand pounds Sterling in his baggage. Arnold claimed American citizenship and gave his name as John Anderson. Believing Arnold a British spy, the French confined him to a prison ship until they could hang him. He kept himself low and his cash lower. Some small change bought information from guards that Jervis's fleet had arrived to blockade the harbour. Arnold, by this time in his fifties, escaped out of a window and slid down a rope to a raft. The ship's watch aboard HMS *Boyne* must have been surprised when he arrived knocking the hull of in the dead of night. Having paddled with his hands, a French boat chased him, but Arnold lost it in the dark. Presented to Grey and Jervis, he remained aboard for nearly a year as a volunteer,

---

19 GRE/A353, 27 June 1794.
20 GRE/A363, Summaries of letters from Lieut.-General Robert Prescott and Du Buc, 17 June–9 July 1794, with observations.
21 GRE/A349, 4 Messidor in the 2nd Year of the French Republic [22 June 1794]. Letter from Victor Hugues (le Commissaire délégué par la Convention Nationale aux Isles-du-Vent) to Grey and Vice-Admiral Sir John Jervis.

acting as quartermaster and organising local planters and merchants into a militia.[22]

It was now the sickly season. Grey knew there was now no time to lose. He had to launch his grand assault on Pointe-à-Pitre whilst he still had at least a few serviceable battalions, but the lack of any serious troop strength consigned him to undertaking the mission as a series of measured steps. On the night of 25 June six companies of grenadiers and the marines under Colonel Fisher were detached to capture the road from Gozier to Fort Fleur d'Epée, which they did at dawn on 26 June without loss. On 27 June Brigadier General Richard Symes attacked and captured Morne Mascotte, just north of and visible from Fort Fleur d'Epée. A small French counter-attack that afternoon was repulsed. Two days later a much more serious effort was made, 1,500 French attacked Morne Mascotte, but were repulsed by the disciplined musketry of the grenadier and light battalions. Symes' garrison had been bolstered by the light companies from the Berville garrison, who had been transported across from Petit Bourg to Gozier the previous night under the command of Major Andrew Ross of the 31st Foot. Only the weakened companies of the 39th and 43rd Foot were now left at Berville. There followed several days of inconclusive skirmishing as the two sides eyed each other from less than two hundred yard's range.

On 29 June about 1,000 black and mulatto troops, wearing what Grey described as the 'National Uniform' – possibly the new French blue infantry uniforms – advanced out of Fort Fleur d'Epée, making for a party of Gomm's light infantry stationed on a rise above Morne Mascotte. They hoped to draw Fisher's grenadiers out of Morne Mascotte in so doing, then rush the fort. As they ascended the hill, singing martial songs and with colours flying, Fisher took the bull by the horns and advanced his men out from the fort, and ordered them to lie down. As the Republican column came within a few yards, he had his grenadiers stand up and deliver a killing volley. They then charged and the fighting evolved into a confused mass, which the French guns in Fort Fleur d'Epée lashed with artillery fire. Fisher was hit three times by grapeshot and his horse killed under him. Captain de Ruvijnes of the Royal Artillery received a musket ball in the neck. Lieutenant Philip Toosey of the 65th Foot was killed and another thirty grenadiers killed and wounded, but the Republicans were repulsed.[23] As ever, Captain William Stewart was at the forefront:

> This night passed over better than we had every reason to expect. It was a night which, I must question, has seldom been exceeded in point of severe

---

22   Nelson, *Sir Charles Grey*, pp.161-162; Milton Lomask, 'Benedict Arnold: The Aftermath of Treason', *American Heritage*, at https://www.americanheritage.com/content/benedict-arnold-aftermath-treason accessed October 2017.
23   Wylliams, *Account*, p.121.

duty by any army in the field. Harassed for six successive days, and now obliged to stand under arms for ten or twelve hours, drenched with the torrents of rain that fell, and expecting every minute a storm of our posts from the enemy, who must have come within fifty yards of our bayonets before we should have perceived them, unless, as I may almost assert, by the assistance of the repeated flashes of lightning which for some hours absolutely seemed to set the whole firmament in a blaze! The effects of this severe duty were sensibly felt next day by our army, many of our men falling upon the doctor's list. However, a hot sun came out, as usual, on the morning of the 1st of July; and our smoking clothes on our backs, with an additional allowance of grog, made us wish for another attack from our friends on the opposite hill as soon as they should please.[24]

That evening the French approached under a flag of truce and asked to be allowed to carry away their wounded and bury their dead. They undertook most of the former but little of the latter.

With Morne Mascotte secure, and with the rains now coming regularly, Grey decided the time was right to deal what he hoped would be a death-blow to Hugues. A French deserter had informed him on 29 June that the Republicans were demoralised. Benedict Arnold supplied similar information based upon his time as Hugues' captive. For this service, Grey offered Arnold's son a commission in the 21st Foot. Arnold refused. Arnold asked to be made a brigadier general; Grey refused. For his attack, Grey used the best troops he had: Fisher's 1st Grenadiers, Gomm's 1st and Ross's 2nd Light Infantry, and the 1st Battalion of Seamen commanded by Captain Robertson RN. It was to be a night attack on the fort at Morne Gouvernement under the command of Brigadier General Symes, and Grey would stay behind at Morne Mascotte with the 2nd Grenadiers, 65th Foot, and Captain Sawyer's 2nd Battalion of Seamen in reserve, in order to attack Fort Fleur d'Epée upon a signal if Symes was successful. Sadly, Symes was not.

The troops moved out from Morne Mascotte at seven o'clock at night on 1 July, and immediately got lost in a coffee plantation in a ravine. The night was pitch-black, and they eventually emerged on the coastal road, where they were joined by two small cannon to be dragged by seamen. Somewhere near the rear of the column there was a commotion. People speaking French had been heard in the jungle. Lieutenant Wolley RN chased after them, but they were gone. No further notice was taken of the incident, to the column's great peril. After a series of stoppages in ravines, during which time Symes issued no specific orders for his force, they found themselves where they did not wish to be. Symes' own account suggests that they had become lost. 'The troops marched with the utmost silence, through deep ravines, in hopes of reaching the enemy undiscovered,' he wrote, 'but our

24 Anon. *Cumloden Papers*, p.13.

guides, whether from ignorance, or the darkness of the night, led us in front to those posts of the enemy which it had been proposed to pass by, and which they assured us was practicable: to effect our purpose by surprise became therefore impossible'.[25]

Perhaps due to panic in the command, the three companies of seamen were unaccountably ordered to advance to the attack, despite being well back in an extended column that was exhausted and had lost much of its cohesion. They had to jog nearly a mile before coming upon the 1st Grenadiers, who were being held as a reserve. A bugle sounded and the seamen were ordered to attack immediately. Their officers, Lieutenants Thomson and Maitland RN, and Midshipman Oswald, could barely rouse 30 fit men into battle formation, the rest being strung-out and panting on the road behind. Lieutenant Wolley was ordered to lead the advance whilst Captain Lewis Robertson remained behind to form up the rest. The seamen ran forward into an inferno. The French defences at Morne Gouvernement were by now the strongest on the island, and the sailors were cut to ribbons by grape-shot. The disorganised mass of seamen veered left, away from the heights and towards the town, and entered into the streets of Pointe-à-Pitre. This exactly what the French commanders, Jean Boudet and Mathieu Pélardy, had intended all along. Enfiladed from the heights, from ships in the harbour, and from hundreds of muskets fired from the windows of homes and shops, the troops lost all order and control in the darkness, loaded their muskets and fired at each other, panicked then retired.

The pre-dawn light illuminated the scale of the disaster. Captain William Stewart, although barely twenty years of age, demonstrated he understood military common sense;

> Daylight began now to open upon us, and with it our eyes were opened to the blunders we bad been all along committing; for, instead of having permitted the whole army to have pursued the route of the fugitives from the first post, the larger body should have kept a road more to the right, and stormed Morne Gouvernement, by possession of which we should have commanded the whole town and harbour. This plan was not adopted, chiefly, I believe, from the loss of our guides, but partly also, I am apprehensive, from the want of regular plan and exact arrangement, which are so essentially necessary in all attacks and operations carried on by night. However this be, it was absolutely necessary to make the best of a retreat out of the town, and rather keep possession of the more distant heights. The works and every spot of the Morne were covered by the enemy, who poured on us an incessant fire of musketry and grape from every part of it; and, to complete our annoyance, one or two of their frigates had so

---

25 *Bulletins and Other State Intelligence*, 1794, p.315.

brought some of their guns to bear upon us, that we were in a manner assailed upon both flanks, and in short found a retreat necessary to save our scattered army.[26]

The French response to the retreat was brutal; Captain William Stewart saw '…the most cruel of all spectacles now before us, without attempting to save our brother soldiers, whom we saw falling before our eyes under the swords and bayonets of a merciless enemy.'[27]

Symes' later published account[28] painted a far rosier picture than actual events. The men had been marching for eight hours before the assault, so were even more exhausted than usual. The light infantry were not the elite flankers of the early campaign. They had been on campaign for nearly four months, sick and exhausted, and their hearts were not in it. Brigadier General Symes tried to rally them from horse-back, was hit in the right arm, fell heavily, and had to be carried to the rear. He had not delegated his orders to any other officer. Lieutenant Colonel William Gomm of the 1st Light Battalion was killed by a sharpshooter. Captain John Burnet of the 43rd Foot had his arm broken by a musket-ball, then was thrown to the ground after an explosion, completely covering him with blackened gunpowder. In this state grenadiers following behind assumed him to be a mulatto and so bayoneted him three times, before his cries put an end to the stabbing: the unfortunate Burnet survived and lived to become a major general. Captain Lewis Robertson RN was killed by an exploding shell. Lieutenant Isaac Wolley RN was shot in the leg and dragged off by his men.

Brigadier General Gerrit Fisher assumed overall command and tried to stem the retreat, aided by Major Robert Irving's 2nd Grenadiers, sent by Grey to cover the retreat. The war-like Captain Stewart was still up for the fight; 'I did not see, in my own opinion, the smallest necessity for this retreat. On the contrary, our men, though, to be sure, already knocked up by marching and fighting from sunset the previous evening, yet were anxious to be led on to the storm, and seemed ten times more sensible of the disgrace which Old England was incurring this day than some of their commanding officers.'[29]

The failure of leadership was evident to all who witnessed the attack. But Grey did not, and blamed the troops. He expressed his frustration over the failed attack in a letter to Evan Nepean, sent to England with Lieutenant Colonel Coote, a week later. 'I fear his[Syme's] mind is not at ease – not that he has any occasion; for no man could do more at the head of a corps than he did… between ourselves they

---

26   Anon. *Cumloden Papers*, p.14.
27   Anon. *Cumloden Papers*, p.14.
28   Report from Symes to Grey written at Gozier 2 July 1794, in *Bulletins and Other State Intelligence,* 1794, pp.315-317.
29   Anon. *Cumloden Papers*, p.15.

[the troops] were so completely worn down that they would not advance when ordered. It is a serious fact. The light infantry refused to make the least exertion, therefore I suppose they could not'.[30] But Grey was right; his corps was completely spent as a fighting force. His elite troops, the grenadiers and light infantry, were effectively hors de combat. A combination of disease and battle casualties had brought them to the point of extinction. From now on, these formerly magnificent battalions could do little more.

The diligent and quietly-spoken Richard Symes, Grey's long-time friend and companion, was shipped to Saint Kitts to recover, but died of his wounds there, probably from gangrene, on 19 July. He would be the highest-ranking British battle casualty of the entire campaign. Grey's losses between 10 June and 3 July amounted to one lieutenant colonel, four captains, seven lieutenants, and 93 non-commissioned officers and privates killed, one major, three captains, seven lieutenants, and 319 non-commissioned officers and privates wounded, and 56 non-commissioned officers and privates missing. The Royal Navy in the same period lost one captain, four seamen, and two private marines killed, one lieutenant, one lieutenant of marines, 24 seamen, and three private marines wounded, and 16 seamen missing. All in all, a total of 543 men from an expeditionary force that was desperately under-resourced in the first place, not even counting the nearly 700 men who died from disease in June. Captain William Stewart summed up the latter part of the campaign before finally leaving for England;

> Thus was finally relinquished that part of Guadaloupe called Grande-Terre, after having sustained, in the attempt to recover it, eighteen or nineteen as severe days of service as were probably ever witnessed in this or any other as unfavourable a climate for military operations. The dispositions made for the success of this last part of our West India campaign were good, and seconded by unusual exertions of our troops; and in every instance success might have been presumed upon, except in that one and final expedition as conducted by Symes. It may appear ungenerous to throw entire blame upon a quarter from whence a defence cannot now be made, by the subsequent death of that officer at St Kitt's in August [July]; but surely no one was witness to the events of the 1st and 2d of July without attributing almost the whole cause of failure upon that occasion to that same quarter.[31]

Jervis summed up the catastrophe. 'I have only to observe, that every possible exertion was made by the army and navy that the debilitated state of the officers

---

30   F. Loraine Petre, *History of the Norfolk Regiment: 1685 to 1913* (Uckfield: Naval and Military Press, 2001), p.122.
31   Anon. *Cumloden Papers*, p.16.

and men would admit of. It is but justice to them to declare, that they were quite exhausted by the unparalleled services of fatigue and fire they had gone through for such a length of time, in the worst climate'.[32] Of Captain Robertson, Jervis wrote, 'the fate of Captain Lewis Robertson, who had distinguished himself highly, fills my mind with the deepest regret: he had long been a child of misfortune, although he possessed talents to merit every success and prosperity: and as I am informed, he has left a widow and infant family unprovided for, I beg leave to recommend them to the protection and good offices of their Lordships to obtain a suitable provision, which will be a great encouragement to officers in similar circumstances to emulate so great an example'.[33]

With the Royal Navy's assistance, Sir Charles Grey retreated from Grande-Terre without molestation on 5 July, being unable to overcome superior French forces on that peninsula. He established a new position between Saint John's Point and Bay Mahault, with his headquarters at Camp Berville, on pestilential low-lying ground west of Pointe-à-Pitre. He left 1,800 men under Colonel Graham of the 21st Foot (whom Grey appointed a local brigadier general, backdated to 26 May) plus about 500 Royalists to fortify the position, and then returned to Saint Pierre on Martinique, to sort out the problems with General Prescott. Before he sailed he received a letter from Henry Dundas dated 21 May, in which the Secretary advised him of the votes of thanks passed by the House of Commons, to himself, Jervis, the major generals, the senior naval officers, indeed every man of the entire force engaged.[34] With the campaign in tatters – Guadeloupe more than half lost, Sir Charles Gordon about to be court-martialled, the garrison on Martinique down to a bare minimum – these words must have sounded hollow, almost surreal. Grey however was ever the man to put on a brave face. Riding the wave of the Parliamentary approbations he wrote to Dundas on 8 July, optimistically requesting 6,000 reinforcements.[35] He should have known better. With Dundas' various earlier plans for reinforcements shot to pieces, any reinforcements might take six months to arrive. Grey did not have that much time. To make matters worse, he received word from Prescott on 9 July that an American ship had spotted a French fleet bound for these islands. The report turned out to be untrue.

Hugues was the man with the benefit of time, of territory, and of numbers. He elevated Colonel Jean Boudet and Captain Mathieu Pélardy to the rank of général de brigade (brigadier general) on 19 June for their leadership at Fort Fleur d'Epée,

---

32 Letter from Jervis to Phillips Stephens, secretary of the Admiralty, in *Bulletins and Other State Intelligence,* 1794, p.318.
33 *Bulletins and Other State Intelligence,* 1794, p.319.
34 GRE/A322a, Letter from Henry Dundas to Grey 21 May 1794. Informing him of the King's satisfaction at the capture of St. Lucia and Guadeloupe.
35 A2243t, Grey to Henry Dundas, 8 July 1794. Concerning his return to England, the uselessness of raw recruits for the West Indies, his intention of leaving Prescott in command, etc.

and added a third battalion to Boudet's Chasseurs.[36] He liked proclamations, and issued them regularly. On 17 July, he told citizens of Guadeloupe that it was not sufficient to merely fight the enemy or to retake territory. 'The one and the other must be purged of the monsters who sullied them and the vices they inflicted'.[37] Whether he considered the monsters the Royalists or the British he did not elaborate.

For all that the British considered Hugue's forces 'brigands and cut-throats', there is no question that his ability to fashion a defending army out of such men speaks volumes for his abilities. Armed with an influx of emancipated slaves – thanks to the French Emancipation law of 4 February 1794 – his army was in the process of completely derailing the British military effort whilst significantly boosting French prospects of retaining the islands. Whatever sense of satisfaction Grey and Whitehall could take from the campaign was about to be sorely tested

---

36   Monica Fouché, *Glory Overshadowed: The Military Career of General Jean Boudet 1769-1809* (Unpublished Doctoral Thesis, Florida State University, 2005).
37   William S. Cormack, 'Victor Hugues and the Reign of Terror on Guadeloupe 1794-1798', p.34.

13

We Have Been Greatly Neglected

'You seem to have totally forgotten us', Grey wrote in a letter to Evan Nepean dated 18 July.[1] He was back at Saint Pierre on Martinique, intending to sit out the rainy months in that pretty town. Jervis sailed HMS *Boyne* into the safe and snug Trois Islets Bay near République-ville in order to do the same. Under intense pressure to provide reinforcements for other garrisons much troubled by brigand actions, Grey accordingly doled out some of his best remaining troops. He sent flank companies hither and thither; those of the 6th and 9th Foot to Saint Lucia, those from the 4/60th to Saint Vincent, those of the 65th to Grenada, the grenadiers of the 21st to Antigua, the light company of the 21st to Saint Kitts. Another battalion company of the 21st sailed to Dominica. He retained one grenadier battalion, Cradock's 2nd, as the permanent guard at Fort George;[2] two of the other three flank battalions were disbanded and the remaining men drafted into other regiments. Even they would not make up for the 552 men dead from disease in August, added to 788 in June and more than 500 in July.[3]

On 20 July, Grey ordered the troops to be assembled once more for another *feu de joie*, this time to celebrate Lord Howe's victory over the French fleet at the Glorious 1st of June. He had spent the day writing a summary of the garrisons necessary for the continued safety and security of the Leeward Islands, and probably needed cheering up. By his own calculations, some 10,800 infantrymen and 740 artillerymen were needed for this task, whereas these islands currently held 6,000 and 450 respectively, of whom only 3,200 and 390 were actually fit for duty. Losses in the artillery arm made necessary an order issued on 1 August, that one sergeant, one corporal and twelve men from each infantry regiment were to be 'instructed

---

1   Fortescue, *A History of the British Army*, Vol. IV Part I, p.376.
2   According to a return in GRE/A390 dated 18 August 1794, Cradock's battalion had 7 officers, 4 staff, 13 serjeants, 7 drummers and 216 other ranks present, of whom only 139 were fit for duty.
3   GRE/A584, Abstract of monthly returns of H.M. Forces in the Caribbee islands, January – November 1794. Abstract of the monthly returns of the Royal Artillery in the Caribbee islands, January – December 1794.

in the exercise of artillery', and that these men, once skilled were perfected, were to be relieved by an equal number to be taught the same, and so on.[4]

Out of the blue, Grey received a letter from his old foe Rochambeau. After arriving in Philadelphia, the Frenchman had compiled his reports on the loss of Martinique and forwarded them to Committee of Public Safety in Paris, then awaited his fate. A summons home did not arrive. So he lived graciously in Philadelphia and Newport, surrounded by old friends and admirers of his famous father. Thus safely and distantly ensconced, Rochambeau wrote a long hectoring letter to Grey on 26 June. 'You are surrounded by a party which without the assistance of the British armies should never have gained the least advantage on such of the Frenchmen as were faithful to the Republic' [sic], he warned. 'The hatred of that party is proportionable to their weakness; Their vengeance to their cowardice; With what a Secret pleasure do they not make of you the direct instrument of their private resentments!' In plainer language, Royalists were using Grey as a tool to settle their private quarrels. Grey must have felt a chill as he read it. 'Yes, Monsieur le General, I say it without disguise; your government in the West Indies will not be of a longer duration than mine..'. Rochambeau finished the letter with one last dig; 'I do then lament very sincerely that you do not take advantage of the fortunate opportunity offered to you, to immortalise your name by your acts of benevolence in the New World, and surround it with the sentiments of gratitude'.[5]

To cap off a bad month, Grey received a letter from Henry Dundas dated 9 June accusing Grey and Admiral Jervis of pecuniary crimes and extortion of prize-money. All prize-money owing as a result of the campaign was therefore cancelled. Grey was appalled, then furious. 'If this army be deprived of its prize money, many of the officers must be ruined', he complained.[6] The history of the matter extended back three months. As early as 14 April 1794, a little over a week after the capture of Saint Lucia, a correspondent on Saint Vincent had written to Messrs. George Baillie & Co., merchants, complaining of 'extraordinary plunder' by the commanders-in-chief.[7] In early June 1794 a committee of the West India Planters in London had meet with Prime Minster Pitt which resulted in a promise from Pitt that the commanders-in-chief would be ordered to give up any property improperly confiscated. Henry Dundas had asked Sir William Scott, the advocate-general, his opinion of the matter, only to be told that the confiscations were

---

4   Willyams, *Account,* Appendix, p.46.
5   GRE/A352, English translation of letter from Lieut.-General Rochambeau to Grey, 26 June 1794. Criticizing Grey's conduct as Governor in the West Indies.
6   Fortescue, *A History of the British Army*, Vol. IV Part I, p.377.
7   GRE/262, Extract of letter to Messrs. George Baillie and Co. from their correspondent at St. Vincent. Concerning the 'extraordinary plunder' under the Commanders-in-Chief at Martinique.

'illegal and without sufficient warrant'.[8] Grey wrote a long letter to Dundas on 28 July explaining his side of the story. 'I always understood the property found in any place taken by Storm or assault became the legal Prize or Booty of the Captor; consequently, neither the Admiral or I found any difficulty or hesitation in considering the produce, Merchandize, &c, found afloat and onshore at St Pierre and Fort Royal as justly forfeited and liable to Confiscation'.[9]

In an effort to defend his conduct Grey plucked out examples from years gone by, 'Almost every village or town taken by Prince Ferdinand in Germany was immediately Paid under his Contribution and the Money distributed amongst the Troops, of which I have shared myself when on that Service, and I believe the Marquis de Bouille levied a Contribution on the Island of Saint Christopher's, when taken by the French in 1782, many more instances may be added.' Feeling justified in his actions, he was sure who was to blame for misrepresenting his actions at home. 'It appears that the English Merchants, particularly those in the West Indies (who had carried on an illicit Trade to the French Islands before they were Captured and had immense sums due to them in consequence of it, which they could not obtain payment till after we had conquered those Islands) have taken the lead in demurring and in misrepresentations or Miss-statement of facts to England, from self-interested motives'.[10] He packaged off the reply on the first available fast frigate, knowing that a response could be two months away, and returned his mind the generally bad state of the campaign on Guadeloupe.

But however bad things were for Grey and his men, the French were not having things all their own way. On 6 July French military commander Général de Brigade Aubert died of fever, and his deputy Général de Brigade Rouyer died of wounds he received from shrapnel two weeks earlier. Hugues promoted field officers to replace them, amongst them Jean Boudet, a future count and général de division under Napoleon. Pierre Chrétien also succumbed to Yellow Fever, meaning that Victor Hugues now had sole authority over Guadeloupe. He started to rule the island like a Grand Vizier, employing various villains as spies and henchmen, whilst on the domestic front creating a coterie of concubines, local women who perhaps were only following the old rule of keeping friends close but enemies closer. Hugues sequestered the goods and private property of departed émigrés at will, but to show impartiality in financial matters, treated the chattels of patriots as equally fair game. As is often the way in such circumstances, Hugues built around him an entourage of brutish and grasping Republican hot-heads who treated any

---

8 GRE/A379a, Copy letter from the Advocate General, Sir William Scott (subsequently Lord Stowell), to Lord Grenville, 2 August 1794. Stating his opinion that the condemnation of American vessels at Martinique was null and void.
9 GRE/A378, Copy of letter from Grey to Henry Dundas, 28 July 1794. Replying to Dundas' letter of 9 June concerning prize goods and contributions, etc.
10 GRE/A378, Copy of letter from Grey to Henry Dundas. Replying to Dundas' letter of 9 June concerning prize goods and contributions, etc.

comment or suggestion from the great man as an order, and always over-extended their authority. As a measure of his perceived self-importance, Hugues actually refused to enact the Constitution of the Year III, issued from Paris in August 1795, stating, 'the constitution which offers such advantages in France, presents only difficulties in these countries to promulgate it; to put it into action today, would mean the next day that the colonies would no longer exist'.[11]

If Hugues was quiet in August and September, it was because he was raising, equipping, training, and motivating a Franco-Guadelupian army. Despite his vices, this was one area in which Hugues excelled. This was arguably the first western army in history to contain men of all colours and classes, ordered to enlist as 'national volunteers'. The first regiment raised was the Bataillon de Sans-Culottes de la Guadeloupe. Artisans fought side by side with former slaves, patriots with *gens de couleur*, although it is fair to say that the officers needed to demonstrate an absolute obedience to Jacobin principles, and many were hand-picked by Hugues himself. Some time in this period additional reinforcements arrived from France and they formed the backbone of the new Guadeloupe armed forces. Hugues enlisted 2,000 black soldiers in late August and early September alone. He declared that any man who brought in twenty recruits would automatically be made a sergeant. Total troop numbers are not known, but could easily have been more than 5,000 men. Nervous about the possibility of the numerous slaves serving with the army resorting to acts of sabotage or assassination –although there had been no such occurrences to date – Grey ordered that all blacks serving with his army be sent to Saint Pierre or République-ville on 3 August, preparatory to their being sent home.

Meanwhile at République-ville on Martinique, Lieutenant General Prescott paced the ramparts and fumed. He penned a letter to Grey on 30 August which stopped only just inches short of insubordination. 'You seemed the middle of last month to signify an intention of my going to Guadeloupe. I shall be glad to know what you have resolved on, as if, I am to go, and stay there, you will so good as to tell how I am to go and to order some vessel to transport our horses'.[12] Prescott did not understand how truly disastrous were the circumstances into which he was entering. Grey responded from Saint Pierre immediately. Prescott was to go. It was not a difficult decision, since the Royalist Baron de Clairfontaine had written to Grey on 18 August advising him of the serious administrative difficulties on Guadeloupe due to the lack of a governor,[13] and in any event Prescott had alienated himself from most of the civil administration on Martinique. Therefore a

---

11 Cormack, 'Victor Hugues and the Reign of Terror on Guadeloupe 1794-1798', pp.31-41.
12 GRE/A408, Letter from Lieut.-General Robert Prescott to Grey. Requesting to know whether he is to be sent to Guadeloupe.
13 GRE/A391, Letter from Baron de Clairfontaine to Grey. Concerning the serious administrative difficulties in Guadeloupe because there was no Governor there.

military posting elsewhere seemed the best use of his talents. Prescott and his horses boarded HMS *Roebuck* and arrived at Basse-Terre on 4 September. He set out on a tour of inspection, and what he found did not please him. He inspected Berville, re-sited a few batteries, then went to Fort Matilda, only to find it in a state of disrepair. The Royal Engineer officer on the spot was ordered to put the fort 'in the best order'. Worst of all, the fort had only seventeen privates fit for duty, plus about sixty convalescents barely fit to stand, not counting the dubious local militia. Prescott ordered Captain Lewis Hay to Trou au Chien, a strong post about ten miles due east as the crow flies, to collect all the local militia he could find. He then ordered the company of the Carolina Black Corps from Fort Matilda to reinforce the garrison at Berville.[14]

Brigadier General Colin Graham's troops remaining in the swampy and malaria-ridden Berville camp on Guadeloupe comprised only three full battalions, albeit depleted by sickness, and bits-and-pieces of others. The complete units were Major Hugh Magan's 39th, James Drummond's 43rd, and Captain John Grant's 65th Foot. Flank companies from the 15th, 58th, and 64th provided some stiffening, as did the battalion companies of the 35th Foot, at least until the remains of the 2nd Grenadiers, just 70 fit men, arrived as a relief at the end of August, wherupon the flank companies of the 15th and 64th sailed to Martinique. The remaining guns were served by detachments of the Royal Artillery and Royal Irish Artillery. Some local Royalist militia, variously attired and armed, added a local flavour if nothing militarily. Most field officers had either gone to England on leave of absence or perished. Lieutenant Colonel Stephen Fremantle of the 39th Foot had died aboard HMS *Vengeance* in August. Lieutenant Colonel Drummond of the 43rd was sick in bed and had been for weeks. The 70 grenadiers who arrived at the end of August were down to 20 fit men within three weeks. By early September things were, of course, worse. Some 330 men had died in the last month, and nearly 1,400 were sick. There were barely 400 men left to defend the long perimeter. Some battalions existed almost in name only. The Light Battalion had 33 men fit for duty out of a total strength of 415; the 39th, 24 fit men out of 308; the 43rd, 23 out of 199. By mid-September the number present and fit for duty had shrunk to 158, with the virtually non-existent 43rd Foot able to put only a single man in the line.[15] Unfortunately the company of Carolina Corps was marched with such exertion as to render them almost unfit for duty when they arrived at Berville.

On 26 September, at Hugues's express order, his new Franco-Guadelupian army went for the jugular. Some new French sloops had arrived, and on a moonless night, his troops under the command of newly-minted Général de Brigade Pélardy

---

14 GRE/A474, Letter from Lieut.-General Robert Prescott to Grey. Defending his conduct in Guadeloupe and giving a detailed account of events there, 4 September – 8 October 1794.
15 Return in GRE/A433, Letter from Brigadier-General Colin Graham to Grey. Reporting from Berville camp, 14 September 1794.

sailed from Pointe-à-Pitre and Fort Louis, disembarked at Goyave and Lamentin, respectively south and north-west of the Berville camp, and commenced their advance. The Goyave Republicans captured Point Bacchus, where Lieutenant Colonel James Drummond of the 43rd Foot was in hospital. Drummond and some convalescents escaped to the waterfront, but the Republicans massacred some who could not flee, and captured Drummond and his pathetic band of 160 men anyway. A large number of Royalists and sick soldiers escaped on a pair of Royal Navy sloops, which sailed away miserably over-crowded. Brigadier General Graham immediately ordered all British and Royalist troops to fall back to Berville, having lost communication with his only supply base at Petit Bourg. Général de Brigade Boudet advanced a second column from Lamentin and combined with a smaller central column under Chef de Bataillon Gaspard de Bures of the 2ème Bataillon des Sans-Culottes de la Guadeloupe.[16]

The combined Republicans were in position to advance against the camp at Berville in great force two days later. Graham considered retiring westward to Rivulet du Coin, a place from where he believed he could not be dislodged, but after discussions with his acting engineer Captain Joseph Walker (of the Royal Irish Artillery) and artillery commander Captain Henry Hutton, decided to fortify the Berville position. Two days of frantic activity followed. Graham was hampered for lack of artillery and engineer officers. Captain Francis de Ruvijnes was wounded and sick aboard ship, and his next choice, Lieutenant George Stackpoole too sick in camp to stand. So he called Captain Henry Hutton back from a leave of absence and set him to work. 'The astonishment of the Enemy on the 30th was great', Graham later wrote, 'to find works and Artillery at a place where they did not expect to find a Gun (notwithstanding the constant Spies in our Camp)'. After putting his few fit men into the posts on the left flank at Morne Savan and Pointe Saint Jean, he divided the rest, including 'every convalescent who could crawl to the works', into two divisions, one attached to Major David Forbes and his grenadiers, the other to Captain Richard Stovin and his light infantry.[17]

Graham's original plan was to have one division in the lines and one in reserve, whilst the French Royalists held the line throughout, but had to abandon the idea due to lack of men. So it was every man to the front line. This line ran along a crest more or less parallel with the coastline south of the Berville farm, with right-angled re-entrants conforming to the twist and turns of the headland. The right flank was anchored by three six-pounders on some rising ground overlooking the Rivulet du Coin; a single gun enfiladed the Rivulet du Coin road from the centre of the line; and two guns on a knoll allowed cross-fire along the whole line. Hugues's response was to site fourteen cannon in the swampy meadows around

---

16 GRE/A2243ee, Colin Graham to Grey, 21 October 1794. Concerning the attack on Berville camp and its capitulation; see also Fouché, *Glory Overshadowed*.
17 Most of the details of the Berville defence taken from GRE/A2243ee.

Rivulet du Coin, and to keep up a harassing fire day and night. Graham had only 250 regulars and 300 untrained Royalists to hold the perimeter. The Republicans captured Bellecour, north-west of Berville and site of the camp of the 43rd Foot on 29 September. The ring was closing.

Lieutenant General Prescott heard of the attacks against Petit Bourg and Berville whilst at Fort Matilda in the morning of 28 September. He awoke on the morning of 29 September to find that about half of the militia had deserted in the night. During the day one Monsieur Poyen arrived with intelligence that 1,200 of Hugues' men had captured Lamentin. 'The consternation amongst all ranks was very great', Prescott recorded.[18] The remainder of the local militia duly evaporated that night. This was surely the point when it was apparent that all Royalist goodwill towards the British had dissolved. Prescott wrote to Rear Admiral Thompson off Basse-Terre the following day. 'Amongst the French the consternation is great, they and the English are embarking, saving what they can, for they see I have no men to protect them'.[19] He ordered Captain Lewis Hay to move the few militia he had collected at Trou au Chien to Saint Marie, on the coast road near Trou au Chien, in order to block any brigands heading south. Hay roused the militia to move but half of them immediately deserted. The wheels were well and truly falling off the defence of Guadeloupe, with much worse to follow.

The alarm went off in Berville camp at four o'clock in the morning of 30 September. The regular garrison of Berville at this time comprised what was left of the flank companies of the 8th, 12th, 17th, 31st, 33rd, 34th, 38th, 40th, 44th, and 55th Regiments of Foot, three companies each of the 56th and 65th, and the remaining whole of the 39th and 43rd.[20] Every man rushed to the works. Somewhere out in the dark, the French were advancing in three columns, two from Bellecour and one from Paul's Plantation, in the vicinity of Rivulet du Coin. Captain Stovin's light infantry were posted on the right flank and were the first into action, pouring volleys into the massed ranks of Republicans. Major Forbes' grenadiers, who had been entirely within the camp, arrived and Graham posted him at right angles to Stovin's men, facing west, to hold the enemy attacking from Bellecour. At that moment Graham received a musket wound that grazed his shinbone, and retired to the camp to have it treated. Major Forbes was hit and collapsed, a wound that next day proved to be mortal, and Captain Stovin assumed command of the entire defence. Captain Henry Hutton commanded the artillery which 'did great execution' until he was hit in the right eye by a musket-ball.[21] The

---

18 GRE/A448, Letter from Lieut.-General Robert Prescott to Grey 29 September 1794. Reporting from Guadeloupe where the enemy had disembarked.
19 GRE/A454b, Letter from Lieut.-General Prescott to Grey, 30 September 1794. Reporting on the situation in Guadeloupe.
20 Fortescue, *A History of the British Army*, Vol. IV Part I, p.375.
21 GRE/A2243ee, Colin Graham to Grey, 21 October 1794. Concerning the attack on Berville camp and its capitulation.

youthful but sick Royal Engineer officer Lieutenant Elias Durnford Junior arrived and offered to command the artillery, there being nothing he could do as an engineer at that moment. Captain Vermont and his company of Royalists evidently behaved with great steadiness. The attack petered out, and the rest of the day was quiet. Five separate Republican suicidal frontal assaults against the earth ramparts had been repulsed at a cost of 400 attackers, including their commander, Jean Boudet, his shoulder fractured by a musket-ball. The defenders lost 25 men killed and 51 wounded.[22]

The following morning, 1 October, a howitzer was moved from Morne Savan to the left flank of the Berville line, in order to be able to blast grape-shot against any fresh attackers. Some French gunboats occupied the harbour south of Berville, and the awful realisation dawned on Graham that these ships completely cut off the only means of communication he had left – by sea. These same gunboats sailed out of Pointe-à-Pitre and daily bombarded the few British ships remaining at Petit Bourg. On 5 October a cannon-ball plunged through the cabin of deputy quartermaster-general, Major Robert Irving of the 70th Foot, killing him whilst escaping Berville aboard HMS *Assurance* as a convalescent. Vice Admiral Jervis aboard HMS *Boyne* sailed into the harbour and anchored of Gozier at ten o'clock in the morning of 2 October, sent to add the weight of shot against whatever Republican defences were within range, and hopefully draw off some attackers from Berville. Despite a barrage of red-hot shot from the ship, the tactic did not work. Hugues applied the tourniquet around Berville mercilessly. He attacked again on 3 October, and again the following day, although these attacks soon descending into desultory sniping. The brave Royalist Vermont was wounded on 4 October and his deputy, Lieutenant De Lisle, killed alongside him. Vermont, an ardent Royalist, had good cause to despise the Republicans, having lost his estate, his mother, his sister, and his pregnant wife to them in the weeks before the arrival of the British. It was only Grey's invasion that saved him from a Fort Saint Charles dungeon and the guillotine.

By 4 October Graham realised that Hugues had commenced to land troops to the north of him, thus blocking his only possible line of retreat. 'When seeing no prospect of Relief, our men dropping off fast, our Wine and Rum expended, seven Barrels of Pork and about Twenty of Flour being only left, two days before the capitulation, and almost all the can[ister] ammunition for the Field Artillery likewise expended, I was induced to follow the opinion of my Officers, who were unanimous in declaring the Post no longer tenable' he later wrote. 'Seeing the great Preparations making from the Sea to attack our Rear, and knowing that the Swamp was penetrable in several places, even all the way from the Gabarre, from whence my information was that they meant to penetrate, not able to guard so extensive a front'. He was by that point defending the southward line at the rate of about 75 fit men per mile. Doubling the frontage was ludicrously out of the question. 'I

---

22 Fortescue, *A History of the British Army*, Vol. IV Part I, p.381.

was under the necessity of listening to Terms of Capitulation, the heads of which I had already prepared, but wishing to postpone the matter as long as possible, I shewed no signs of a desire to capitulate, as from their real knowledge of our State of Provisions, I expected a summons, which coming from them, I was in hopes of getting better terms'.[23] With Lieutenant Colonel Drummond a prisoner and Major Magan too sick to attend, Graham had only nine captains and twenty lieutenants left, and many of those were incapacitated. He had lost his second-in-command, Major David Forbes, as well as Lieutenant John Cochran of the 39th Foot, killed. Captain Henry Hutton of the Royal Artillery was blinded in one eye. The senior remaining officer of the 43rd, Captain John Cameron was badly wounded. Any decision other than surrender would have led to the camp being over-run, and the garrison massacred. The French regulars might have shown mercy, but they were in the minority.

Finally, in the morning of 6 October, a subaltern walked out of the lines carrying a white flag. Brigadier General Graham asked for the terms of capitulation. They were agreed on the spot between Graham and Hugues as follows:

> Art. I. That, in consideration of the gallant defence the garrison has made, they shall be allowed the honours of war.
> *Answer. Granted.*
>
> Art. II. That the inhabitants of the island now co-operating with the army, whether white or free people of colour, being British subjects, having taken the oaths of allegiance to his Britannic Majesty, shall be considered and treated as such.
> *Answer. Not admissible: but a covered boat shall be allowed to the general, which shall be held sacred.*
>
> Art. III. That the troops, and such of the inhabitants as do not wish to become subjects of the French Republic, shall he sent to Great Britain, as soon as transports can be provided for that purpose.
> *Answer. The troops shall be sent to England, as soon as transports are ready: But as to the inhabitants, it is answered in Article II.*
>
> Art. IV. That the baggage of the officers and inhabitants in camp shall be allowed to them.
> *Answer. The troops shall be allowed their baggage.*

---

23 GRE/A2243ee, Colin Graham to Grey, 21 October 1794. Concerning the attack on Berville camp and its capitulation.

Art. V. That the sick and wounded, who cannot be sent on board transports, shall be allowed British surgeons to attend them.
Answer. Agreed to.

Art. VI. That the ordnance and stores of every denomination shall be given up in their present state.
Answer. Agreed to.

Art VII. If any difficulties in settling the above shall happen hereafter, they shall be amicably adjusted by the respective commanders.
Answer. Admitted. [24]

With the words 'not admissible', over 300 Royalists faced their doom. Twenty-five men only could be accommodated in a covered boat. Thus, the Royalist officers sailed to HMS *Boyne* and safety. The rest were to be left to their fate. With the terms agreed, 125 skeletal redcoats, the remnant of 46 companies, staggered out of the lines. The rest, over 1,000 men, were sick. Everyone was taken into captivity, but many died within weeks. A party of officers of the 39th Foot, and some convalescents, escaped to the Inner Harbour, found some open boats, and escaped with their colours. They eventually reached the Saintes. The remainder, not so lucky, were marched aboard prison hulks. They included 46 officers, Brigadier General Graham chief amongst them, the valiant Captain Stovin, the ill Lieutenant Colonel Magan of the 39th, the thrice-wounded Lieutenant Henry Keating of the 33rd Foot, the ailing Lieutenant Durnford of the Royal Engineers, and virtually every remaining officer of the 43rd Foot. In theory they were to sail for England within twenty-days of the surrender, on the condition that they would not serve against France again during the present war. Hugues had no intention of honouring such a deal. As far as he was concerned, they could sit aboard the hulks in the harbour until they all died. Then Hugues demonstrated what he intended by the word 'inadmissible'. He massacred all the Royalists in the garrison, many with a makeshift guillotine. According to one account, the first 27 heads came off in seven-and-a-half minutes. A single machine could only do so much; perhaps the blade went dull. So most of the rest were tied together in roped batches of fifty or so, forced to stand at the edge of a giant pit, then fired into by a company of infantry. Those hit fell into the pit and dragged those unhurt in with them. This was a technique Hugues had seen used at Lyons, Toulouse, and in the Vendée, and was useful for processing large batches of executions quickly without using up too much ammunition. Once all victims were in the pit, the company of infantry filled the hole, tamping the dirt down until the last muffled

---

24   Quoted in Anon. *A Collection of State Papers Relative to the War against France*, 1795, p.159.

noises from under the ground faded away. The job done, Hugues then sent 2,500 men south, burning plantations as they went. [25]

Ten miles to the south, Lieutenant General Prescott was as yet unaware of this development, and ironically had just received a letter from Grey ordering him to take command at Berville. 'My Dear General', the letter ran, 'we have been greatly neglected'.[26] His minuscule force had been boosted on 1 October by the arrival of HMS *Woolwich* with Captain John Douglas RE and 49 infantrymen of the 56th Foot, raising the spirits of the inhabitants. Prescott implored Commander William Charles Fahey of the *Woolwich* to stay, pointing out that the locals were disaffected by the present government, 'from the severe unjustifiable rigour of arrests and from numbers being sent away'.[27] His troops spent 3 and 4 October destroying all guns and batteries that occupied the high ground above Fort Matilda, and the mood in the town so improved that about thirty of forty militiamen returned to the fort. English merchants in the town were seen to be hiding their effects, and Prescott asked them to keep their arms with them at night in case of any insurrection. On 5 October Prescott sent a lieutenant, two sergeants and 42 privates to Saint Marie to bolster the militia there and to stop plundering that had been reported.

On 6 October, the day that Berville fell, Prescott found himself with as small a garrison as he had on 30 September, and was probably feeling quite depressed about the state of affairs. 'Without any reinforcements and no news whatsoever, nor was the communication opened by Vice Admiral Sir John Jervis with the Camp'.[28] Any misgivings or anxieties Prescott had were laid wide open at eight o'clock on the night of 7 October, when a letter arrived from Jervis informing him that the troops at Berville had capitulated. He was now alone. He sent to the only ship in dock, Captain Charles Davers' HMS *Bulldog*, for twenty men, or any he could spare, but got none. No doubt the night was a sleepless one. The following day was all chaos with townspeople, French and English, boarding any vessel they could get onto, laden with trunks and bundles of possessions. Prescott's garrison was too small to keep any kind of order amid the panic. All they could do was stand on the ramparts and watch. Scattered shots from sentries in the hills overlooking Fort Matilda announced the arrival of the first of Hugues' troops on the night of 9 October, but the ravine-covered mountainous country slowed their final approach, and it was a few days before they were in position on the heights.

25   Willyams, *Account,* pp.137-138.
26   GRE/A2242a, Grey to Lieut.-General Robert Prescott, 29 September 1794. Ordering him to take command of Berville camp, Guadeloupe, and concerning the impossibility of providing reinforcements from St. Lucia or Martinique, payment of spies, and the militia of St. Lucia and Martinique.
27   GRE/A474, Letter from Lieut.-General Robert Prescott to Grey. Defending his conduct in Guadeloupe and giving a detailed account of events there, 4 September – 8 October 1794.
28   GRE/A474, Letter from Lieut.-General Robert Prescott to Grey, 9 October 1794. Defending his conduct in Guadeloupe and giving a detailed account of events there, 4 September – 8 October 1794.

Prescott commenced an earnest and almost daily correspondence with Grey, which grew increasingly shrill as the odds lengthened against him. 'I received a private message from Sir John Jervis acquainting me… that His Majesty has been graciously pleased to grant me permission to return to England', Prescott wrote on 4 October. 'I was just going to inform you that I no longer find myself able to act in this country'.[29] Grey was furious. 'No such permission has come into my hands', he replied two days later, a reply that indicated he realised the worst might ultimately come to pass. 'Should Berville unhappily fall, I am confident you will defend the remaining part of Guadeloupe as long as possible, and finally Fort Matilda'.[30] Prescott was shocked at the response and drafted a long letter explaining his actions since he had arrived on Guadeloupe. He pointed out that he believed he needed 1,500 men to properly garrison Fort Matilda, with 500 fit men as an absolute minimum. He in fact almost exactly that number, but half of them were sick absent.[31] Grey replied on 15 October to say that he had received a letter from Henry Dundas advising that the long-promised reinforcements were at last on their way under Lieutenant General Lake and Major General Leigh.[32] This was followed by another letter three days later passing on Dundas' news that 7,000 men had sailed from Portsmouth on 7 September, the 17th, 31st, 34th, and 85th Foot; also the 46th, 61st, and 68th could be expected from Gibraltar.[33] In fact only the latter part of this summary was true, and the 2,200 troops from Gibraltar could not arrive until December. The rest, especially the over-inflated strength figure, was fantasy; the 85th, for example, was then serving in Europe.

Grey had added a footnote; 'You will excuse not writing myself, but really have not the power, being quite worn down and weakened by a flux for some days past'.[34] For a man like Grey to admit to being ill suggested he was very sick indeed. In fact, he had dysentery. From the middle of October until the end of November he was bed-bound at Saint Pierre, too sick to stray from his quarters. News received in September that his wife and daughter had been gravely ill but had recovered must have given him trepidation. '[I am] nearly done for, and by no means equal to another campaign', he wrote to his son-in-law. 'I assure you I need no addition

---

29 GRE/A2242b, Prescott to Grey, 4 October 1794. Requesting permission to return to England by the next convoy as the King had given him leave to return home.
30 GRE/A2242c, Grey to Prescott, 6 October 1794. Refusing to allow him to return to England and concerning his expectation that Prescott had gone to the assistance of Berville camp.
31 GRE/A474, Letter from Lieut.-General Robert Prescott to Grey, 9 October 1794. Defending his conduct in Guadeloupe and giving a detailed account of events there, 4 September – 8 October 1794.
32 GRE/A2242n, Grey to Prescott, 15 October 1794. Concerning reinforcements, the question of the effect of the arrests of dangerous persons, the surrender of Berville camp, and the defence of Fort Matilda. In fact, neither Lake nor Leigh sailed for the West Indies.
33 GRE/A2242n, and GRE/A2242p, Grey to Prescott, 18 October 1794. Concerning news of reinforcements for the British forces in the West Indies, and promising men for Guadeloupe when they arrived.
34 GRE/A2242p, Grey to Prescott, 18 October 1794.

to my uncomfortable situation, amongst the Death of all my friends, and Deaths even now daily announced'.[35] Jervis was sick and worn down also, but his station aboard his flagship helped mask this fact from the men on the ground.

On 12 October Grey received accounts of the actions of brigands at Grande Riviere, on Martinique, and detached Soter's Island Rangers, a locally raised light infantry formation commanded by a Royalist planter, and thirty light dragoons under Captain Hare to suppress them. It was the first time that Grey had used primarily local troops for active service. The first colonial militia regiment of the new administration had actually been formed at Saint Pierre in August, the Royal Martinico Volunteers, the commanding officer being a wealthy customs collector, Captain James Bontein. Twelve months later this force had grown to six battalions with components of artillery and light dragoons, some 2,200 Frenchmen and 250 expatriate Britons dressed in red with black top-hats and grey pantaloons. The experiment worked well, but only in very limited instances, but it was much too little too late to be of use in the present campaign. To discourage locals from joining such units, Hugues instigated a policy to have any captives from these regiments executed on the spot.

Arriving too late to help the Berville garrison were a company each from the 21st Foot (sent from Saint Christopher's) and the 4/60th (from Saint Vincent's) which landed in mid-October at Fort Matilda, it being obvious that a landing at Berville was out of the question. Prescott added them to his meagre garrison, which at this time comprised detachments of virtually every British regiment that had taken part in the campaign – the 15th Foot (33 men), 21st Foot (107), 33rd Foot (9), 35th Foot (61), 39th Foot (21), 56th Foot (43), 4/60th Foot (119), together with 62 Royal Artillerymen, 65 Royal Navy seamen, 36 Rangers, 5 Royal Engineer officers and 9 staff.[36]

Hugues completely outwitted Prescott on 12 October. A schooner bearing a flag of truce hove into view at Basse-Terre, carrying aboard a high-ranking Republican officer and the captured Captain George Eiston of the 35th Foot. Eiston explained what had happened at Berville, and requested money and supplies for the benefit of the captured British soldiers at Pointe-à-Pitre.[37] Eiston was returned with the necessaries two days later, but of course the British prisoners saw none of it. However the French officers and crew of the schooner had seen at first-hand how weak the garrison of Fort Matilda truly was. Hugues' ordered his 2,500-man force to tighten the noose. By this time Prescott had made peace with Jervis, referring to 'Sir John Jervis's unaffected politeness and attention' in a letter on 25 October,[38]

---

35 Nelson, *Sir Charles Grey*, p.149.
36 Anon., *Bulletins and Other State Intelligence*, 1795, p.35.
37 Willyams, *Account*, p.140.
38 GRE/A487, Letter from Lieut.-General Robert Prescott to Grey, 25 October 1794. Reporting from Guadeloupe.

and he needed every bit of assistance he could get. Things were so dire that he was reduced to writing statements such as 'Captain King arrived with twelve men – a most capital reinforcement'.[39] That his tiny army was on its last legs must have been obvious to Grey. His total force in these islands on 1 November consisted of 85 regular officers, 1,166 rank-and-file infantrymen fit for duty, 193 fit artillerymen, and 28 artificers. His strongest regiment was the 15th Foot on Martinique with 279 men and the weakest the 64th Foot, also at Martinique, with just 51 fit men in the ranks. He was effectively trying to defend seven widely-dispersed islands with the equivalent two full-strength infantry battalions.[40]

From his prison hulk in the Outer Harbour, Brigadier General Graham penned a long letter of explanation concerning the surrender of Berville to Grey on 21 October. It is a clear and logical account of the defence, of the overwhelming odds against him, of the wretched state of his men and supplies towards the end. He had written a much shorter account of events to Jervis immediately after the surrender, and Grey had expressed some displeasure at his report, so Graham took pains to include as much detail as possible. Reading it today, it is hard to see how any course other than surrender was possible. Almost 550 British prisoners-of-war were aboard ships in the Outer Harbour, and Hugues wrote to Jervis to make him aware that a French supply ship *Prevoyante* had loaded them. As agreed with Hugues, Jervis wrote a letter guaranteeing safe passage to the vessel on its voyage to England, as per the terms of capitulation at Berville. The ship sailed, but full of loot, bound for France, with its letter of safe passage. But the prisoners remained hidden below-decks in stinking hulks off Pointe-à-Pitre. In early January a group of officers of the 35th and 43rd Foot managed to escape, by waiting for a small supply boat to pull alongside, then overpowering the guard and rowing off into the night. They eventually were picked up and made it back to Martinique.

Hugues' siege batteries overlooking Fort Matilda opened fire on 20 October, but the early bombardments were weak and sporadic. Prescott ordered his men not to return fire. 'So they may fire and be d____ed', he wrote.[41] But as time went by, more and more enemy batteries came into action, closer and better served. One cannon-ball took off the fore-end of Prescott's cocked hat, to which he merely said, 'a miss is as good as a mile!'[42] Difficult he may have been, but never lacked for bravery. He was in very bad health by 25 October,[43] writing again to Grey imploring to

---

39 GRE/A87, Letter from Lieut.-General Robert Prescott to Grey, 25 October 1794. Reporting from Guadeloupe.
40 GRE/A501, State of the garrisons in the Windward and Leeward Islands. Total of men in the general return of 1 November 1794, and total of the above return with the addition of sick, prisoners, etc.
41 GRE/A485, Letter from Lieut.-General Robert Prescott to Grey, 20 October 1794. Reporting from Guadeloupe.
42 Willyams, *Account*, p.147, fn.
43 The Republicans cut off the fort's water supply during the night of 23 October, which cannot have helped the sanitary conditions in the fort.

Lieutenant General Robert Prescott. Undeniably valiant, but one of the most difficult subordinates to ever serve a field commander. (National Portrait Gallery)

be allowed to go to England immediately.[44] But Grey, struck down himself, had no-one he could send in his place. Thomas Dundas and Symes were dead, Francis Dundas gone home, Graham a prisoner. All his battalion commanders either dead, sick, captured or returned to England. The highest-ranking officers he could offer were a pair of majors, Innes of the 64th and Evatt of the 70th, and both of them were sick. No, Prescott would have to fight it out.

It was therefore probably a very ailing Prescott who received a peremptory letter from Victor Hugues on 28 October, dated 7 Brumaire in the 3rd Year of the French Republic, addressed from Victor Hugues, Commissaire Délégué par la Convention Nationale aux Îles du Vent, to Prescott himself, as usual full of seemingly outrageous allegations:

---

44 GRE/A488, Letter from Lieut.-General Robert Prescott to Grey, 25 October 1794. Declaring himself totally unfit for further service in Guadeloupe and requesting that he be allowed to return home when reinforcements arrive. The handwriting is very shaky.

> In hearing that you commanded at Fort St. Charles, I expected to find a chief in whose reputation for honour and probity was already clear to me; However many assassinations have been committed upon Women and peaceable inhabitants and that for the purpose of robbing them. The Public Edifices consecrated by humanity for the succour of all sick people have been burnt by you, also certain houses and huts… I demand justice for the assassination committed upon a person named Renoue by a Dragoon of your Garrison.[45]

But Hugue's accusations were not outrageous; they were true. Prescott had indeed ordered carcasses from the mortar battery to be thrown into the hospital and for the building to be set on fire to prevent the attackers gaining lodgement. Even as a professional soldier with fifty years' service under his belt, Prescott was having to fight savagery with savagery.

The end-game commenced at dawn on 6 November. Having constructed two new batteries and rebuilt three damaged ones, the French opened fire at twenty past six in the morning and continued a heavy bombardment for five hours. The hundreds of shells and cannon-balls killed and wounded nine men inside the fort, but more importantly damaged and weakened several of the main buildings. At eleven o'clock an envoy came down under a flag of truce, and handed Prescott a message:

> I summons you sir to deliver to me the fort and your command in three hours; that is to say, from this hour until two o'clock, after which time, no propositions will be listened to, or quarter given. I have also to inform you that the leaders of the English not apprehended in the capitulation will answer for any fire or pillage which may be committed in the fort in the case of evacuation.[46]

Prescott replied immediately, declaring that he would defend Fort Matilda 'to the last extremity'.[47] And so the siege continued. All the while Prescott kept up a stream of correspondence to Grey, demanding reinforcements, and to be allowed to go home due to illness.[48] Exasperated by Prescott's constant calls for reinforcements,

---

45 GRE/A496b/c, 7 Brumaire in the 3rd Year of the French Republic [28 October 1794]. Copy letter from Victor Hugues, Commissaire Délégué par la Convention Nationale aux Îles du Vent, to Prescott. Complaining of assassinations, robbery, pillaging and destruction by members of the British forces or persons associated with them.
46 GRE/A506b, Letter from Victor Hugues to Prescott, 16 Brumaire in the 3rd Year of the French Republic [6 November 1794], calling on him to surrender the fort that he was defending in 3 hours.
47 GRE/A506c, Letter from Prescott to Hugues, declaring that he would defend Fort Matilda to the last extremity, 8 November 1794.
48 GRE/A2442, Grey/Prescott correspondence. Refer to letters dated 5, 8, 9, 10, 15, 25 October, and 1, 8, 11 November 1794.

Grey added a footnote to his letter on 13 November. 'PS. I have only left here 14 artillery men, and 29 at Fort George and Fort Edward, and the soldiers here have [had] barely one night in bed'.[49] Grey was laid low with dysentery, so was in fact probably sicker than Prescott. He issued his last General Order of the campaign on 7 November, condemning Hugues' barbarity at Berville, and reminding Royalists that they were subject to the laws of Great Britain and were to be treated as such; subsequently 'no place is to be surrendered before this is expressly and explicitly acknowledged and subscribed to by the enemy'.[50]

On 9 November Prescott received the last of any possible reinforcements, a sergeant and twenty men of the Royal Artillery. 'Our walls are greatly shook, and chiefly from our own fire', Prescott advised Grey on 11 November in handwriting shaky from illness. 'Sandbags [we] are making, in order to thicken and support the works. Traverses we have been obliged to throw up, as their shot come[s] in on all sides, and we have been obliged to have as many men as could be spared for these and other works, which keeps us all fully employed'.[51] In the mid-morning of 14 November a great alarm went up in Jervis' squadron, as three enemy men-of-war had been spotted. Had more French reinforcements arrived? At length the three ships hove into view, and the Royal Navy tars cheered. They were British: the flagship, HMS *Majestic* with Vice Admiral Benjamin Caldwell aboard, HMS *Theseus*, and HMS *Bellona*. Caldwell arrived with the news that Lieutenant General Sir John Vaughan had arrived at Saint Pierre, and that Sir Charles Grey had handed over command in these islands to him. The tired and sick Sir John Jervis was to hand over the naval command to Caldwell, then to report to the Admiralty in London for further instructions.

Jervis collected his seamen from Fort Matilda – to Prescott's chagrin – and sailed for Saint Pierre. There, on 27 November, after saying their farewells, Grey and Jervis sailed for home. Shortly before their departure, Grey had received a letter from Shelburne, advising him that his and Jervis' reputations were under attack at home. He also received Dundas' reply to his 'booty' letter dated 28 July. The letter contained a long reply from advocate-general Sir William Scott stating that Pitt, and all the cabinet ministers, agreed with his ruling that the ship seizures and confiscations were illegal. Legal claims could only be judged in a legally assembled court of the admiralty and in any event, property other than military items belonged to the Crown, and could only be given to the victors with the King's assent.[52] No doubt these letters gave Grey and Jervis much to ponder about during the long voyage home.

---

49 GRE/A2242dd, Grey to Prescott, 13 November 1794. Concerning reinforcements for Fort Matilda.
50 Willyams, *Account,* Appendices, pp.53-54.
51 GRE/A516, Letter from Lieut.-General Robert Prescott to Grey, 11 November 1794. Reporting on the siege of Fort Matilda.
52 Nelson, *Sir Charles Grey*, p.140.

On 29 November, Captain William Cockburne of the Royals, aide-de-camp to Sir John Vaughan, arrived by sea at Fort Matilda with the unwelcome news that no more reinforcements were possible. If the men at Berville had been the lost battalion, Prescott's 500 men were the legion of the damned. Hugues forces on the other side of the hill had swollen to a figure approaching 7,000. A week later Prescott despatched his aide-de-camp, Captain John Thomas, who, due to a yawning insufficiency of fit officers, was actually second-in-command, to Vaughan to advise his that the bastion facing the Galion was in ruins and was about to tumble into that river. Thomas returned on 7 December to find the bastion facing the town on the point of giving way also. Prescott had given up all hope of defence. It was time to withdraw. The gallant Captain Thomas sailed away again, this time to Rear Admiral Charles Thompson, the senior Royal Navy man on the Guadeloupe station, to arrange a plan for evacuation.

Three days later, from his headquarters overlooking Fort Matilda, Victor Hugues declared that 'the body of Thomas Dundas, interred in Guadeloupe, shall be taken up and given as prey to the birds of the air', presumably well aware that Dundas was buried in the ramparts of the fort.[53] Whether this was an intention, or just fighting talk, and whether the deed was ever actually carried out, we will never know for sure. One account has Dundas' corpse being mutilated then thrown into the River Galion. Given Hugues' track record and propensity to do whatever he threatened, it seems likely that the unfortunate Dundas fed the wildlife of Basse-Terre.

On 11 December Thompson wrote to his new superior, Vice Admiral Caldwell:

> Yesterday morning Captain Bowen of his Majesty's ship *Terpsichore*, accompanied by Captain Thomas, aide-de-camp to lieutenant general Prescott, brought me a letter from the general, saying, that he had held out at Fort Matilda as long as possible; (indeed from the ships, we could perceive that the walls of the fort were much shattered, and many of the guns dismounted), and requested that I would make an arrangement for taking off the troops, who would be ready at the water-side by seven o'clock that evening.[54]

Thus with Royal Navy help courtesy of Thompson, Prescott and his garrison escaped to Martinique in the dead of night without loss. Troops from the 15th and 21st Foot manned the defences as the rest boarded Royal Navy ships starting at seven o'clock in the evening, then joined them aboard at ten o'clock. The only injury was Captain Richard Bowen, struck by a musket-ball in the face while bringing off, in his own boat, the last man of the garrison.

53 Quoted in *The Gentleman's Magazine,* Vol. 174, p.255.
54 Anon. *A Collection of State Papers,* 1794, pp.44-45.

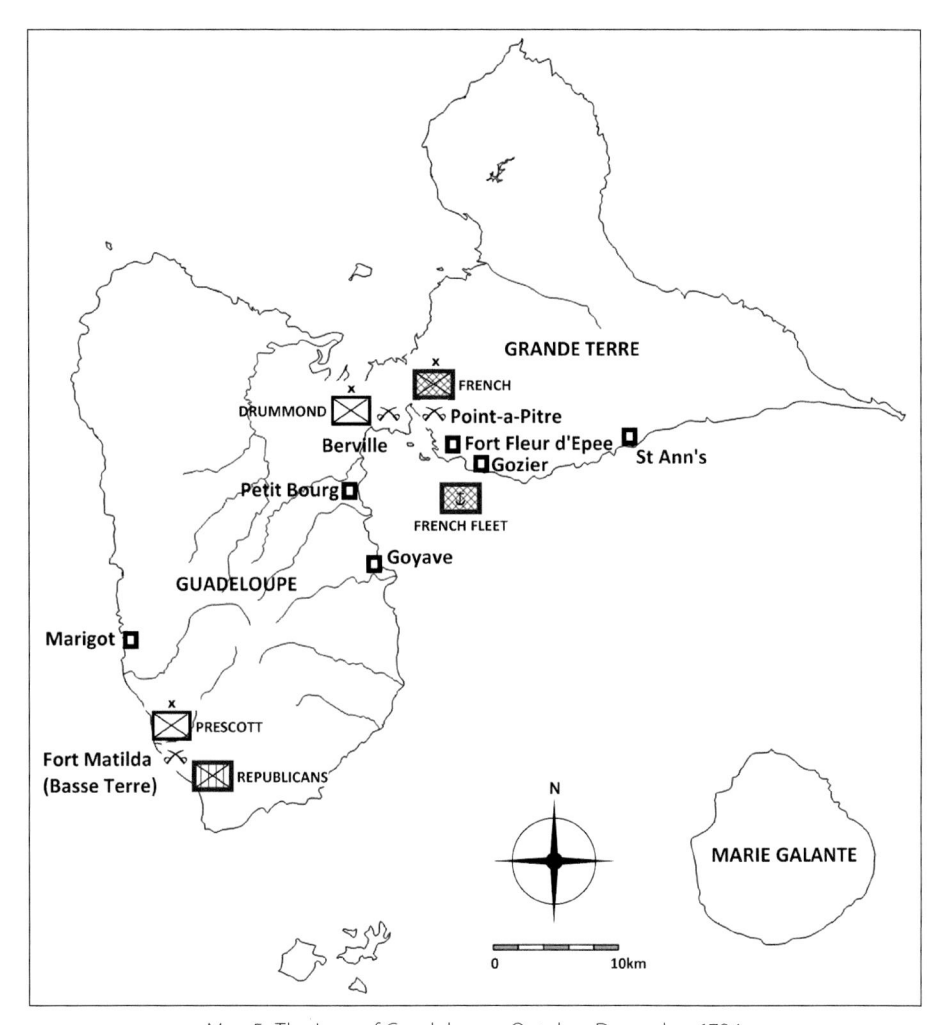

Map 5 The Loss of Guadeloupe, October-December 1794.

Robert Prescott had the last word:

> One company of the 21st regiment occupied the ramparts, whilst the light infantry of that regiment were posted on the right flank on the beach which led to the town, and the third remaining company of that regiment, under the command of Captain Mackay, a most confidential officer, was posted along the Gallion river to cover our left.[55] The fifteenth took

---

55 Captain Robert Mackay; resigned from the Army as a captain in 1800.

post along the circular battery towards the sea, and to the barrier near the town, which was quite open to the enemy, and which position was necessary to protect the sally port we marched through to reach the shore. The enemy from the water-side near the town, fired some small arms soon after our men began to embark, but were checked by the light company of the 21st regiment, under the command of Lieutenant Patterson,[56] a steady gallant officer, as well as by a boat from the *Terpsichore* frigate, into which Captain Bowen, who inspected and regulated the embarkation, had, as unexpectedly as judiciously, put a gun, and by the fire of which I imagine the enemy were very much surprised; at the same time all possible aid was given from the ramparts by such guns as bore on the town, and on that particular spot where the enemy fired from. The embarkation continued with little or no interruption, and was happily completed about ten o'clock at night, without its being discovered by the enemy, who continued firing as usual on the fort till two or three o'clock in the morning of the 11th, as we could plainly perceive from the ships. My satisfaction was great at having thus preserved my brave garrison to their king and country.[57]

Thus Guadeloupe was given up. Prescott's skeletal force arrived at République-ville on 13 December, adding his less than 500 convalescents to the 1,500 men left on Martinique, only half of whom were present for duty. Undoubtedly there was not a man amongst them who would never care if he did not see Guadeloupe again.[58]

---

56 Lieutenant William Paterson; later commanded a brigade in the Mediterranean and at New Orleans in 1815, subsequently a lieutenant general.
57 Anon. *Bulletins and Other State Intelligence*, 1795, pp.32-33.
58 That said, one of Prescott's aides, Captain William Henry Beckwith of the 56th Foot, must have felt enormous satisfaction when his older brother George Beckwith recaptured Guadeloupe in February 1810, as lieutenant general commanding British forces in the Windward and Leeward Islands.

14

Prize Money

Grey and Jervis arrived at Plymouth on 8 January 1795 aboard HMS *Boyne* after sailing through a French fleet blockading the mouth of the Channel.[1] Several carriage-rides later they were in London, as heroes with soiled reputations, the whole issue of prize money still hanging over their heads. Worse, they found themselves suspended from active service. The issue of the legality of their confiscations, particularly the American vessels, remained to haunt them. They had been required to hand back all American confiscations, but they had long before sold such property, keeping poor records and pocketing the proceeds. The eminent merchant banker Sir Francis Baring made a memorial to Henry Dundas on 30 December in their defence. On the other side of the ledger, the West India Planters and Merchants presented a memorial to the Duke of Portland on 6 February 1795, requesting him to 'represent to the King the probable dangerous consequences of the measures taken in the West Indies and calling for an enquiry into the public conduct of Grey and Jervis and a public disavowal of the principles on which they acted'.[2] This was swiftly followed by a similar memorial by the merchants of Liverpool, and another from the agents on behalf of the principal inhabitants and proprietors on the island of Martinique. The Duke of Portland was forced to hold a conference with the West India planters and merchants on 12 February 1795 to placate them.

On 26 February 1795, Foster Barham, Member of Parliament from Pembroke, who had financial interests in Jamaica, rose in the House of Commons and laid before the house a motion condemning Grey's and Jervis' proclamations:

> That an humble address be presented to His Majesty, representing that it appears to this House that certain proclamations were, issued by Sir Charles Grey and Sir John Jervis in the island of Martinique, and dated May the 10th and 21st, 1794, which this House conceives to contain principles not

---

1 Nelson, *Sir Charles Grey*, p.169.
2 GRE/A555, Memorial from the West Indian Planters and Merchants to the Duke of Portland.

warranted by the law of nations, and of dangerous precedent in all future cases of hostility, and which occasioned great alarm and dissatisfaction in His Majesty's colonies; and therefore humbly praying His Majesty, that he will be graciously pleased to take such measures for recalling the same, and. removing the apprehension of his faithful subjects, as to His Majesty shall seem good.[3]

The government was keen to put the whole matter behind them. At the end of April Portland formally responded to all, playing the complaints with a dead bat:

In answer to the memorials which have been transmitted to me from the West-India planters and merchants, on the subject of certain proclamations issued during the command of Sir Charles Grey and Sir John Jervis in the West Indies, I beg leave to inform you, that his Majesty's ministers, the moment they were informed of the nature of those proclamations, sent directions respecting them, in consequence of which no further proceedings were had upon them; and information has since been received, that those directions were so clearly understood, that the money which had been paid as contribution has already been returned; so that the proclamations in question cannot but be considered to be, as in fact they are, annulled.[4]

Foster Barham brought a motion against the two commanders on 2 June 1795; it was defeated by 57 votes to 14. Henry Dundas weighed in, providing his views in a letter to Lord Penrhyn:[5]

I am well aware that the present warfare is, in almost every respect, different from any that ever existed; and that there is too much reason to apprehend, that the object of the enemy with whom we are engaged is rather a plan of savage devastation, than of conquest beneficial to themselves: but I cannot admit that such a plan originated in any of the transactions of Sir Charles Grey and Sir John Jervis: it being an absolute certainty that the system is the natural consequence of the principles on which the present Government in France is founded, and existed long before either Sir Charles Grey or Sir John Jervis were employed in the West Indies.[6]

---

3   Anon. *A Collection of State Papers 1794*, pp.44-45.
4   Anon. *A Collection of State Papers, 1795*, p.164.
5   Richard Pennant, 1st Baron Penrhyn (1737-1808) was a major plantation owner and slaveholder in Jamaica; also a staunch anti-abolitionist.
6   Anon. *A Collection of State Papers, 1795*, p.202.

Robert Prescott arrived in London in mid-February, and immediately accused his former commander of prejudicing him; Grey had sent a cabinet minister copies of Prescott's orders from the previous June concerning the disregarding of all orders given by Jervis. Grey, who had tried to always maintain a conciliatory tone with Prescott – which cannot have been easy – resented the tone of Prescott's letter. It was obvious Prescott was out to end the friendship; Grey did not make any efforts to dissuade him. The two never spoke again.

With the matter of booty and the relationship with Prescott behind them, Grey and Jervis could at least look forward to the settlement of prize money. Prize payments (known as dividends) for the campaign were made in 1796 and 1797. As commander-in-chief, Sir Charles Grey received £11,229.4.9, a sum equivalent to about £1.1 million today, whilst general officers Prescott and Whyte received £3,616.14.0 each. Thomas Dundas' estate and Prince Edward received the same, the former for giving his life, the latter for several weeks of organising and attending drill parades. Serving field officers or their next-of-kin – Richard Symes, Henry Grey, Francis Dundas, William Gomm, William Lyon, and Frederick Maitland – received £1,101.7.8 each. At the other end of the scale, a typical private or drummer received fifteen shillings and four-pence – about £80 today – for what was, in the end, a ten-month campaign. All told, some eleven field officers, 57 captains, 155 lieutenants and ensigns, 270 sergeants and 4,942 other ranks (or their next-of-kin) received prize money between 1795 and 1806.[7] Naval men received similar payments in proportion.

Two senior naval officers of the campaign did not get to share in the spoils. Captain Robert Faulknor was killed in action in a close-quarter battle between HMS *Blanche* and the French frigate *Pique* off Marie Galante near Guadeloupe on the early hours of 5 January 1795. After an epic exchange of broadsides, which left both frigates without small boats and largely dismasted, Faulknor attempted to lash the bowsprit of the French vessel to his main-mast, during which he was shot through the heart. He has a memorial in Saint Paul's Cathedral. The equally gallant Captain Josias Rogers died of Yellow Fever on Grenada on 24 April 1795, aged 40. A memorial to him, his brother and his nephew is in Lymington, Hampshire.

A study of Grey's accounts for the campaign shows some interesting expenses. On 31 March, a few days after the capture of Martinique, a sum of £21.15.7 was paid to Captain Conyngham 'for Rochambeau's mistress' without further explanation.[8] In June Grey paid the grand sum of £98.5.1 to Colonel Myers for the procurement of 'Madeiras, Claret, etc'. which suggests that his headquarters were always well-lubricated, a supposition borne out by the purchase of seven-and-a-half dozen bottles of wine at Colonel Gomm's auction on 29 August for £14, although there

---

7   Series WO 164/37-55, /66, /484 – Royal Hospital Chelsea: Prize Records. National Archives.
8   Madame de Tully. Financial details from GRE/A532/2, Account between Grey and Lieut.-Col. Fisher, his secretary, 1793 – November 1794 [endorsed 7 December 1794].

is every likelihood this auction was for the benefit of the kin of the late Colonel, killed on 2 July. The French Royalists who served Grey did very nicely out of the expedition; on 4 June 1794 a total of £1,753 was paid to Monsieurs Courignon, Charton, Soter, Serin, Bexon, Goudreville, Lirow, Legrange, and Sence 'for secret services', an amount equal to about £20,000 each today, although given the consequences if they were caught by Hugues and his men, perhaps the rewards equalled the risk.[9]

One must not think that all these arrangements provided a tidy conclusion to the campaign, however. For in the islands themselves, the upheavals wrought by Grey's campaign were turning the Antilles into hell on earth.

---

9   Various details from GRE/A532/2, Account between Grey and Lieut.-Col. Fisher, his secretary, 1793 – November 1794 [endorsed 7 December 1794].

15

Daily Expected

The first day of 1795 saw little cause for celebration in the Antilles. At the northern end, Victor Hugues and his sizable force of French regulars and *gens de couleur* exercised complete control over Guadeloupe and Marie Galante. For all intents and purposes, Guadeloupe had become an outpost of Jacobin France, with all the same freedoms and terrors. Hugues's official title was Commissaire Délégué par la Convention, but he ruled liked a Viceroy, with powers of jurisdiction that were far-ranging. He was a strong-man about to get stronger. Five frigates and ten transports, carrying a colonial battalion (500 white and 200 black infantry) commanded by Chef de Bataillon Cottin, 120 gunners, and a battery of field guns sailed from Brest on 17 November 1794, and arrived at Pointe-à-Pitre on 10 January 1795 after suffering only minor interception by the Royal Navy.

The centre of British military power, or what remained of it, lay across the water southwards on Martinique. Lieutenant General Sir John Vaughan, a 63-year-old Irishman, had arrived at République-ville aboard HMS *Ramillies* on 10 November 1794 and assumed command of His Majesty's forces in the Leeward Islands. Vaughan had served in the Seven Year's War and as a major general in the American War of Independence, but carried the stigma of having been implicated with Admiral Rodney during the capture of Saint Eustatius in 1781, after which it was controversially alleged that Vaughan and Rodney had used the opportunity to enrich themselves and thus neglected more important military duties. He had with him his suite – one of his aides was a certain Captain Thomas Picton, overseas on his first campaign – but no general officers or troops, who were 'daily expected'.[1]

Daily turned into six weeks. The long-promised reinforcements finally arrived from Gibraltar on 21 December. These were the 46th (South Devonshire) Regiment of Foot, the 61st (South Gloucestershire) Regiment of Foot, and the 68th (Durham) Regiment of Foot. In addition to these 2,200 fresh but raw troops, Vaughan had maybe 2,500 of Grey's exhausted veterans on Martinique and Saint Lucia, of whom

---

1 GRE/A2242ee, Grey to Prescott. Concerning the arrival of Sir John Vaughan at Martinique.

nearly half were sick, and all were virtually militarily useless without a long period of rest. The entire situation had been exacerbated by a condition of near-famine that had existed on the island since mid-August, caused by the break-down of traditional industries, employment of slaves by the army, loss of planters and plantation managers, and the needs of the army and fleet. Fish was being purchased from American ships to feed the slaves when it could have been caught locally in the rich tropical waters.

Militarily, events were in an equal state of disrepair. Until the arrival of the three fresh regiments just before Christmas, Vaughan had been defending ten islands with 1,200 fit men, whereas he estimated he needed 7,500. He could not count upon the battered remnants of Grey's army, many of whom were already earmarked to go home. The process started just before Christmas when the 56th Foot drafted all its fit privates into the 6th, 9th, and 15th Foot, leaving the surviving non-commissioned officers and officers to pack up and depart on 3 January. The 6th then recycled these same men and its own fit men into the 9th Foot. Five fresh battalions arrived from home at the start of April, which gave Vaughan some breathing-space. The 2/2nd Foot (Queens) was a freshly raised battalion, commanded by the same George Ramsay who had served under Grey; and the 45th was returning to the West Indies after recruiting up to strength in England from the shell that had earlier returned home. Both therefore contained green troops. The 25th and 29th had both just done two years' service aboard ships as marines, but had seen little conventional combat; only the 34th had spent some time in the islands to acclimatise.[2]

Vaughan sent the 25th and 29th to Grenada, and the 34th to St Lucia. The pathetic remnants of Grey's wonderful flank battalions were drafted into the 45th Foot, and destined to serve on in the West Indies until 1802. In return, the cadres of the 35th, 39th, 43rd, 56th, 58th, 64th, 65th, and 70th boarded ships for home. Only the 9th and 15th Foot, present in the West Indies since well before the campaign began, stayed behind having soaked up all the 'fit' men from the other regiments. There cannot have been many men left in the ranks of those regiments who had been present with either the 9th or 15th when they arrived in the West Indies five years earlier. The advent of the 1795 'sickly season' only exacerbated the problems. Fever was once again rampant on Martinique. There were 1,300 effectives on 23 July, plus another 764 sick. 177 soldiers died during the month.[3] To make up the losses, fresh troops arrived. The newly-raised 83rd Foot landed at the end of July, and in late September four battalions of veterans from the Duke of York's Flanders campaigns, under the command of Major General Peter Hunter

---

2   Based upon data in the author's own series, 'British Regiments and the Men who led them 1793-1815'. https://www.napoleon-series.org/military/organization/Britain/Infantry/Regiments/c_InfantryregimentsIntro.html
3   Fortescue, *A History of the British Army*, Vol. IV Part I, p.451.

– the 40th (2nd Somersetshire), 54th (West Norfolk), 59th (2nd Nottinghamshire), and 79th (Cameronian Volunteers) Regiments of Foot.[4]

Some of the gaps were made up by the raising of local regiments. Malcolm's Royal Rangers was raised in April 1795, under the command of Captain Robert Malcolm of the 41st Foot. More followed, commanded by some of Grey's trusted veterans. In May, Whyte's Regiment of Foot, under the command of Colonel John Whyte; and Myers' Regiment of Foot, under the command of Colonel William Myers. Expediency was changing British military thinking. In June, Vaughan received official approval from Henry Dundas to raise two regiments of ex-slaves, something unthinkable six months prior.[5]

Vaughan's new naval equivalent was Vice Admiral Sir Benjamin Caldwell aboard his flagship HMS *Majestic*. Caldwell was a 55-year-old Liverpudlian who nursed a grievance at being omitted from the official despatches for the great naval battle of the Glorious First of June; he had even been denied a commemorative medal issued to the captains who had fought at the battle. Caldwell brought with him a much more powerful squadron than had been afforded Jervis, including nine ships-of-the-line. Again, it was too little, too late. Caldwell found almost all the warships left on the station to be unserviceable. Most needed major refits and were grossly undermanned, due to deaths and desertions. Neither of these deficiencies could be remedied in the West Indies. A surgeon in Caldwell's squadron, Leonard Gillespie, made some alarming observations about the state of Jervis' fleet:

> On November 21st our little squadron, commanded by Vice-Admiral Caldwell, joined that of Sir John Jervis, off Guadeloupe, consisting of three ships of the line, and eight or nine frigates or sloops. This latter squadron we found pretty healthy, though weak from the loss of men; having lost, as was conjectured, during the six months only preceding this, about a fifth part of their crews, by the malignant epidemic fever… The frigates and sloops had been so fatally affected by this disease before the hurricane months, that the Admiral prudently had sent several of them to Halifax, whence they had returned with the remains of their crews in good health. The epidemic proved still more fatal to the seamen on board of transport ships, than to those of King's ships; whilst its ravages amongst the land-forces were so destructive, that we found, on our arrival in the islands, the fine army of Sir Charles Grey, which left Portsmouth in the latter part of 1793, in a considerable degree annihilated.[6]

---

4   Fortescue, *A History of the British Army*, Vol. IV Part I, p.440.
5   Fortescue, *A History of the British Army*, Vol. IV Part I, pp.442-443.
6   Gillespie, *Observations on the diseases*, p.8.

Saint Lucia, the next island southward from Martinique was nominally British, but with a skeletal garrison. Drawn inexorably into the vacuum created by the departure of the Royalists and destruction of Grey's force, this small island was about to become the epicentre for subsequent events. The success of Victor Hugues on Guadeloupe had caused a sensation. Civil unrest spread quickly, as slaves realised that there had been a precedent to liberty. Hugues's Jacobin hordes had risen, but had not yet started to migrate in any appreciable numbers.

Saint Lucia had been a major sugar cane producer since 1765, from which time the number of slaves on the island ballooned from about 4,000 to over 25,000. A famine in 1777 and a destructive hurricane in 1780 created conditions leading to the escape of many thousands of slaves into the interior of the island. The volcanic peaks, swampy valleys, and myriad of caves dotted throughout the lush jungles made concealment easy. The runaways started calling themselves Maroons, a corruption of the Spanish cimarrón, meaning fugitive or feral animal. Maroon incursions against plantations grew so bad that in 1784 Governor Baron de Laborie resorted to offering amnesties to all Maroons, offering freedom from prosecution to all who returned voluntarily. Many who returned escaped again and again – freedom being a powerful tonic – and in doing so created a greater desire amongst all those remaining as slaves. The British called them 'brigands'. To deal with the brigand problem, Sir John Vaughan retained the fresh but inexperienced 61st Foot on Martinique and sent the 46th and 68th to support the 9th on Saint Lucia, where trouble seemed to be brewing. The regimental digest of the 68th summed up the situation the men found upon arrival; 'A great body of runaway negroes and others of colour assembled in the wood, procured arms and became a daring enemy. They were called Brigands and said to be about 7,000 men'.[7]

In early March Vaughan withdrew 150 men of the 46th Foot from Saint Lucia to sail to Grenada to quell the growing rebellion there, then had to send further reinforcements from Barbados to Saint Lucia a month later upon hearing about local unrest. Victor Hugues was once again in the thick of it, and had despatched a sizable force from the newly-arrived reinforcements on Guadeloupe to help the Saint Lucians cast off the British yoke. Hugues gave up on re-capturing Martinique, as he felt he had insufficient men to do so. He sent all his available forces to Dominica and Saint Vincent instead, thus inciting the Carib revolt. Vaughan's own reinforcements were substantial; the flank companies of the 9th and 68th, the entire 61st Foot, Malcolm's Royal Rangers (later the 1st West Indian Regiment), and the Carolina Corps, plus a detachment of Royal Artillery.

The officer commanding on Saint Lucia, Lieutenant Colonel (local Brigadier General) James Stewart of the 68th Foot gratefully received the reinforcements from Vaughan. Leaving the 34th Foot in garrison at Castries, he set sail for

---

[7] S.G.P. Ward *Faithful: The Story of the Durham Light Infantry* (London: Nelson & Sons for Durham Light Infantry, 1963), p.63.

Vieuxfort at the southern tip of the island to flush out some brigands on 13 April. His force disembarked near Vieuxfort two days later, stormed and captured the brigand camp there. The following day was spent skirmishing with brigands, but he advanced north-west towards Soufriére as sweating seamen from HMS *Blanche* dragged four artillery pieces over the hills. In such dense jungle country, with narrow winding roads over steep hills, ambushes were always likely. The whole of 20 April was spent fighting off two such attacks at a pass called Choiseul, in which pickets of the 9th Foot and Malcolm's Royal Rangers were heavily engaged. The going was getting tougher.

Finally, at a place called Rabot on 22 April, Stewart found the road through the hills near Fond Doux blocked by a heavy barricade. As they reconnoitred to discover a means of attack, they were attacked themselves on three sides. The battle soon dissolved into messy and prolonged sniping in thick jungle. The fight went on for seven hours during which time the brigands behaved with 'the greatest coolness and trepidity'.[8] Evidently the training regime instigated by Hugues, and bolstered by the recapture of Guadeloupe, was making soldiers to be reckoned with. Hampered by lack of ammunition, Stewart decided to retreat, and luckily the brigands did not follow. But it had cost him the lives of one officer and 29 men killed, with eight officers and 144 men wounded, mainly in the leading unit, the 61st Foot. The following day he left 200 Black Rangers as a garrison at Vieuxfort and sailed the rest of his force northward, to the safer haven of Morné Fortuné near Castries.[9]

May was the start of the sickly season, and, as it had done the year before, Yellow Fever struck the garrison hard, especially amongst the newly-arrived regiments. Stewart's force spent virtually all of May inert and sickly, whilst the brigands grew stronger in numbers and more daring in activity. Sir John Vaughan made a tour of inspection at the start of June and estimated them at 6,000 men on Saint Lucia alone, whereas regiments on the islands were losing anything up to 40 men each per month to fever.[10] The noose was tightening. Brigands attacked and captured Pigeon Island, commanded by Major John James Barlow of the 61st Foot, and the post at Gros Islet, nine kilometres north-east of Castries, on 6 June. Vaughan was scathing of the fighting spirit exhibited by the defenders, stating that 'this backwardness was too general'.[11] The brigands commenced a bombardment of Vigie, a promontory just north of Castries, during the night of 17 June, threatening the use of the harbour. They swarmed over and captured the place against feeble resistance. The fort was manned by marines and seamen 'depressed and worn out with

---

8   Ward *Faithful*, p.66.
9   Ward *Faithful*, p.67.
10 Petre, *History of the Norfolk Regiment: 1685 to 1913*, p.126; also Col. H.C. Wylly, *History of the 1st and 2nd Battalions The Sherwood Forest*ers (Printed by the Regiment, 1929), pp.103-104.
11 Ward *Faithful*, p.63.

fatigue'.[12] The end was nigh, and Stewart knew it. He convened a council of war on the morning of 18 June and all agreed that evacuation was the only option. The troops marched down to a bay close to Fort Edward and embarked between midnight and 5:00 a.m. on 19 June. Some 53 officers and 740 fit men of three regiments were taken off, along with 625 sick and convalescents. The 61st and 68th returned to Martinique, whilst the 34th went to Saint Vincent. The 68th Foot left 126 men behind on Saint Lucia as prisoners or missing, most of whom were never seen again.[13] No doubt Sir John Vaughan watched the returning troops arrive on Martinique with a heavy heart, but did not have to dwell on the matter too long. He died of fever on 30 June, to be replaced by Major General Paulus Æmilius Irving.

So, Saint Lucia was lost, as was Guadeloupe; Martinique, at least, remained safe. The brigands only made a single attempt at a landing on Martinique, at Vauclin, in December 1795. A boatload from Saint Lucia landed on the south-eastern coast of the island, organised by Citizen Goyrand. A detachment of the 2/2nd Foot under Lieutenant Colonel George Ramsay, with attendant militia, attacked the brigands in their entrenched positions, and forced them to retire. Black Rangers who had been following up in support cut them off and captured them. Thereafter the brigands made no serious attempt to capture this last bastion of British sovereignty in the Antilles.[14]

12 Ward, *Faithful*, p.68.
13 Ward, *Faithful*, p.68.
14 Fortescue, *A History of the British Army*, Vol. IV Part I, p.454.

16

The Cost

Grey's campaign was over, although events morphed into another grisly campaign later in 1795, as the entire eastern Caribbean boiled over into revolt, actions as prefigured by the events described in by the preceding chapter. Those details are for another book, another time.

It is hard not to feel sorry for Grey. At the time of his appointment to command the expedition he was arguably Britain's most experienced and forward-thinking field commander, with a suite of tactical motions of his own devising entirely suited to the campaign ahead. He deserved to receive the best resources available; the best subordinates, the best regiments, the best commissary, the best naval support. In these, he got only the last, and even then for only the first half of the campaign. Instead, he found himself tossed about in the wake of political and foreign policy bumblings from September to November 1793, watching helplessly as regiments were added then subtracted from his force. The troops he finally received were far too few to carry out the mission, less than 7,000 men, and he was made to believe reinforcements would come, although, as we have seen, only one batch arrived during the entire course of the campaign. He had to shout down the objections of his subordinates, all of whom believed he had too few men to capture Martinique and that he should concentrate on Saint Lucia and Guadeloupe only. Perhaps they were right.

A total of 7,000 men would have been too few even if they were all fit and well. The British Army had served in the West Indies for over a hundred years by this time, and wastage from disease was well known. Losing fifty percent of a force to fever should have been an obvious fact to the planners. Using this logic, Grey was being asked to capture and hold the three islands with effectively 3,500 men. In the longer term, all he could hope for was to garrison the major forts, ports and towns, leaving the countryside free of troops and therefore fertile territory for Republicans and the disaffected to gather and hide. He later arrived at a plan showing a requirement for 10,800 men, as a minimum, to garrison the Leeward Islands, and capturing them would require more – perhaps 15,000 all told.

On 28 April 1796, Henry Dundas arose from his bench in the House of Commons and gave a speech, an elaborate defence of his conduct during the West

Indies campaigns. A transcript exists today and it runs for 59 pages, so, allowing for interruptions, the speech must have run for more than an hour. Part of the speech related to the disclosure of official efforts to improve the health of the army in that quarter. Public sentiment must have rendered this necessary, since in 1796, it was claimed in the House of Commons that 'almost every person in the country knew someone who had died in the military campaigns then being fought out in the Caribbean'.[1] The papers presented to the House to support his case included detailed lists of all hospital stores, bedding, tents and stationery sent to those islands; copies of letters received from Sir Charles Grey on campaign; letters from the Chief Surgeon; detailed shipping returns, showing tonnage; every a diary showing the 'state of the winds'. It was the extraordinary performance of someone trying to paint a picture of a campaign that they had built up, then cut down, then under-manned the force whilst over-expecting the results.

The planners at Whitehall let Grey down badly in their expectation that his meagre force could provide the resources to administer the islands. Grey therefore was forced to allocate his second-in-command and three brigadiers to the task, leaving only field officers to control the troops. Prescott, a valiant man with fifty years soldiering behind him, was manifestly unsuited to the governorship of a conquered island. Thomas Dundas, steady and sensible, but dead too soon. Charles Gordon, too easily corrupted. Much of the detailed administration was left to Royalists, most of whom soon fell into in-fighting and the settling of old scores, or jockeying for position under the new regime. Most had no intention of looking after the interests of the islanders.

The Royal Navy provided sterling support up to the capture of Guadeloupe, then became too dispersed to effectively conduct further operations. The fact that Hugues' fleet arrived undetected is an example of this. Like the army, the navy was being expected to do too much with too little. Seamen were as fallible to Yellow Fever as the soldiers; more so, perhaps, since they spent their time in close confinement aboard ships. Notwithstanding, the close relationship between Grey and Jervis was pure gold in the early phases of the campaign, and Jervis was blessed with some outstanding subordinates – Rogers, Faulknor, and Robertson in particular stand out – and it is a tragedy that none of these three survived the campaign, for they would surely have gone far indeed.

In terms of regiments and commanders, Grey was well-served by his staff and brigadiers, notwithstanding Prescott's tetchiness, and had many men of genuine merit in the field and company officer grades. Alas, too many of them died of disease during the campaign. Of those who survived, the fact that five of them went on to command divisions, another two to command the Royal Artillery and one the Royal Engineers in Wellington's field armies speaks volumes for their

---

1   David Geggus, 'The Cost of Pitt's Caribbean Campaigns, 1793 to 1798' in *The Historical Journal*, Vol. 26, No. 3 September 1983 (Cambridge: Cambridge University Press), p.699.

professional skill. Far and away the pick of Grey's troops were the flank battalions, the grenadiers and light infantry, who despite being young soldiers at the outset, soon developed into Grey's shock troops and found themselves at the forefront of every action in February, March, and April. Despite being detached from their parent regiments they seem to have developed an internal *esprit de corps*. By June they were exhausted and withering away, and never as effective thereafter. The use of converged flank battalions was only practised sporadically by the British army after Grey's retirement, most notably at Maida in 1806. The lesson to be learnt from 1794 was that they could be extremely effective if used sparingly, for shock or specialist rather than general action.

Five lessons learned from the campaign allow us to see what might have happened with the benefit of hindsight. Firstly, an expeditionary force of perhaps 10,000 men was required at the outset, with another 5,000 guaranteed reinforcements by April. Interestingly the first figure is what Grey believed he had in September 1793, before Whitehall stripped part of his force for other purposes. The 5,000 fresh reinforcements at the time of the invasion of Guadeloupe would have ensured the defence of that island.

The second lesson was that Jervis required a reinforcement of frigates before June. It was this type of ship which would have intercepted Hugues and his men long before reaching Guadeloupe, and created a naval encirclement ensuring the security of the force.

The third lesson was that at least three senior civil administrators, with staffs, were needed to take over the running of the captured islands. The general officers needed to be free to concentrate on military matters, which they were paid for, and good at.

The fourth lesson concerns age. Grey and Jervis should have been required to hand over the running of the campaign to younger men by about June 1794, at which point they should have returned home for rest. Men in their forties, not in their sixties, were required to superintend the proceedings from that time on.

And last, the sickly season would have afflicted troops no matter the state of play militarily. However, rates of Yellow Fever would have been lower if the troops had been fresher. The idea of raising islander regiments, with men more or less immune to local diseases, was in its infancy at the time, but it proved of great benefit to the British army in later years.

As for the French commanders, Rochambeau was superb; Ricard hopelessly outnumbered; Collot timid. Observers watching Rochambeau's vanquished force trailing out of Fort Bourbon after capitulation could not believe that he had done so much with so few men. In holding up Grey and Jervis for 47 days, he had ensured that the British campaign would almost certainly extend into the 'sickly season', something Grey hoped earnestly to avoid. Had he surrendered Martinique within a week or ten days, as did Collot of Guadeloupe, Saint Lucia could have been taken by late February, and Guadeloupe by early March; five or six weeks earlier than actually happened. Grey's force could have occupied Guadeloupe much less exhausted than were the tired men who did so on 20 April. Exhausted men were so much more vulnerable to disease.

The principal French hinge-point was of course, the arrival of Hugues in early June. Hugues was the classic example of what political fanaticism combined with enormous personal energy can achieve. Although no soldier, he completely galvanised the Republicans and islanders into a common cause, and despite losing most of his regular officers to disease early on, had a superb subordinate in Boudet who used his regular experience to give Hugues' motley army some semblance of order and discipline. The re-capture of Guadeloupe was a pivotal moment in the campaign – and the island was effectively captured once Berville fell – since it gave Hugues a military and naval base from which to spread foment and Jacobin ideals. This dispersal of 'brigandage' across the islands really took hold in 1795 and caused the British Army untold difficulties, all of which stemmed directly from the actions described in this book.

Of the expeditionary force that Grey created, Michael Duffy has written; 'It was probably the finest British strike-force assembled in the whole war and Grey used it in brilliantly successful shock-tactics, storming with the bayonet wherever possible and demoralising opponents into submission'.[2] But by December 1795 this strike force had been destroyed, mostly by disease. The loss in officers on campaign was considerable. Some 27 officers were killed or died of their wounds; but 170 died of Yellow Fever and other sicknesses. Only two officers were killed in action on Martinique, Colonel Campbell and Captain Mackewen, underlining the stellar success of that portion of the campaign. All other losses in action had occurred on Guadeloupe, progressively more of them as the situation deteriorated and ultimate success seemed less likely. The most senior casualty was the 'quiet hero' Brigadier General Symes. Lieutenant Colonel Gomm, Major Irving, eight captains, and fifteen lieutenants rounded out the list of killed. But deaths from sickness made this list look positively minuscule. Some regiments were stripped of many of their best officers. The 39th Foot lost Lieutenant Colonel Fremantle, three captains, five lieutenants, three ensigns, two adjutants, and their surgeon; a total of fifteen out of the thirty-two officers listed as serving in the 39th in the 1794 Army List.[3] The 43rd (thirteen officers), 56th (ten officers), 58th (ten officers), 64th (eleven officers), 65th (ten officers), and 70th (nine officers) suffered nearly as badly. The 39th (Fremantle), 58th (Stewart), 64th (Buckeridge), and 65th (Close) all lost their commanding officers to fever.

---

2 Michael Duffy, 'The Caribbean Campaigns of the British Army 1793-1801' in Alan James Guy, *The Road to Waterloo: The British Army and the Struggle Against Revolutionary and Napoleonic France,1793-1815* (London; Alan Sutton Publishing, 1990), p.28. This statement may have been true for the flank battalions, but the author is not convinced this is true for the force as a whole, based upon the weak state of many of the battalions as outlined in Chapter 7.
3 Anon. *A List of the Officers of the Army and Marines, with an index, a succession of Colonels, and a list of the Officers of the Army and Marines on Half-Pay* (London: War Office, 1794).

Things were just as bad in the supporting forces, sickness robbing the Royal Engineers of their commander (Durnford), the Royal Artillery of three battery commanders (Shewbridge, Tyrell, Smith), and the hospital service of three doctors, two apothecaries and six hospital mates. In addition to the thirteen dead officers, the 43rd Foot also had commanding officer Lieutenant Colonel James Drummond and ten officers held prisoner by Victor Hughes at Point a Pitre, leaving a mere handful of officers to conduct the shattered remnants of the regiment home. Some of the captive officers were imprisoned aboard a French hulk for fifteen months before being sent to France, and forced to swab the decks along with the privates in order to learn Republican principles. Two of them were Captain Richard Stovin of the 17th Foot and twenty-year-old Lieutenant Francis Skelly Tidy of the 43rd: after being released on parole in March 1796 both returned to England and resumed their military careers after three years away, only to find their regiments officered by complete strangers who had leap-frogged over them in rank whilst they sweltered and swabbed aboard hulks off Pointe-à-Pitre.

Total British army losses in the Windward and Leeward Islands for 1794 were 4,110 men. Sadly, this was nowhere near the worst year. 1796 saw 6,630 men rolled into Caribbean graves. Total losses for the period 1793 to 1798 were 19,000 men died, 545 deserted, and 4,100 discharged due to sickness, usually never to serve again. If Jamaica and Saint Domingue are added to the equation, and foreign troops in British pay included, the numbers are staggering; 40,500 dead, 1,800 deserted, and 7,100 discharged, or a shade under 50,000 men all told. [4]

The Royal Navy suffered less in the same period, losing perhaps 12,500 men. Confining losses to Grey's campaign, nearly 50 masters of transport vessels perished, as did 1,100 of their crewmen. No exact figures are available for the Royal Navy, although if we use surgeon Leonard Gillespie's estimate of one-fifth of crew strengths lost to disease, that would equate to approximately 1,500 seamen lost to all causes aboard the King's ships during the campaign, and this figure is probably much too low.

These horror statistics amplify the relatively minor casualty figures suffered by Grey's force in the taking of Martinique. In addition to the two officers noted as killed, 92 other ranks died, whilst 10 officers and 218 were wounded; only three men went missing in the entire six-week campaign. The magnificent grenadier and light battalions bore the lion's share of the casualties, maybe 70 percent of the total. Losses in the taking of Saint Lucia were nil, but the toll escalated dramatically once the force reached Guadeloupe.

The financial cost of the campaign was great. But that cost was recouped very quickly in terms of trade and taxation. Customs duty paid on brown sugar imported into Britain grew by 50 percent between 1793 and 1798. In the British Leeward Islands, sugar made up 97 percent of exports. Sugar changed the way

---

4 Figures contained in tables within Geggus, 'The Cost of Pitt's Caribbean Campaigns', p.703.

Europe ate. Prices fell due to volume. By 1800 all levels of society had become common consumers of the former luxury product. One of the most popular uses in Britain was in tea, and in Europe for coffee, but later confectionery and chocolate became extremely popular, and also jams. An ironic viewpoint might be that all Grey's and Jervis' men suffered and died so that Britons could enjoy a better-tasting cup of tea.

Hugues' capture of Guadeloupe had significant implications in the years that followed. With a secure base, the island became the focal point of all French activities in the islands. Guadeloupe became a base for regulars, irregulars, brigands, and privateers, capable of radiating efforts out to all surrounding islands whilst being reinforced from home. For as Sanderson later wrote:

> The harsh truth had to be faced in 1794 that, in spite of British naval supremacy in the area an inferior enemy force had succeeded in reaching Guadeloupe undetected, landed and taken complete possession. Unlike earlier wars, France did not need to send a fleet to ensure success; because the seas were wide, the islands numerous and the patrolling cruisers too few, the door was wide open to all who came.[5]

The Great War between France and much of the rest of Europe lurched erratically along until 1801, having directly or indirectly affected North and South America, the East and West Indies, the Mediterranean, Egypt and South Africa. Then, after eight years of warfare, weariness set in. The preliminary articles of peace were signed in London on 1 October 1801. William Pitt had been replaced as Prime Minister by Lord Addington, who did not believe, as Pitt had, that Britain and France were traditional enemies. The emerging Napoleon took advantage of this to gain diplomatic ground. Austria had recognised the French Helvetic (Switzerland), Batavian (Holland), and Ligurian and Cisalpine Republics (Italy), giving Napoleon a large slice of Europe, and thus the upper hand at the peace table. Amiens, the capital of Picardy, was chosen as the site for the signing of 'A Treaty of Universal Peace'. The treaty was signed in the town hall there on 27 March 1802. Napoleon's brother, Joseph Bonaparte, signed for France, Lord Cornwallis for England. London and Paris celebrated, for a time; but the Treaty of Amiens was not cause for celebration. Under the terms agreed, Britain was to hand over most of its conquests, including islands in the West Indies and the Mediterranean, whilst France was to give up Naples and return Egypt to the Ottoman Empire. But Great Britain could not survive without trade, and Napoleon had other plans. And so, hostilities were soon to begin again.

---

5   Michael William Bristowe Sanderson, *English Naval Strategy and the Maritime Trade in the Caribbean, 1793-1802* (Unpublished Doctoral Thesis, London University, 1968), p.37.

Martinique was handed back to France in 1802, and remained in French hands until February 1809, when it fell to a British expeditionary force commanded by Lieutenant General Sir George Beckwith. One of the divisions involved was commanded by Major General Frederick Maitland, Grey's aide from the 1794 campaign. Muskets shots, not the bayonet, were the rule in this campaign. The British Army had undergone a considerable improvement in training and discipline since 1794. Aided by Beckwith having a much larger invasion force, the island fell in a mere 25 days. The returning Bourbons took back the island for France in 1814. In 1902 Mont Pelée erupted and completely destroyed Saint Pierre, a town Thomas Dundas had described as being the finest in the West Indies, killing 30,000 people. It remained a ghost town for many years, and today is little more than village on an island that remains an overseas department of France. Saint Lucia likewise went back to France in 1802, but Britain regained control in 1803, restored slavery, and then acquired permanent sovereignty after the Conventions of 1814. After being part of several West Indian federations, the island finally achieved independence in 1979. Although English is the first language, most place-names remain French, and the locals speak a French-tinged creole dialect.

Guadeloupe was also formally reinstated to France in 1802. The mulatto leader Louis Delgrès led an uprising which was brutally put down the same year, after which slavery was re-instated. Britain took control again after an invasion under Beckwith that lasted eight days in February 1810, then it was given to Sweden in 1813, but had been returned to the new regime in France following Napoleon's first abdication in April 1814. Admiral Charles-Alexandre Léon Durand Linois had been appointed by King Louis XVIII as Governor in 1814, but news of Napoleon's return from exile in Elba in February 1815 forced him to reconsider his political stance. Linois vacillated, but then declared his support for Napoleon on – ironically – the day Waterloo was fought, 18 June 1815. Peninsula hero Lieutenant General Sir James Leith, commander of British forces in the West Indies, promptly despatched an expeditionary force made up of regiments then available in the Leeward Islands, with naval support under the command of Rear Admiral Sir Philip Charles Durham. The British expeditionary force landed on 8 August 1815 – the day after Napoleon set sail for St Helena – and within 48 hours secured a complete capitulation over this last bastion of support for Napoleon, with relatively few casualties. Six weeks after Waterloo, the Emperor's last battle was over. Leith then handed the island back to the representative of the French King. France rewarded Leith with the Order of Military Merit. Guadeloupe remains an overseas territory of France to this day.

17

The People

Sir Charles Grey's active soldiering days were almost over. From 1798 to 1799 he served in a desk job as Commander of the Southern District in England, in which capacity he organised a raid on Ostend in May 1798. Earlier that year, the French army earmarked for the invasion of Britain had departed for the Orient; however, a large force remained on the north coast of France, and reports of boat-building in the vicinity of Flushing and Antwerp began trickling back to London. These reports also mentioned the fact that the canals leading to Ostend and Dunkirk had been enlarged to permit the passage of larger vessels. Royal Navy intelligence also picked up the fact that large sluice gates to control the canal flow had been constructed just behind Ostend. Grey put forward the idea that these gates could be destroyed in a raid. The concept received the support of the Secretary of State for War. Grey was immediately placed in overall charge of the expedition, and drew selected troops from his local command area. Ever the champion of the set-piece action, he put together plans for what would have been considered, in later parlance, a commando raid. Grey planned the Ostend Raid as a quick smash-and-grab. But in their usual fashion, the government saddled him with all manner of secondary targets, so that his final mission had five objectives. It was just like the West Indies all over again; too many tasks to perform and not nearly enough men. After some early success, the weather changed, and the French arrived in force. Rough seas meant the men on the beach could not re-embark, and most of the expeditionary force was taken prisoner on the beach. Grey was not publicly condemned after the Ostend raid. Although he had not taken part personally, it must have been a bitter blow, and probably precipitated his retirement the following year at the age of 70.

Between retirement and 1807 he held the position of Governor of Guernsey in the Channel Islands, a position that was mostly honorary and did not entail any significant workload. In acknowledgement of his military service, he was created Baron Grey of Howick in the County of Northumberland in January 1801. In 1806, he was created Earl Grey and Viscount Howick in the County of Northumberland. He died at home in Fallodon on 14 November 1807 at the age of 78, after days of agony due to a blocked urinary tract. He was given a simple burial in his local parish. Colonel Henry George Grey inherited Fallodon, and Sir Charles' wife Elizabeth lived there for another fifteen years until her death in 1822. Sir Charles' eldest son, also Charles, became the 2nd Earl Grey, Prime Minister of the United Kingdom from 1830 until 1834, and had sixteen children, of whom two became admirals, one a general, and two clergymen; a grandson became Governor-General of Canada. Captain George Grey RN, Sir Charles's third son, was great-grandfather to Sir Edward Grey, British Secretary of State, the man who famously said in 1914 that 'the lights are going out all over Europe'.

Sir Charles Grey's name not often mentioned amongst the likes of Wellington, Moore, and Abercromby, his whole career within the timespan of the Great War with France devolving upon a single campaign, and one that was ultimately only partially successful. He deserves better; he was a man well ahead of his time. In terms of personal qualities, his outstanding trait was his ever-sunny optimism, an air of cheerful confidence that boosted the morale of his troops at every turn. His outstanding military trait was his aggressiveness: his country gentleman demeanour concealed a ruthless streak that found expression in his insistence on silent night attacks with the bayonet only, in order to discomfit and scatter an unwary enemy. There were many in contemporary military circles who discredited these tactics, pointing out that they were a recipe for creating disorder and atrocity – how could the troops be kept under discipline after first contact? – but there is no question they were brutally effective. His use of military intelligence was likewise outstanding. He invaded Martinique and Saint Lucia knowing more about the French defences than did the defenders, and his early efforts on Guadeloupe were compromised only through the want of troops; nonetheless he was aided considerably by the timidity of the French commander. On the debit side, his overt avariciousness and nepotism rankle modern sensibilities. One can only imagine how horrified we would be to read of a 21st century general taking such liberties. Grey made no effort to conceal the favouritism given his sons in terms of promotions, civil posts and perquisites, some even for life. His understanding of the advantages accrued by 'booty' belong to an earlier age – indeed, he used examples from the Seven Years War in his defence – so perhaps it is inappropriate to judge his actions from a contemporary viewpoint. That he was a career soldier who knew that he was conducting his last campaign, and who wished to benefit as much as possible both financially and for his family's legacy, is abundantly clear.

Of Grey's senior officers, Robert Prescott became governor-in-chief of British North America in 1796, and, applying his typical peppery behaviour, fell out with the French-Canadians and was recalled to England in 1799, although he retained the post until 1807. He died at home in Sussex just before Christmas in 1815, aged 89. HRH Prince Edward lived in Canada until 1800. His military career did not progress, at least, not in the field, and today he is remembered principally as the father of Queen Victoria. The prince died of pneumonia in January 1820 aged 52, less than a year after Victoria was born. Charles Gordon outlived his dismissal from the Army for more than forty years, and died at home in London in March 1835, aged 79. Francis Dundas went to the Cape of Good Hope in 1796 as commander-in-chief and later governor, and returned to England in 1803. He held only staff positions thereafter and died at Dumbarton in January 1824, aged 65. The veteran warhorse John Whyte commanded British forces in the terrible campaigns on Saint Domingue, then thereafter filled staff positions as colonel of the 1st West India Regiment and of the 46th Foot. He died at home in Arundel in 1816. The unfortunate Colin Graham, the brigadier who had tried to hold back the attackers at Berville with a bare handful of half-sick men, was exchanged in March 1796, went home to Inverness and did not hold field command again. He died at home in August 1799, sick and worn out from his years of service and subjection to Caribbean fevers. He is little remembered today except as the man who surrendered at Berville. He too, probably deserves better.

It was long assumed that Sir Thomas Dundas' body had been given up to 'the birds of the air' as Hugues threatened. However, years later a marble urn and tablet were discovered in a remote corner of a neglected garden in Trinidad, and upon the tablet was the following inscription;

> To the memory of MAJOR GENERAL THOMAS DUNDAS, who, with great professional abilities and with a mind generous and brave, fell a sacrifice to his zeal and exertion in the service of his King and country, on the 3rd day of June 1794, in the forty fourth year of his age. His remains were interred in the principal bastion of Fort Maltide, in the island of Guadeloupe, in the conquering of which he bore a most distinguished share, and which he commanded at his death. This tablet was erected by his brother officers as a mark of their high esteem for his many valuable qualities, and their regret for his loss.

Did Dundas' remains remain intact, later to be removed to Trinidad? We will never know for sure. Great outrage was evinced in England over his treatment by Hugues, and by a vote in the House of Commons it was agreed that a monument should be erected in Saint Paul's Cathedral to his memory. His son, also Thomas, who last saw his father at the age of eighteen months old in November 1793, became a captain in the 15th Hussars and served under Wellington for much of the Peninsula War.

Only three of the flank battalion commanding officers survived the campaign. John Francis Cradock served in the army for another 45 years; firstly in the Irish Rebellion, then in Egypt in 1801, then India in 1805. In 1808 he commanded the British garrison in Portugal prior to the arrival of Wellesley, then became Governor of the Cape Colony in 1811. Ennobled as Baron Howden in 1819, he changed his surname to Caradoc the following year. He died in Yorkshire in July 1839 aged 79. William Myers became a lieutenant general, commander-in-chief of the Southern District of Ireland, and eventually a baronet. He died on Barbados on 29 July 1805 aged 55. His son William James Myers commanded the Fusilier

Brigade at the Battle of Albuera in 1811, where he was killed. Eyre Coote fought on for many years; in the West Indies again in 1795, Ostend in 1798, Helder in 1799, Egypt in 1800, and the West Indies yet again in 1805. He returned home after this last, saying the years of service and hot climate had affected his mind. This unfortunately turned out to be true, as his actions in the disastrous Walcheren campaign of 1809 proved. In 1815 he offered to pay some schoolboys if he was allowed to flog them, and they he; after a court-martial he was dismissed from the Army for conduct unworthy of an officer and a gentleman. He died in December 1823 aged 61.

The veteran artilleryman Thomas Paterson did not survive the campaign by long, dying at Blackheath in January 1796. His deputy Orlando Manley eventually became a major general and died at Dublin in December 1808 aged 66. Haylett Framingham, a lieutenant in 1794, served as second-in-command of the Royal Artillery in Portugal in 1809, then Commander Royal Artillery under Wellington in late 1812 before going home. His successor, in the Peninsula, George Bulteel Fisher, was also a 'Grey' man. Fisher served in Portugal and Spain as a lieutenant colonel during the Peninsular War, and assumed command of Wellington's artillery following the siege of Burgos in the autumn of 1812. Unfortunately, he was forced to return to England in July 1813 following a misunderstanding with Wellington.

Grey's great friend Sir John Jervis went on to be commander-in-chief of the Mediterranean Fleet, and was made Earl Saint Vincent for his victory at that engagement in February 1797. Between 1795 and 1799 he introduced a series of severe standing orders to avert mutiny. He applied those orders to both seamen and officers alike, for example hanging two mutineers on the Sabbath, Sunday 9 July 1797, a policy that made him a controversial figure. He took his disciplinarian system of command with him when he took command of the Channel Fleet in 1799. In 1801, as First Lord of the Admiralty he introduced a number of reforms that, though unpopular at the time, made the Navy more efficient and more self-sufficient. He introduced innovations including block-making machinery at Portsmouth Royal Dockyard. He was known for his generosity to officers he considered worthy of reward, and his swift and often harsh punishment of those he felt deserved it. It was later said of Jervis that 'his importance lies in his being the organiser of victories; the creator of well-equipped, highly efficient fleets; and in training a school of officers as professional, energetic, and devoted to the service as himself'.[1] 'Old Oak' died at his country estate, Rochetts, near Brentwood in Essex, on 14 March 1823 aged 88.

Rear Admiral Charles Thompson continued to serve with Jervis, acting as second-in-command at the Battle of Cape St Vincent, but the two did not get on

---

1 P. K. Crimmin, 'Jervis, John, Earl of St Vincent (1735–1823)', *Oxford Dictionary of National Biography*, online edition, January 2006.

particularly well. Jervis accused Thompson of ignoring a tacking signal in order to counter a Spanish attacking move, potentially risking the loss of the battle. Jervis fumed privately but chose not to bring the matter into public, even when he and Thompson were rewarded with an earldom and baronetcy respectively. Thompson's next disagreement with Jervis, over the Sabbath hangings, led to Jervis insisting that the Admiralty recall Thompson, which they did. Thompson was then given a sedentary post as third-in-command of the Channel Fleet, which he held until failing health led to a return to England, home, and an early death at Fareham on 17 March 1799 aged 58.

Henry Dundas, the Secretary of State for War, was a sounder politician than the tumult surrounding the arrangement of Grey's force and objectives might suggest. Hard-working and pragmatic, he lacked the guidance at his elbow that a strong military man – the Commander-in-Chief – might have provided. In later eras, Lloyd George had Robertson and Churchill had Alanbrooke to provide them sound military advice. But Dundas had Amherst, and William Pitt had this to say of the latter: 'his age, and perhaps his natural temper, are little suited to the activity and the energy which the present moment calls for'.[2] The fact that the Army was completely run down was not Dundas's fault; it was Amherst's. Created Viscount Melville in 1802, Dundas was appointed First Lord of the Admiralty in 1804 but his career suffered a reverse in 1806 when he was impeached for the misappropriation of public money. He was acquitted. He retired to Scotland and died in May 1811, aged 69.

Victor Hugues did not suffer the violent fate often reserved for tyrants, and in fact died peacefully in his bed many years later aged 65. After the re-capture of Guadeloupe he reconquered the islands of Marie-Galante, Les Saintes, La Desirade, and Saint Martin, restoring the latter to its former owners, the Dutch, in 1795. Lieutenant General Sir Ralph Abercromby sailed to attack him in early 1796 with a force of nearly 20,000 men, but in his usual ruthless fashion Hugues enforced conscription in the islands, raising 15,000 men, and sent them out to all the adjoining islands to practise their irregular tactics on all the British garrisons. He also sent out privateers, and captured over 150 merchant vessels over a two-year period. These included United States vessels. Although not the main cause, Hugues's corsairs were contributory towards the undeclared 1798 'Quasi War' between the United States and France. Embarrassed, the Directory recalled Hugues to France. Hugues left the governorship of Guadeloupe to General Edme Étienne Borne Desfourneaux, one of his most trusted military subordinates. In 1799 General Bonaparte appointed him governor of Cayenne, giving him instructions to deal with the inhabitants 'in a milder way' than he did on Guadeloupe.

---

2   Arthur Aspinall, *The Later Correspondence of King George III* (Cambridge: Cambridge University Press, 1963), Vol. II p.298.

Hugues, by this time married and with four daughters, seems to have mellowed. He held the governorship for ten years, until 12 January, 1809, the day he signed a capitulation surrendering the colony to Captain James Lucas Yeo RN, commanding an Anglo-Portuguese expeditionary force. He returned to France, accused of incapacity and treason, and was tried by a court-martial, which in 1814 acquitted him. Then Hugues, the enemy of all things Royalist, clergy and noble, showed that he was, in the end, merely an opportunist. Following the re-acquisition of Cayenne by the Bourbons in 1815, Hugues was sent again as a special commissioner of King Louis XVIII, and governed the colony until 1819. Following the expiration of his term of office he remained in Cayenne as a private citizen, devoting his time to his immense estate and his grandchildren. According to some reports went blind in his final years. He died in Cayenne on 12 August 1826.

Louis-François Du Buc served on as Administrator of Martinique until August 1795 when he became a member of the Privy Council of the British colonies, then President of the Sovereign Council. Following the 1802 Treaty of Amiens which restored Martinique to France, he was sent by colonists to represent their interests to the First Consul – Napoléon. The Consul quite rightly suspected Du Buc of being an Anglophile, and treated him with disdain, despite Du Buc being a distant cousin of his wife, Josephine de Beauharnais. In 1803 Du Buc was elected as deputy to the Chamber of Agriculture on Martinique, a posting the new Emperor Napoléon reluctantly agreed to. Du Buc eventually came into the Emperor's good graces and was even allowed to touch the salaries that had been granted him by the colony. In 1814 King Louis XVIII appointed him steward of Martinique and made him a Knight of the Royal and Military Order of St. Louis. Du Buc retired in 1821, was elected deputy of Martinique in 1827, but died in Paris in December 1827 at the age of 68 before serving in the post.

After fleeing Martinique in 1793, Jean-Pierre-Antoine de Béhague went to Trinidad, and later gravitated to England where he joined the British Loyal Emigrants. On 9 May 1798 he was appointed the commander of the émigré Catholic and Royal Army of Brittany, but arguments with fellow expatriate Georges Cadoudal kept him out of any field command. He died in London in 1813. Chevalier Jean-Louis Alexandre Gédéon Ridouet de Sancé, who had proved himself extremely useful on Martinique, spent the Napoleonic era exiled in England, but returned to France to be made a count by the returned King Louis in January 1815.

General Rochambeau was feted around the United States for the rest of 1794 as a guest of honour, on account of his famous father, whose reputation ran deep. His parole ended when he was exchanged for the captured British Lieutenant General Sir Charles O'Hara in late 1795. Being at the disposal of the Convention, he was appointed Governor of Saint Domingue in 1796. Facing opposition from the civil commissioners there, he was dismissed and returned to France where he was imprisoned for some time. Luckily, the rising General Bonaparte came to his rescue. In 1800 he was appointed a divisional commander in the Italian campaign, and returned to Saint Domingue in 1802 as commander-in-chief. He stirred the mulattoes to a general uprising. Besieged by the British forces, he was captured in 1803 and was taken to England as a prisoner-of-war. Released in 1811 following an exchange, he returned to French service. In October 1813 this brave and proud old officer was killed in action at Leipzig.

Nicolas Xavier de Ricard sailed to Le Havre at Christmas 1795 and was allowed to retire in January 1804. He died in Paris on 30 May 1812, aged 86. Georges Henri Victor Collot arrived in North America in late 1794 and by 1796 was on an expedition down the Ohio and Mississippi Rivers, playing the wide-eyed tourist for the Americans whereas he was in fact in the employ of the French Republic, making maps and observing fortifications. After being arrested by the Spanish in Louisiana he returned to France, where he died in May 1805, aged 55.

This story would not be complete without recounting the future exploits of a number of Grey's company-level officers who later went on to high command, although most have melancholy endings. The after-effects of the campaign of 1794 hung over these men like a spectre, and most suffered from either prolonged poor health, or depression, or both.

Two who were lucky were Cole and Oswald. Galbraith Lowry Cole, a company commander in the 70th Foot on Martinique, went to Portugal in 1809 to be given command of the 4th Division, which he commanded for much of the Peninsula War. He missed Waterloo, being married in England the day the campaign started. Wellington considered him one of his most reliable subordinates. He later became the Governor of the Cape Colony and died in Hampshire in 1842 at the age of 70. John Oswald, commander of the grenadiers of the 35th Foot, served for many years in Egypt and the Mediterranean before assuming command of the 5th Division in the Peninsula in 1812. He went home in 1813 to attend to domestic affairs; his military career at that point was effectively over. A popular general, well-read and often in-demand as an after-dinner speaker, 'Jack' Oswald died in Scotland in 1840 aged 68.

The Honourable William Stewart, the young man who commanded the grenadiers of the 22nd Foot, arguably one of the most intelligent and dashing young officers in the campaign and well-liked by Grey, later became the first lieutenant colonel of the famous 95th Rifles. He served with Oswald in Egypt in 1807 then commanded troops at Cadiz before joining the field army in the Peninsula. He commanded the 2nd Division in 1811 and then the 1st Division for a time in 1812, but Wellington felt him an officer who needed close supervision, so he posted him to the 2nd Division again, serving under Rowland Hill for the remainder of the war. Thus despite his early promise, Stewart never entered the front rank of Peninsula generals. He died in Scotland in 1827 aged just 52.

George Ramsay, Earl of Dalhousie, the bold captain commanding the sole company of the 2nd Foot on Martinique, served in the Irish Rebellion and in Egypt. In 1812 he went out to Spain to command the 7th Division of Wellington's army, a command he held until the end of the war. In 1816 he became lieutenant-governor of Nova Scotia, then governor of British North America, a post that saw him fall out with the colonists. He was shuffled off to India but poor health saw him return home within two years; he suffered badly from depression. He died in Edinburgh in 1838 aged 68.

Grey's indispensable deputy adjutant-general Frederick Maitland returned to the West Indies in 1796 as secretary to General Sir Ralph Abercromby, and was appointed quartermaster-general in the West Indies in 1800. He commanded a brigade at the capture of The Saintes in 1801, and was second-in-command at the taking of Surinam in 1804. In 1805 Maitland was appointed Governor of Grenada at the express orders of King George. In 1809 he commanded a brigade during the invasion of Martinique, which must have been cause for great reflection. In 1811 he was appointed second-in-command of the Army in Sicily under Lord William Bentinck, then led a diversionary army to the east coast of Spain. But with his health impaired after many years' service in the West Indies, Maitland fell ill and returned to England. He was later appointed lieutenant-governor of Dominica. He died in Kent in 1848 at the age of 84.

Rufane Shaw Donkin of the 44th Foot gained promotion to major in 1796, then to lieutenant colonel the following year at the age of 25. He gained a reputation as one of the most gallant young field officers in the British Army after he led a light battalion with distinction in the raid on Ostend in 1798. He served at Copenhagen in 1807, and in 1809 was in command of a brigade in Wellesley's army in Portugal. On the night prior of the Battle of Talavera, an advance French force surprised Donkin's brigade on the Cerro de Medellin: Donkin fell back, rallied the men at the main line and led the brigade throughout the battle, but his star had waned. He found himself transferred in the role of quartermaster-general to the Mediterranean command. He served there from 1810 to 1813, taking part in expeditions to the east coast of Spain, but it was a side-show to Wellington's campaign in Spain. In 1815 he received a posting to India, where he once again distinguished himself as a divisional commander and was knighted in reward. He went to the Cape of Good Hope following the death of his young wife and administered the Cape Colony as acting Governor. In poor health and suffering from depression, he hanged himself in 1841 aged 69.

John Leveson-Gower, a twenty-year-old captain in the 9th Foot, became a lieutenant colonel before he was 21 and a major general at the age of 31. His career was curtailed after serving as second-in-command to the infamous General John Whitelocke in the disastrous expedition to Buenos Aires in 1807. He died in 1816 aged just 42. His wife died a year later, leaving two small orphans.

Frederick Philipse Robinson, the young lieutenant of the 38th Foot, spent many years as an Inspecting Field Officer in the English Home Counties, watching the events in Portugal and Spain from afar and hoping for a posting. In September 1812 Colonel Robinson joined the army in Spain as a brigadier general and six months later was a major general. He made up for the years of relative inactivity by commanding his brigade with great zeal in the battles of Vitoria, San

Sebastian, Nive, and the blockade of Bayonne, after which he found himself temporary commander of the 5th Division. Wellington hand-picked him from his army as one of four brigade commanders to go to North America in June 1814. In November 1814 he was appointed commander-in-chief and provisional governor of the Upper Provinces in Canada, a posting he held until June 1816, when he returned to England. He afterwards became governor and commander-in-chief of Tobago from 1816 to 1828. Sir Frederick Philipse Robinson survived to become the oldest living soldier in the British service, and died at Hove on the first day of 1852, aged 88.

Richard Fletcher, the junior officer of the Royal Engineers who went so close to losing his life on Saint Lucia, became Wellington's indispensable Chief Royal Engineer in Portugal and Spain until his unfortunate death in the trenches at San Sebastian in 1813, aged 45. His wife having predeceased him, he left a son and five young daughters behind. A monument was later erected to his memory in Westminster Abbey.

Robert Dale, an 18-year-old ensign in the 39th Foot from Derbyshire, captured at Berville and imprisoned on a hulk until 1796, eventually ended up as lieutenant colonel commanding the 93rd Highlanders. Fearing a premonition of his own death, he was killed in the abortive diagonal attack on the American redoubts at New Orleans in January 1815.

Several officers of the valiant 43rd Foot, a regiment which was virtually destroyed on the campaign, survived captivity and later resumed their careers. All had been imprisoned aboard a French hulk, some spending fifteen months in intolerable conditions before being sent to France to be paroled. Lieutenant Colonel James Drummond was one of the lucky ones. He escaped in early 1795. After another stint commanding on Saint Lucia in 1797-1798 he served on the staff at home and in Gibraltar as a brigadier general, and eventually became a general, but saw no more service, and died in 1831. Captain John Cameron served throughout the Peninsula War as commanding officer of the 9th Foot, being once severely and twice slightly wounded. He commanded a brigade in the Army of Occupation in France after Waterloo. He died on Guernsey in 1844 aged 71. His fellow captive Lieutenant Edward Hull commanded the 43rd Foot in the Peninsula between 1808 and 1810 but was killed in action on the Coa River on 24 July 1810 aged 39. Francis Skelly Tidy, a young ensign, returned to England and ended back in the West Indies as aide-de-camp to Sir George Beckwith. In September 1807 he became major of the 14th Foot, serving as assistant adjutant-general in the expedition to Spain under Sir David Baird in late 1808. In 1814 he was appointed lieutenant colonel of the newly-raised 3/14th Foot, which he commanded at Waterloo. The vast experience of 'Colonel Frank' helped his young battalion to survive the ordeal of that terrible day with credit. He died in Kingston, Canada, in 1836 aged 61.

Thus were the roots of Wellington's army planted, many years earlier, in those beautiful, terrible Leeward and Windward Islands.

Appendix I

British Forces in Windward & Leeward Islands June 1793

Based upon a return in GRE/A134 of the Grey Papers.
Number of rank & file present and fit for duty at the following stations in June 1793.

Station	Regiment	Number of Companies	Men Fit for Duty	In West Indies Since
St Kitts	9th (East Norfolk) Regiment of Foot	8	256	February 1788
Barbados	21st (Royal North British Fusiliers) Regiment of Foot	10	283	June 1793
	32nd (Cornwall) Regiment of Foot	8	264	June 1793
	45th (1st Nottinghamshire) Regiment of Foot	2	52	June 1784
	48th (Northamptonshire) Regiment of Foot	2	60	February 1788
	3/60th (Royal American) Regiment of Foot	2	48	November 1788
	4/60th (Royal American) Regiment of Foot	2	63	November 1788
	67th (South Hampshire) Regiment of Foot	2	64	Early 1785
Dominica	15th (Yorkshire East Riding) Regiment of Foot	10	305	Late 1790
	48th (Northamptonshire) Regiment of Foot	1	27	February 1788
	4/60th (Royal American) Regiment of Foot	1	29	November 1788

Station	Regiment	Number of Companies	Men Fit for Duty	In West Indies Since
Tobago	32nd (Cornwall) Regiment of Foot	2	73	June 1793
	4/60th (Royal American) Regiment of Foot	7	203	November 1788
Grenada	45th (1st Nottinghamshire) Regiment of Foot	8	192	June 1784
	67th (South Hampshire) Regiment of Foot	8	232	Early 1785
St Vincents	48th (Northamptonshire) Regiment of Foot	7	189	February 1788
Antigua	3/60th (Royal American) Regiment of Foot	7	140	November 1788
Montserrat	3/60th (Royal American) Regiment of Foot	1	20	November 1788
Various Garrisons	Royal Artillery / Royal Irish Artillery	6	429	Varies
Locally Raised Troops	Black Dragoons	1	44	
	Black Pioneers	1	157	
	Black Artificers	1	46	
	Militia of Grenada	8	855	
	TOTAL		4,093	

The 6th (1st Warwickshire) and 65th (2nd Yorkshire North Riding) Regiments of Foot sailed from Halifax for Barbados on 1 July 1793, with 339 and 208 men fit for duty respectively.

The above totals are for rank & file (corporals and privates) fit for duty only; add about another 10 per cent for officers, sergeants and drummers. Numbers of men sick are not shown.

Appendix II

Return of Troops Embarked at Barbados 1 February 1794

Return of troops embarked at Barbados for the invasion of Martinique, based upon a return in GRE/A200, Grey Papers.

Regiment	Number of Companies	Officers	Rank & File Present	Rank & File Sick	Comments
Royal Artillery / Royal Irish Artillery	9	30	499	40	
Light Dragoons	1	2	33	8	Detachment only
Royal Engineers	1	10	–		
Military Artificers	1	–	132		
Flank Battalions					
1st Grenadiers	9	30	593	32	Companies from 6th, 8th, 12th, 17th, 22nd, 23rd, 31st, 41st, & 58th Foot
2nd Grenadiers	9	28	580	13	Companies from 9th, 33rd, 34th, 35th, 38th, 40th, 44th, 55th, & 65th Foot
3rd Grenadiers	8	24	395	85	Companies from 15th, 21st, 39th, 43rd, 56th, 60th, 64th, & 70th Foot
1st Light Infantry	9	28	586	6	Companies from 6th, 8th, 9th, 12th, 17th, 22nd, 23rd, 35th, & 70th Foot

Regiment	Number of Companies	Officers	Rank & File Present	Rank & File Sick	Comments
2nd Light Infantry	7	23	453	12	Companies from 15th, 31st, 33rd, 34th, 38th, 40th, & 41st Foot; Companies from 44th & 55th Foot not yet arrived
3rd Light Infantry	8	24	428	59	Companies from 21st, 39th, 43rd, 56th, 58th, 60th, 64th, &65th Foot
1st Brigade (Gordon)					
15th (Yorkshire East Riding) Regiment of Foot	8	15	256	84	
39th (East Middlesex) Regiment of Foot	8	15	247	217	
43rd (Monmouthshire) Regiment of Foot	8	13	365	75	No field officers present
2nd Brigade (Dundas)					
2nd (Queen's) Regiment of Foot	1	4	68	1	Serving aboard ship as marines
58th (Rutlandshire) Regiment of Foot	8	5	146	11	No field officers present
64th (2nd Staffordshire) Regiment of Foot	8	8	150	274	No field officers present
65th (2nd Yorkshire North Riding) Regiment of Foot	8	16	325	49	
3rd Brigade (Whyte)					
6th (1st Warwickshire) Regiment of Foot	8	14	318	73	No field officers present
9th (East Norfolk) Regiment of Foot	8	14	277	56	
70th (Surrey) Regiment of Foot	8	15	369	103	
TOTALS		318	6,220	1,198	

360 sergeants and 202 drummers to be added to the above totals, of whom 50 were sick.

Of the officers presents, there were 10 lieutenant colonels, 12 majors, 90 captains, 156 lieutenants, and 40 ensigns – a very low tally to command the 146 companies present. There were also 14 adjutants, 14 surgeons, and 10 hospital mates.

Appendix III

French Garrison of Martinique February 1794

Based upon a return estimate in GRE/A513 of the Grey Papers.

Location	Unit	Strength
République-ville	Regular Artillery	
	Officers	1
	Sous-officers and cannoniers	20
	Ouvriers	5
	Regular Infantry	
	37e Régiment d'Infanterie (formerly Turenne)	
	Officers	5
	Sous-officers and soldats	125
	32e Régiment d'Infanterie (formerly de Bassigny)	
	Sous-officers and soldats	15
	52e Régiment d'Infanterie (formerly de la Fère)	
	Sous-officers and soldats	8
Saint Pierre	Island Militia	
	- Whites	700
	- *Gens de Couleur*	300
République-ville	Island Militia	
	- Whites	150
	- *Gens de Couleur*	200
Other parts of the island	Island Militia	
	- Whites	800
	- *Gens de Couleur*	600
TOTAL		**About 3,000**

Appendix IV

Returns of British Forces in Windward & Leeward Islands in 1794

Return of British troops present and fit for duty during 1794, based upon a return in GRE/A534 of the Grey Papers.

Date	Artillery Present & Fit for Duty	Artillery Sick	Artillery Dead since last return	Infantry Present & Fit for Duty	Infantry Sick	Infantry Dead since last return
1 January 1794	260	19	–	2,326	99	71
1 February 1794	494	126	–	6,334	1,755	76
1 March 1794	485	123	–	5,889	2,385	150
1 April 1794	416	176	17	5,948	2,092	131
1 May 1794	493	85	6	4,984	2,682	222
1 June 1794	371	100	19	4,007	2,873	788
1 July 1794	371	100	19	3,275	2,903	565
1 August 1794	371	100	19	2,471	3,346	552
1 September 1794	363	106	15	2,065	3,245	613
1 October 1794	331	129	11	1,641	1,706	214
1 November 1794	193	91	16	1,166	1,742	195
TOTALS			122			3,577

The above totals are for rank & file (corporals and privates) only; add about another 10 per cent for officers, sergeants and drummers.

Total number of officer deaths was 197, or about 52 per cent of those participating. Assuming similar losses amongst sergeants and drummers, the total death toll would be in the order of 4,200 men.

Appendix V

State of Martinique Garrison in November 1794

Based upon a return in GRE/A517 of the Grey Papers.

Location	Regiment	Officers & Staff	Present Fit for Duty	Sick
Saint Pierre	Light Dragoons	3	30	41
	Artillery	1	14	4
	15th Foot	10	240	232
	56th Foot	11	9	5
	Convalescents from regiments on other islands	–	22	41
	Carolina Black Corps	–	6	–
République-ville	Military Artificers	1	5	9
	Artillery	4	38	76
	58th Foot	9	85	148
	64th Foot	11	47	232
	70th Foot	15	11	18
Point Negro	Carolina Black Corps	–	50	29
Marin and elsewhere	Island Rangers (3 co.)	12	151	36
TOTALS		77	708	871

Only three field officers (included above) were present for the entire garrison. 124 sergeants and 74 drummers to be added to the above totals.

209

Appendix VI

Grey's Officers

A partial list of British officers known to have participated in the campaign, based upon paybooks in the WO 164 series, and other sources. Known to be incomplete in some cases.

As the 3rd battalions of grenadiers and light infantry were made up principally of men from complete regiments also serving in the theatre, these officers have been shown attached to their parent regiments. Officers are shown in the highest rank they are known to have held during the campaign.

(f) died of Yellow Fever
(k) killed in action
(w) died of wounds
(p) prisoner of war in January 1795
(d) dismissed from the service.

Staff

Commander-in-Chief
Lt. Gen. Sir Charles Grey KB

Second-in-Command
Lt. Gen. Robert Prescott

Brigade Commanders
Maj. Gen. HRH Prince Edward
Maj. Gen. Thomas Dundas (f)
Brig. Gen. John Whyte
Col. Sir Charles Gordon (d)

Field Officers on the staff
Brig. Gen. Richard Symes (w)
Lt. Col. William Gomm, 55th Foot (k)

Commanders Royal Artillery
Lt. Col. Thomas Paterson
Lt. Col. James Sowerby

Commander Royal Engineers
Col. Elias Durnford (f)

Adjutant-General
Brig. Gen. Francis Dundas

Deputy Adjutants-General
Maj. Frederick Maitland, 60th Foot
Maj. William Lyon, 55th Foot (f)
Capt. John Conyngham, 43rd Foot

Quartermaster-General
Brig. Gen. William Myers, 15th Foot

Deputy Quartermaster-General
Lt. Col. Henry George Grey, 18th Light Dragoons
Lt. Col. Robert Irving, 70th Foot (k)

Assistant Quartermasters-General
Capt. John Burnet, 43rd Foot
Capt. Francis Lewis de Ruvijnes, Royal Artillery
Lt. Henry Watkins, 15th Foot

Military Secretary
Lt. Col. Gerrit Fisher, 60th Foot

Majors of Brigade
Capt. Alexander Loraine, 9th Foot
Capt. John J Vischer, 65th Foot
Capt. James O'Callaghan, half-pay 10th Foot
Capt. Rufane Shaw Donkin, 44th Foot
Lt. George Stracey Smyth, 7th Foot

Aides-de-camp to Grey
Maj. Finch Mason, 32nd Foot
Maj. Thomas Grey, Independent Company
Capt. James Hare, 10th Light Dragoons
Capt. Newton Ogle, 70th Foot (f)
Capt. Hon William Stewart, 22nd Foot
Capt. William Grey, 21st Foot

Aides-de-camp to Prescott
Capt. & Lt. Lewis Hay, RE
Capt. John Thomas, 28th Foot
Capt. William Henry Beckwith, 56th Foot
Lt. Richard Westerman, 35th Foot

Aides-de-camp to HRH Prince Edward
Capt. Frederick Augustus Wetherall, 11th Foot
Capt. John Agmond Vesey, 11th Foot

Aides-de-camp to Thomas Dundas
Capt. Charles Maitland, 17th Light Dragoons
Capt. Robert Malcolm, 41st Foot

Naval Attaché
Lt. Thomas Tilt RN (f)

Captain of Guides
Chevalier Jean-Louis Alexandre Gédéon Ridouet de Sancé

Adjutant Generals Department – Clerks
Thomas Monk
William Craig

Commissary General
John Jeoffray

Commissary Department – Deputies
John Carmody
Alexander Jeoffray

Royal Artillery

CRA
Lt. Col. Thomas Paterson

Deputy CRA
Lt. Col. James Sowerby
Maj. Orlando Manley

Commissary of Stores
Lt. Thomas Sowerby

Appendix VI

Assistant Commissary
Lt. Elias Walker Durnford RE

Company Officers, RA
Capt. Charles Robison
Capt. Francis Lewis de Ruvijnes
Capt. Henry Hutton
Capt. Robert Hope
Capt. Robert King
Capt. Francis Whitworth
Lt. Robert George Suckling (p)
Lt. Brook Young
Lt. Haylett Framingham
Lt. Edward W. Drozier
Lt. George Bulteel Fisher
Lt. Edward Pritchard
Lt. Lucius O'Brien
Lt. Thomas Franklin
Lt. John Sheldrake
Lt. George Stackpoole (p)
Lt. Edward Barnes

Company Officers, RIA
Capt. John Pratt
Capt. Joseph Shewbridge (f)
Capt. William Smith (f)
Capt. John Bouchier
Capt. Arthur Tyrrell (f)
Capt. Joseph Walker
Lt. Richard Thornhill (f)
Lt. Thomas Cathcart Harris (f)
Lt. Edmund Nugent (f)
Lt. Joshua George (f)
Lt. John Baggot
Lt. Hon Benjamin Jones (f)
Lt. Edmund Maloney (f)
Lt. George Dawson (f)
Lt. James Coulson (f)

Royal Engineers

CRE
Col Elias Durnford

Commissary
Capt. Mark Warcup

Assistant Commissary
John Fowler

Paymaster
Capt. Thomas James Rudyard

Naval attaché
Capt. William Ross RN

Royal Engineers
Capt. John Chilcott (f)
Capt. John Robert Douglas
Capt. William Johnston
Capt. William Kersteman
Capt. James Fiddes
Capt. Lewis Hay
Capt. William G Hall
Lt. Richard Dowse (f)
Lt. Douglas Lawson (f)
Lt. Richard Fletcher
Lt. Henry Evatt
Lt. Elias Walker Durnford (p)

Assistant Engineers as Lieutenants
Jacques de Grondeville
Francis Duchat
Pierre Albert Delarcut
Monsieur Legrange
Josiah Gannaway
Monsieur Brunett
Louis Leron
Monsieur Polaster
Monsieur Laurent

1st Battalion of Grenadiers

Lt. Col. Richard Henry Buckeridge, 64th Foot (f)
Lt. Col. Robert Stewart, 58th Foot (f)
Maj. and Brevet Lt. Col. Robert Irving, 70th Foot (k)

8th Foot
Capt. Durell Saumerez (f)
Lt. & Adjt. Bryce McMurdo
Lt. George J. Reeves
Ens. J.R.M. Caulfield (f)

12th Foot
Capt. Adam Tweedie (f)
Lt. John Matthews
Lt. William Newport (k)
Lt. Wright (f)

17th Foot
Capt. Henry Hamilton
Lt. John Augustus Hitchman
Lt. William Cane (f)

22nd Foot
Capt. Hon. William Stewart
Lt. William Riddick
Lt. Robert Kelso

23rd Foot
Capt. Charles Apthorpe
Lt. Alexander Hackett
Lt. Evan Jones

31st Foot
Capt. George Pigot
Lt. Peter Thomas Robertson
Lt. William Sorrell

41st Foot
Capt. John Grey
Lt. Robert Malcolm
Lt. John Hardy

2nd Battalion of Grenadiers

Lt. Col. John Francis Cradock, QMG in Ireland
Maj. Jonas Watson, 65th Foot

33rd Foot
Capt. James Leigh Harvey (f)
Lt. Henry J Keating (p)

34th Foot
Capt. David Forbes (k)
Lt. James Innes (f)
Lt. William Forrester (f)
Lt. Nath (f)

35th Foot
Capt. John Oswald
Capt. George Eiston
Lt. Frederick Mukins (f)
Lt. Aldworth Phaire (f)
Lt. Philip Saunders (f)

38th Foot
Capt. John Mackewan (k)
Lt. Frederick Phillipse Robinson
Lt. Richard Mytton (f)
Lt. James Oughton Clarke (f)

40th Foot
Capt. John George Hood (f)
Capt. William Danser (p)
Lt. John Zephaniah Holwell (p)

44th Foot
Capt. John Lee
Lt. Henry Holland
Lt. John Charles Phipps (p)

55th Foot
Capt. George Taggart (f)
Lt. Richard Mayne (f)
Lt. Poyntz McKenzie (f)
Lt. Henry Dixon (p)
Lt. Thomas Hamilton (p)

1st Battalion of Light Infantry

Col. Eyre Coote, 70th Foot
Lt. Col. Farnham Close, 65th Foot (f)
Maj. Coote Manningham, 105th Foot

8th Foot
Capt. Thomas Armstrong (k)
Lt. James Booth (k)
Ens. Lorenzo Toole
Vol. John Armstrong (f)
Vol. Mark Kirby

12th Foot
Maj. John Perryn (f)
Lt. William O'Brien
Lt. John Lyster (k)
Lt. James Milner (f)
Lt. Wallace (f)

17th Foot
Capt. Richard Stovin (p)
Lt. James Ritchie (f)
Lt. R Ardesois Auchmuty (k)

22nd Foot
Capt. John Gustavus Crosbie
Lt. David Hamilton
Lt. Alexander Campbell
Lt. McDonald (f)

23rd Foot
Capt. John Henry Campbell
Lt. William Polhill (f)
Lt. William Wynne Garnons (k)

35th Foot
Capt. John Clarke
Lt. James FitzGerald (f)
Lt. William Clapham
Lt. George Charles Barry (f)
Ens. William Fitzgerald

2nd Battalion of Light Infantry

Lt. Col. Bryan Blundell, 44th Foot (f)
Maj. Andrew Ross, 31st Foot

31st Foot
Lt. John Maurice Davies (f)
Lt. John Thomas Williams (f)
Lt. Murdoch McKenzie (f)

33rd Foot
Capt. George Stewart
Lt. Andrew D Beatty (f)

34th Foot
Capt. James Roche (f)
Lt. Robert Owen
Lt. Charles Wattell (f)

35th Foot
Capt. Charles Grove (k)
Lt. Charles Strickland (p)
Ens. Thomas Holmes (p)

38th Foot
Capt. Hon. Alexander Douglas (f)
Lt. Robert Barclay (p)
Lt. Edmund Bower (f)
Lt. Brown (p)

40th Foot
Capt. Waldegrave Pelham Clay
Lt. Joseph Thompson
Lt. Daniel Manson (k)

41st Foot
Capt. William Douglas
Lt. Hon. George Colville
Lt. Richard Nugent

44th Foot
Capt. Rufane Shaw Donkin
Lt. Montagu Thorley
Lt. Charles Phillips (p)

<u>55th Foot</u>
Capt. John Lindsay
Lt. Godfrey Taylor (f)

10th (Prince of Wales' Own) Regiment of (Light)Dragoons

Lt. James Shadwell (f)
Cor. John Locke
Cor. Charles Payne Galway (p)

2nd (Queen's) Regiment of Foot

Capt. George Ramsay
Lt. William Gray
Ens. Thomas Edward Hunt

6th (1st Warwickshire) Regiment of Foot

Maj. William Scott
Capt. Thomas Welsh
Capt. Arthur Forbes
Capt. Alexander Adolphus Dalley (f)
Capt. Michael Impey
Capt. Walter Shairpe
Lt. Edward Thong (k)
Lt. Thomas Carnie
Lt. Hamilton Leonard Earle
Lt. Thomas Molyneux
Lt. Thomas Gale (f)
Lt. John Ekins (w)
Lt. William Hamilton
Ens. James Carter
Ens. Charles Wyndham Burdett
Ens. Richard Wallis Johnson
Ens. John Bristow Devenish
Ens. William Hague

9th (Norfolk) Regiment of Foot

Col. John Campbell (k)
Maj. Alexander Baillie
Capt. Alexander Buchanan
Capt. Archibald Campbell (f)

Capt. John Sandieman
Capt. Alexander Houston
Capt. John Leveson Gower
Lt. Archibald McLean
Lt. James Rose
Lt. Henry Stopford
Lt. John Nugent Smyth (p)
Lt. William Burbridge
Lt. Abraham Newenham
Lt. Alexander Gifford Nesbitt
Lt. David Campbell
Lt. Hercules Renny
Ens. Thomas Lancaster
Ens. Peter Buchanan

15th (Yorkshire East Riding) Regiment of Foot

Capt. Mungo Paumier
Capt. James King Coombe (k)
Capt. Charles, Lord Sinclair
Capt. Richard Hindson
Capt. Duncan Macdonald
Capt. John Bathe
Capt. Lt. James Gillespie
Lt. Samuel Madden
Lt. Dunbar Hammond Price
Lt. Henry Watkins
Lt. Henry Green Barry
Lt. Charles Atkinson
Lt. George Croker (k)
Lt. Francis Willoughby
Lt. Charles C Costley
Lt. Robert Manners
Lt. George Robertson
Ens. Henry Roberts
Ens. Thomas Edward James (f)
Ens. Robert Napier (f)

21st Regiment of Foot

Maj. George Rowley (f)
Capt. John Macdonald (k)
Capt. Robert Mackay

Capt. Lt. Alexander Francis Taylor
Lt. William Paterson
Lt. Alexander Dunbar
Lt. William Neate (f)
Lt. Samuel Knollis (k)
Lt. Edward Barnard King
Lt. Harry Foley Price (k)
Lt. Samuel Ward Stanton (f)

39th (East Middlesex) Regiment of Foot

Lt. Col. Stephen Fremantle (f)
Maj. Hugh Henry Magan (p)
Capt. George Bell
Capt. George Wilson
Capt. Alexander Buchanan
Capt. Love Albert Parry
Capt. Aeneas Shaw (f)
Capt. Robert Johnston (f)
Capt. Lt. William Purdie (f)
Lt. John Burslem (f)
Lt. Boyd Horsbrough (p)
Lt. John Cochran (k)
Lt. Birkenhead Glegg
Lt. Francis Scanlan (f)
Lt. Daniel Corneille
Lt. William Proby Hutchinson (f)
Lt. James Patterson (f)
Lt. Edmund Reynell (f)
Ens. William Humphries
Ens. Robert Dale (p)
Ens. Richard Tyldesley (f)
Ens. Hamilton Gorge
Ens. Michael Creagh (f)
Ens. Atkins (f)
Ens. de Ruvijnes (p)
Adjt. Simpson (f)
Adjt. McKenzie (f)

43rd (Monmouthshire) Regiment of Foot

Lt. Col. James Drummond (p)
Capt. Charles H Vignoles (f)

Capt. William Shireff Bayard (f)
Capt. Edmond Affleck (f)
Capt. John Burnet
Capt. Lt. James Fenton (k)
Capt. John Cameron (p)
Lt. John Alexander MacDowall (f)
Lt. William Jones (f)
Lt. John Butler (f)
Lt. Edward Hull (p)
Lt. Henry Spencer (f)
Lt. Joseph Graham (f)
Lt. Philip Crofton (k)
Lt. Charles Cameron (p)
Lt. Montagu Thorley (p)
Lt. Adrian de Yonge (p)
Ens. Francis Skelly Tidy (p)
Ens. James Grey Denniston (f)
Ens. Theophilus Boulton
Ens. A.D. Cameron
Ens. Christopher Mitchell
Ens. S Barwell Adams
Ens. Charles Criggan
Ens. George William Daniel (f)
Ens .Kirwan (f)
Ens. Peter Deshon (p)

56th (West Essex) Regiment of Foot

Capt. James Barrington
Capt. Richard White (f)
Capt. Edward John Fancourt (f)
Capt. Arthur Cuthbert
Capt. Richard Buckby
Capt. Robert Owen (p)
Capt. Lt. Allen Stevenson
Lt. Robert O'Neil
Lt. Hugh Taylor (f)
Lt. Fletcher Barclay (p)
Lt. Henry Cole Johnson (p)
Lt. Saunders McCausland (p)
Lt. William Stawell (f)
Lt. Warren (f)
Lt. O'Hara (f)

Adjt. John Perry (f)

58th (Rutlandshire) Regiment of Foot

Capt. Caesar Morrison (k)
Capt. James Ingram (f)
Capt. John Crowgey
Capt. Philip Brampton Gurdon
Capt. Francis Flood (f)
Lt. Alexander Mawdsley (f)
Lt. Anthony van Homrigh
Lt. Anthony Hennis (k)
Lt. Edward Hamilton Smith (f)
Lt. Hon. Robert King
Lt. Hon. Richard Tonson (f)
Lt. James Hamilton (f)
Lt. Thomas Holmes
Lt. William Hamilton
Lt. Charles Snell
Ens. George Berford (f)
Ens. J Somerville Murray (f)
Ens. Henry Bouchier (f)
Ens. Thomas Deane
Ens. William Collis
Ens. Richardson (p)
Ens. David Delisle (p)
Adjt. William Royall

3/60th (Royal American) Regiment of Foot

Capt. John De Lancy
Capt. Lt. William Robins
Capt. James Ecuyer
Lt. John Campbell
Lt. C. Frederick Picquett
Lt. William Henry Bunbury
Lt. Jacob Tonson
Lt. F G de Montmollin (f)
Lt. Benjamin K Lavicount
Lt. Mar. Foulkes Edgell
Ens. Lewis Schneider (f)
Ens. William Cooke (f)
Ens. William Bell (f)

4/60th (Royal American) Regiment of Foot

Capt. John Randall Forster
Lt. P. Luay Conway (k)
Ens. William Cunningham (f)

64th (2nd Staffordshire) Regiment of Foot

Maj. Robert Compton (f)
Maj. James Innes
Capt. George Rowley
Capt. James Mercer
Capt. David Boswell
Capt. George Johnston
Lt. Sir Richard McGuire (f)
Lt. Charles Miller
Lt. Lancelot Knight (f)
Lt. William Usher (f)
Lt. Anthony D Cudmore (p)
Lt. William Ambrose Wilson (f)
Lt. Henry Carey
Lt. John Ewing
Ens. John Stratford (f)
Ens. Thomas Paul Usher
Adjt. John Wilkinson (f)

65th (2nd Yorkshire North Riding) Regiment of Foot

Maj. John Herbert Dalrymple (f)
Capt. Alexander Macgregor (f)
Capt. John Grant
Capt. Lt. Henry Blacker (f)
Lt. George Oliver (f)
Lt. Robert Douglas
Lt. William Clarke
Lt. Philip Denton Toosey (k)
Lt. Thomas Kennedy (f)
Lt. Hon. James Stopford
Lt. James Adams (f)
Lt. Edward Bullock
Lt. Ralph Bates
Lt. Capel Bringlow (f)
Ens. Henry Dixon

Ens. Daniel Millward (f)

67th (South Hampshire) Regiment of Foot

Capt. Adam Gordon
Lt. Edward Gayer
Lt. Daniel Cudmore
Lt. William Huey
Lt. Arthur Edward Dobbs
Lt. Thomas Fairclough

70th (Surrey) Regiment of Foot

Maj. and Brevet Lt. Col. Boulter Johnson
Maj. John Evatt
Capt. Thomas Dunbar
Capt. George Strange Nares (f)
Capt. Galbraith Lowry Cole
Capt. James Eiston (f)
Capt. Lt. James Bruce (f)
Lt. Henry Elliott
Lt. John Grueber
Lt. Henry Gifford (f)
Lt. William Cox (f)
Lt. William Cepton Longford
Lt. Henry Loader
Lt. John Floyer (f)
Lt. John Scott
Lt. Usher Boate
Lt. Patrick Crawford
Lt. Edward Grove
Lt. Henry Thornhill
Adjt. Benjamin Lawrence

Carolina Black Corps

Lt. Col. James Chalmers
Capt. James Green
Lt. Francis Miller
Lt. James Hamilton
Lt. S.D. Crosier
Lt. William Miller
Lt. Charles C. Shilton

Appendix VII

Royal Navy Squadron at Martinique, February 1794

Vice Admiral of the Blue Sir John Jervis, K.B. commanding

Vessel	No. Guns	Rating & Type	Officer Commanding	Comments	Killed/ Wounded
Boyne	98	Second rate ship-of-the-line	Vice Admiral of the Blue Sir John Jervis, K.B Capt. George Grey	Flagship	0/6
Vengeance	74	Third rate ship-of-the-line	Commodore Charles Thompson, Esq. Capt. Harry Powlett		2/2
Irresistible	74	Third rate ship-of-the-line	Capt. John Henry		1/5
Veteran	64	Third rate ship-of-the-line	Capt. Charles Edmund Nugent		1/4
Beaulieu	40	Fifth rate frigate	Capt. John Salisbury		0/0
Solebay	32	Fifth rate frigate	Capt. William Hancock Kelly		0/0
Blonde	32	Fifth rate frigate	Capt. John Markham		0/0
Quebec	32	Fifth rate frigate	Capt. Josias Rogers		1/3
Terpsichore	32	Fifth rate frigate	Capt. Samson Edwards		?
Rose	28	Sixth rate frigate	Capt. Edward Riou	Wrecked off Jamaica on 28 June 1794	0/0
Nautilus	16	Unrated ship-sloop	Commander James Carpenter		2/0
Rattlesnake	16	Unrated ship-sloop	Lt. John William Spranger		0/0

APPENDIX VII

Vessel	No. Guns	Rating & Type	Officer Commanding	Comments	Killed/ Wounded
Zebra	16	Unrated ship-sloop	Commander Robert Faulknor		1/5
Avenger	16	Unrated ship-sloop	Commander James Milne	Captured 17 February; previously French privateer corvette *La Marseillaise*	1/0
Seaflower	16	Unrated cutter	Lt. William Pierrepont		0/0
Vesuvius	8	Unrated bomb vessel	Commander Charles Sawyer		0/0
Experiment	20	Unrated troop ship	Commander Simon Miller	Armed en flûte	
Woolwich	24	Unrated storeship	Commander John Parker	Armed en flûte	
Dromedary	24	Unrated storeship	Commander Sandford Tatham	Armed en flûte	2/2
Joined the squadron during the siege of République-ville					
Asia	64	Third rate ship-of-the-line	Capt. John Brown		3/5
Santa Margarita	36	Fifth rate frigate	Capt. Eliab Harvey	Captured from Spain in 1779	0/0
Ceres	32	Fifth rate frigate	Capt. Richard Incledon		0/0
Winchelsea	32	Fifth rate frigate	Capt. George Stewart. Lord Garlies		1/0
Assurance	22	Unrated troop ship	Capt. Velters Cornewall Berkeley		0/0
Roebuck	-	Unrated Hospital Ship	Capt. Alexander Christie		

Sources:

Isaac Schomberg, *Naval Chronology: Or, An Historical Summary of Naval & Maritime Events, from the Time of the Romans, to the Treaty of Peace, 1802*, (London: T. Egerton, 1802), Volume 4.

Appendix VIII

Royal Navy Squadron at Guadeloupe, April 1794

Vice Admiral of the Blue Sir John Jervis, K.B. commanding

Vessel	No. Guns	Rating & Type	Officer Commanding	Comments
Boyne	98	Second rate ship-of-the-line	Vice Admiral of the Blue Sir John Jervis, K.B. Capt. George Grey	Flagship
Irresistible	74	Third rate ship-of-the-line	Capt. John Henry	Went down to Jamaica
Veteran	64	Third rate ship-of-the-line	Capt. Lewis Robertson	
Santa Margarita	36	Fifth rate frigate	Capt. Eliab Harvey	
Winchelsea	32	Fifth rate frigate	Capt. George Stewart, Lord Garlies	
Solebay	32	Fifth rate frigate	Capt. William Hancock Kelly	
Quebec	32	Fifth rate frigate	Capt. Josias Rogers	Sent with Capt Rogers to take possession of the Saintes
Ceres	32	Fifth rate frigate	Capt. Richard Incledon	Sent with Capt Rogers to take possession of the Saintes
Blanche	32	Fifth rate frigate	Capt. Robert Faulknor	Sent with Capt Rogers to take possession of the Saintes
Terpsichore	32	Fifth rate frigate	Capt. Sampson Edwards	Joined after the taking of Grande-Terre

Vessel	No. Guns	Rating & Type	Officer Commanding	Comments
Rose	28	Sixth rate frigate	Capt. Mathew Henry Scott	Sent with Capt Rogers to take possession of the Saintes Wrecked off Jamaica 28 June 1794
Zebra	16	Unrated ship-sloop	Commander Richard Bowen	Joined after the taking of Grande-Terre
Bulldog	16	Unrated ship-sloop	Commander Edward Browne	Joined after the taking of Grande-Terre
Inspector	16	Unrated ship-sloop	Commander Wyndham Bryer	Joined after the taking of Grande-Terre
Woolwich	24	Unrated storeship	Commander John Parker	Armed en flûte
Assurance	22	Unrated troop ship	Capt. Velters Cornewall Berkeley	Armed en flûte ; joined after the taking of Grande-Terre
Experiment	20	Unrated troop ship	Commander Simon Miller	Armed en flûte
Roebuck	–	Unrated hospital ship	Capt. Alexander Christie	
Joined the squadron before June				
Vanguard	74	Third rate ship-of-the-line	Commodore Charles Thompson, Esq. Capt. Charles Sawyer	
Vengeance	74	Third rate ship-of-the-line	Capt. Richard Incledon	
Resource	28	Sixth rate frigate	Capt. James Ross	
Nautilus	16	Unrated ship-sloop	Capt. H W Bayntum	
Avenger	16	Unrated ship-sloop	Captain Edward Griffith	

Sources:

Isaac Schomberg, *Naval Chronology: Or, An Historical Summary of Naval & Maritime Events, from the Time of the Romans, to the Treaty of Peace, 1802*, (London: T. Egerton, 1802), Volume 4.

Bibliography

Archival Sources

British Library
Liverpool Papers, Add MS 38353, Volume CLXIV.

Digital Library of the Caribbean
Rochambeau, Donatien. (1793). *Journal du Blocus et du Siège de la Martinique.*
Rochambeau, Donatien. (1794). *Journal du Siège de la Martinique par l'armée et la flotte Anglaise commandées du g.al Grey et du vice amiral Joh. Jervis.*

The National Archives, Kew
MPG 1/572 – Plan of the British lines near Berville Camp at the time of the capitulation to the French. Reference table. Signed by Frederick Maitland.
Series WO 164 – Royal Hospital Chelsea: Prize Records
    WO 164/37 – Martinico, Royal Artillery.
    WO 164/39 – Martinico, 56th Foot.
    WO 164/40 – Martinico, 1st Grenadiers.
    WO 164/41 – Martinico, 1st Grenadiers.
    WO 164/42 – Martinico, 2nd Grenadiers.
    WO 142/43 – Martinico, 2nd Grenadiers.
    WO 164/44 – Martinico, 1st Lights.
    WO 164/45 – Martinico, 1st Lights.
    WO 164/46 – Martinico, 2nd Lights.
    WO 146/47 – Martinico, 2nd Lights.
    WO 164/48 – Martinico, 6th Foot.
    WO 164/49 – Martinico, 9th Foot.
    WO 164/50 – Martinico, 15th Foot.
    WO 164/51 – Martinico, 39th Foot.
    WO 164/52 – Martinico, 58th Foot.
    WO 164/53 – Martinico, 64th Foot.
    WO 164/54 – Martinico, 65th Foot.
    WO 164/55 – Martinico, 70th Foot.

WO 164/66 – Martinico, 43rd Foot.
WO 164/484 – Martinico, Staff.

Palace Green Library, Durham University
Papers of Charles, 1st Earl Grey. Collection code: GB 033 GRE-A. Date range: 1725-1807 (predominantly after 1786). Papers in chronological order (1-2236), followed by volumes (2237-2257)
    1793 – Papers A129 to A188b
    1794 (Part 1) – Papers A189 to A294/14
    1794 (Part 2) – Papers A295 to A409
    1794 (Part 3) – A410 to A535
    1795 (Part 1) – A536a to A668b
    A2242 – Correspondence, largely with Robert Prescott, 29 September – 16 November 1794.
    A2243 – Correspondence, largely with Henry Dundas, 18 December 1793 – 18 January 1795
    A2244 – The West-India Atlas: or a Compendious Description of the West-Indies: illustrated with forty correct charts and maps taken from actual surveys. Together with an Historical Account of the Several Countries and Islands which compose that part of the world. By Thomas Jefferys. (London 1775.)
    A2245 – Book containing printed maps of the West India islands. The maps vary in date between 1758 and 1794.
    A2246 – Book in which are mounted forty plans and maps (mostly manuscript but a few printed) of West India islands (mainly Martinique, St. Lucia and Guadeloupe) and strategic points on them. The plans vary in date between 1762 and 1794.

Surrey History Centre
ESR/25/NARE/. Camp Diary kept by Captain George Strange Nares, including a Description of Invasion and Battle of Martinique.

Printed Primary Sources

Anon., *Anthologia Hibernica: Or Monthly Collections of Science, Belles-lettres, and History*, (Dublin: R.E Mercier & Co, 1793)
Anon., *Bulletins of the campaigns of 1793, 1794, 1795, extracted from accounts in the London Gazette* (London: A. Strachan, 1794 to 1796).
Anon., *A Collection of State Papers Relative to the War against France* (London: John Stockdale, 1795 to 1802).
Anon., *Cumloden papers [letters &c. relating to the Hon. Sir W. Stewart and others, with an account of his life].* (Edinburgh: Printed for private circulation, 1871) [Contains extracts of Stewart's campaign journal].

Anon., *A List of the Officers of the Army and Marines, with an index, a succession of Colonels, and a list of the Officers of the Army and Marines on Half-Pay* (London: War Office, 1791 to 1818).

Aspinall, Arthur, *The Later Correspondence of King George III* (Cambridge: Cambridge University Press, 1963).

Dundas, M. I. (ed.), *Dundas of Fingask: Some Memorials of the Family* (Edinburgh: D. Douglas, 1891).

Gillespie, Leonard, *Observations on the diseases which prevailed on board a part of His Majesty's Squadron on the Leeward Island Station between Nov. 1794 and April 1796* (London: G. Auld for J. Cuthell, 1800).

Grehan, John and Mace, Martin (eds.). (2013). *British Battles of the Napoleonic Wars, 1793-1806* (Barnsley: Pen and Sword 2013).

Hoffman, Frederick, *A Sailor of King George* (London: John Murray 1901).

James, Bartholomew, *Journal of Rear Admiral Bartholomew James, 1752-1828* (London: printed by Spottiswoode for the Navy Records Society, 1896).

Willyams, Cooper, *An Account of the Campaign in the West Indies in the Year 1794 Under the Command of their Excellencies Lieutenant General Sir Charles Grey, K.B., and Vice Admiral Sir John Jervis, K.B.* (London, T. Bensley, 1796).

Printed Secondary Sources

Anon., *The British Military Library: Comprehending a Complete Body of Military Knowledge, and Consisting of Original Communications* (London: J. Carpenter, 1799 to 1801).

Anon. *Facts relative to the conduct of the war in the West Indies; collected from the speech of the Right Hon. Henry Dundas, in the House of Commons, on the 28th of April, 1796, and from documents laid before the House upon that subject* (London: J. Owen, 1796).

Anon., *The Field of Mars: Being an Alphabetical Digestion of the Principal Naval and Military Engagements of Great Britain and Her Allies, From the Ninth Century to the Peace in 1801* (London: G. & J. Robinson, 1801).

Baines, Edward, *History of the Wars of the French Revolution: From the Breaking Out of the War in 1792 to the Restoration of a General Peace in 1815; Comprehending the Civil History of Great Britain and France During that Period* (London: H. Light, 1823).

Baker, Anthony, *Battle Honours of the British and Commonwealth Armies* (London: Ian Allen Ltd., 1986).

Baring, Evelyn, *Political and Literary Essays*, (Cambridge: Cambridge University Press, 2010),

Brenton, E. P., *Life and Correspondence of John, Earl of St. Vincent, etc.* (London: Henry Colburn, 1838).

Bunbury, Sir Henry Edward, *Narratives of Some Passages in the Great War with France, from 1799 to 1810,* (London: R. Bentley, 1854).

Chartrand, René, *Emigre and Foreign Troops in British Service 1793-1802* (Botley: Osprey, 1999).
Chartrand, René, *British Forces in the West Indies 1793-1815* (London: Osprey, 1996).
Chichester, Henry Manners and Burgess-Short, George, *The Records and Badges of Every Regiment and Corps in the British Army* (London: William Clowes and Sons Ltd., 1895).
Cormack, William S., 'Victor Hugues and the Reign of Terror on Guadeloupe 1794-1798', in Johnston, A. J. B., *Essays in French Colonial History: Proceedings of the 21st Annual Meeting of the French Colonial Society* (East Lansing: Michigan State University Press, 1997) pp. 31-41.
Devaux. Robert J., *They Called Us Brigands* (Castries: Optimum Printers, 1997).
Edwards, Bryan, *An Historical Survey of the French Colony in the Island of St. Domingo* (Cambridge: Cambridge University Press, 2010, facsimile of 1797 edition).
Fortescue, Hon. J.W., *A History of the British Army* (Uckfield: The Naval and Military Press Ltd., 2004).
Fortescue, Hon. J.W., *The British Army 1783 To 1802*. (London: Macmillan & Co., 1905).
Fouché, Monica, *Glory Overshadowed: The Military Career of General Jean Boudet 1769-1809* (Unpublished Doctoral Thesis, Florida State University, 2005).
Geggus, David, 'The Cost of Pitt's Caribbean Campaigns, 1793 to 1798' in *The Historical Journal*, Vol. 26, No. 3 September 1983 (Cambridge: Cambridge University Press), pp.699-706.
Gilpin, W., *Memoirs of Josias Rogers, esq. Commander of His Majesty's Ship Quebec*. (London: T. Cadell and W. Davies, 1808).
Guy, Alan J. (ed.), *The Road to Waterloo*. (London: National Army Museum, 1990).
Haynsworth, James Lafayette IV, 'Donatien Rochambeau and The Defence of Martinique, 1793-1794', *Consortium on Revolutionary Europe 1750-1850*, 1997, pp.180-190.
Haynsworth, James Lafayette IV, *The Early Career of Lieutenant General Donatien Rochambeau and The French Campaigns in the Caribbean, 1792-1794* (Unpublished Doctoral Thesis, Florida State University, 2003).
Howard, Martin. *Death Before Glory : The British Soldier in the West Indies in the French Revolutionary and Napoleonic Wars 1793 -1815.* (Barnsley: Pen & Sword, 2015).
James, William, *The Naval History of Great Britain: From the Declaration of War by France, in February 1793, to the Accession of George IV. in January 1820* (London: Harding, Lepard & Company, 1826).
Kopperman, Paul E., '"The Cheapest Pay": Alcohol Abuse in the Eighteenth-Century British Army'. *The Journal of Military History Vol. 60 No. 3* (1996), pp. 445-470.

Langdon, Jarvis, *The French Revolution in Martinique and Guadeloupe* (Unpublished Thesis, Cornell University, 1897).
Lémery, Henry, *La Révolution Française à la Martinique* (Paris: Larose, 1936).
Longford, Elizabeth, *Wellington: The Years of the Sword*, (London: World Books, 1969).
McGregor, John James, *History of the French Revolution and of the Wars Resulting from that Memorable Event*, (London: G.B. Whittaker, 1828).
McKenna, Michael G., *The British Army – And Its Regiments and Battalions* (West Chester, Ohio: The Nafziger Collection, 2004).
Miller, J. R., *The History of Great Britain from the Death of George II to the Coronation of George IV*, (London: M'Carty & Davis, 1829).
Nelson, P. D., *Sir Charles Grey, First Earl Grey: Royal Soldier, Family Patriarch* (Madison New Jersey: Fairleigh Dickinson University Press, 1996).
Norman, C.B., *Battle Honours of the British Army* (London: David and Charles Reprints, 1971).
Philippart, John, *The Royal Military Calendar, or Army Service and Commission Book* (London: A.J. Valpy, 1820).
Ralfe, James, *The Naval Biography of Great Britain: Consisting of Historical Memoirs of Those Officers of the British Navy who Distinguished Themselves During the Reign of His Majesty George III* (London: Whitmore & Fenn, 1828).
Reid, Stuart, *Wellington's Officers* (Leigh-On-Sea: Partizan Press, 2008-2011).
Sanderson, Michael William Bristowe, *English Naval Strategy and the Maritime Trade in the Caribbean, 1793-1802* (Unpublished Doctoral Thesis, London University, 1968).
Schomberg, Isaac, *Naval Chronology: Or, An Historical Summary of Naval & Maritime Events, from the Time of the Romans, to the Treaty of Peace, 1802*, (London: T. Egerton, 1802).
Southley, Thomas, *Chronological History of the West Indies*. Three volumes. (London: A&R Spottiswoode, 1827).
Tucker, Jedediah Stevens. *Memoirs of Admiral the Right Hon[orabl]e the Earl of St. Vincent.* (London: R. Bentley, 1844).

Regimental Histories

Cannon, R., *Historical record of the First, or Royal Regiment of Foot: containing an account of the origin of the regiment in the reign of King James VI of Scotland and of its subsequent services to 1846* (London: Parker, Furnivall, & Parker, 1847).
Cannon, R., *Historical record of The Second, or, Queen's Royal Regiment of Foot: containing an account of the formation of the regiment in the year 1661 and of its subsequent services to 1837* (London: Clowes, 1838).

BIBLIOGRAPHY

Cannon, R., *Historical record of the Sixth, or Royal First Warwickshire Regiment of Foot: containing an account of the formation of the regiment in the year 1674, and of its subsequent services to 1838* (London: Longman, 1838).

Cannon, R., *Historical record of the Eighth, or the King's Regiment of Foot: containing an account of the formation of the regiment in 1685, and of its subsequent services to 1841* (London: Parker, Furnivall and Parker, 1844).

Cannon, R., *Historical record of the Ninth, or the East Norfolk Regiment of Foot: containing an account of the formation of the regiment in 1685, and of its subsequent services to 1847* (London: Parker, Furnivall, & Parker, 1848).

Cannon, R., *Historical record of the Twelfth, or the East Suffolk Regiment of Foot: containing an account of the formation of the regiment in 1685 and of its subsequent services to 1847* (London: Parker, Furnivall, & Parker, 1848).

Cannon, R., *Historical record of the Fifteenth, or the Yorkshire East Riding, Regiment of Foot: containing an account of the formation of the regiment in 1685, and of its subsequent services to 1848* (London: Parker, Furnivall, & Parker, 1848).

Cannon, R., *Historical record of the Twenty-first Regiment, or the Royal North British Fusiliers: containing an account of the formation of the regiment in 1678 and of its subsequent services to 1849* (London: Parker, Furnivall & Parker, 1849).

Cannon, R., *Historical record of the Twenty-second or the Cheshire Regiment of Foot: containing an account of the formation of the regiment in 1689, and of its subsequent services to 1849* (London: Parker, Furnivall & Parker, 1849).

Cannon, R., *Historical record of the Twenty-Third Regiment, or, The Royal Welsh Fusiliers: containing an account of the formation of the regiment in 1689 and of its subsequent services to 1850* (London: Parker, Furnivall, & Parker, 1850).

Cannon, R., *Historical record of the Thirty-first, or, The Huntingdonshire Regiment of Foot: containing an account of the formation of the regiment in 1702, and of its subsequent services to 1850, to which is appended an account of the services of the Marine Corps, from 1664 to 1748: The Thirtieth, Thirty-First and Thirty-Second Regiments having been formed in 1702 as Marine Corps, and retained from 1714 on the establishment of the army as regiments of regular infantry* (London, Parker, Furnivall, & Parker, 1850).

Cannon, R., *Historical record of The Thirty-Fourth, or, The Cumberland Regiment of Foot: containing in account of the formation of the regiment in 1702, and its subsequent services to 1844* (London: Parker, Furnivall and Parker, 1844).

Cannon, R., *Historical record of The Thirty-ninth, or, The Dorsetshire Regiment of Foot* (London, Parker, Furnivall and Parker, 1853).

Carter, Thomas, *Historical record of the Forty-fourth, or the East Essex Regiment of Foot* (London, W.O. Mitchell, 1864).

Cannon, R., *Historical record of the Fifty-Sixth, or the West Essex Regiment of Foot: containing an account of the formation of the regiment in 1755, and of its subsequent services to 1844* (London: Parker, Furnivall and Parker, 1844).

Cannon, R., *Historical record of the Sixty-first, or, the South Gloucestershire Regiment of Foot: containing an account of the formation of the regiment in 1758, and of its subsequent services to 1844* (London: Parker, Furnivall and Parker, 1844).

Cannon, R., *Historical record of The Sixty-Seventh, or, The South Hampshire Regiment: containing an account of the formation of the regiment in 1758 and of its subsequent services to 1849* (London: Parker, Furnivall & Parker, 1849).

Cannon, R., *Historical record of the Seventieth, or, The Surrey Regiment of Foot: containing an account of the formation of the regiment in 1758, and of its subsequent services to 1848* (London: Parker, Furnivall & Parker, 1849).

Laws, M.E.S., *Battery Records of the Royal Artillery, 1716-1859.* (Woolwich: Royal Artillery Institute, 1952).

Forbes, Archibald, *The Black Watch: The Record of an Historic Regiment.* (New York: Charles Scribner & Sons, 1910).

Petre, F. Loraine, *History of the Norfolk Regiment: 1685 to 1913* (Uckfield: Naval and Military Press, 2001).

Jones, Robert John, *A History of the 15th (East Yorkshire) Regiment, the Duke of York's Own, 1685 to 1914* (Beverley: East Yorkshire Regimental Association, 1964).

Ward, S.G.P. *Faithful: The Story of the Durham Light Infantry* (London: Nelson & Sons for Durham Light Infantry, 1963).

Wylly, Col. H.C., *History of the 1st and 2nd Battalions The Sherwood Foresters* (Printed by the Regiment, 1929).

Magazines and Periodicals

The Naval and Military Magazine (London: T. Clerc Smith, 1827 to 1833).

The New Annual Register, or General Repository of History, Politics and Literature (London: G.G. & J. Robinson, 1794 to 1815).

The Royal Military Chronicle or British Officers' Monthly Registers and Mentor (London: J Davies, various years, 1811 to 1814).

The United Service Journal and the Naval and Military Magazine (London: Henry Cole Byrne and Richard Bentley, 1830 to 1833).

Websites and Online Resources

17th-18th Century Burney Collection Newspapers. National Library of Australia. https://www.nla.gov.au/app/eresources/item/3304

18th Century British Newspapers Online. National Library of Australia. https://www.nla.gov.au/app/eresources/item/4314

British Regiments and the Men who led them 1793-1815. https://www.napoleon-series.org/military/organization/Britain/Infantry/Regiments/c_InfantryregimentsIntro.html

History of Parliament. http://www.historyofparliamentonline.org
The House of Commons Parliamentary Papers online. National Library of Australia. http://www.nla.gov.au/app/eresources/item/1642
The *Times* digital archive. http://gale.cengage.co.uk/times-digital-archive/times-digital-archive-17852006.aspx

Index

Abercromby, Lt. Gen. Sir Ralph 195, 198, 201
Amherst, General Lord 15, 17, 25, 69, 198
Anse d'Arlet 77-8
Anse du Cap 118
Anse du Choc 118
Antigua 17, 43-4, 144-5, 157, 204
Arnold, Benedict 149-151
Aubert, Général de Brigade Claude 141-2, 159

Baie du Galion 71, 74-5, 101
Baillie, Maj. Alexander 54, 56, 71, 88, 125
Barbados 17-8, 38, 40-1, 43-4, 48-51, 53-4, 57, 59-60, 62, 64-6, 68, 71, 76, 95, 101, 137, 144, 148, 184, 196, 203-5
Barham, Foster 177-8
Baring, Sir Francis 177
Basse-Terre 11, 127, 129, 131-3, 138-9, 143-5, 161, 163, 169, 172, 174
Béhague, Lieutenant Général Jean-Pierre-Antoine de 46-8, 51, 199
Bellegarde, Lt. Col. Louis de 50-1, 53, 73-6, 80-2, 86, 92, 94, 97-8, 113
Berville 12, 144, 150, 155, 161-5, 167-170, 173-4, 190, 196, 202, 230
Blundell, Lt. Col. Bryan 60, 63, 118, 132, 139, 144
Bontein, Capt. James 115, 169
Booty 36-7, 90, 122, 159, 173, 179, 195
Boudet, Général de Brigade Jean 141, 143, 152, 155-6, 159, 162, 164, 190
Bowen, Capt. Richard RN 71, 101, 103, 174, 176, 229
Boyd, Lt. Gen. Sir Robert 138

Bright, Maj. Richard 55
Brown, Capt. John RN 106, 109
Bruce, Maj. Gen. the Hon. Thomas 49-53, 59
Buckeridge, Lt. Col. Richard Henry 63, 93-4, 190
Bures, Chef de Bataillon Gaspard de 162
Burnet, Capt. John 153

Caldwell, Vice Admiral Benjamin 173-4, 183
Cameron, Capt. John 165, 202
Campbell of Blythswood, Col. John 62-3, 75, 82, 86-8, 104, 190
Case de Navire 51-2, 71, 79
Castries (Felicitéville) 44, 116, 120, 184-5
Cayenne 45, 136, 198-9
Chrétien, Pierre 142-3, 145, 159
Close, Lt. Col. Farnham 63, 74, 76, 108, 118, 130, 190
Clugny, Governor Marc-Antoine, Baron de 44
Cochran, Lt. John 165
Cole, Capt. Galbraith Lowrey 78, 200
Collot Governor Georges Henri Victor 132-4, 189
Conyngham, Capt. John 40, 99, 110, 179
Coote, Lt. Col. Eyre 63, 75-6, 82, 93-4, 108, 118-9, 132, 139, 146, 153, 197
Cradock, Lt. Col. John Francis 63, 75-6, 82, 146, 157, 196
Cuyler, Maj. Gen. Cornelius 17, 54-7

Dale, Ensign Robert 202
Davers, Capt. Charles RN 167

INDEX

Dominica 17, 43-4, 97, 157, 184, 201, 203
Donkin, Capt. Rufane Shaw 63, 201
Douglas, Capt. John 134, 167
Drummond, Lt. Col. James 126, 142-3, 161-2, 165, 191, 202
Du Buc, Louis-François 48, 124, 148-9, 199
Ducassou, Commandant Jean 83, 85
Dundas, Col. Francis 33, 39, 41, 139, 145, 171, 179, 196
Dundas, Henry 28, 32-9, 48-9, 53-4, 65-6, 104, 112-3, 115, 122, 131, 137-8, 155, 158-9, 168, 173, 175, 178, 183, 187, 198
Dundas, Maj. Gen. Thomas 37-40, 59-63, 66, 68, 71, 74-7, 79, 81-3, 85-91, 95-6, 100, 103-4, 110, 115, 118, 120-1, 126, 130, 132, 134-5, 138-9, 144, 171, 174, 179, 188, 193, 196, 206
Durnford, Col. Elias, 68, 78, 118, 143, 191
Durnford, Lt. Elias Walker 143, 164, 169

Edward, Major General HRH Prince 61, 100, 103-5, 110-2, 116, 118, 120, 127, 130, 132-5, 179, 195
Eiston, Capt. George 169
Evatt, Maj. John 76, 171

Fahey, Cdr. William Charles 167
Fancourt, Capt. Charles 68
Faulknor, Capt. Robert RN 75, 90, 101, 103, 106-7, 109-110, 112-3, 130, 134, 179, 188, 227-8
Fiddes, Capt. James 50, 55, 57
Fisher, Lt. Col Gerrit 40, 145, 149-151, 153
Flank Battalions, 38, 62, 68, 81, 94, 119-120, 132, 134, 136, 145-6, 150, 154, 157, 182, 189, 191, 196, 205; 1st Grenadiers 63, 79-80, 108 110-2, 118, 126, 130, 132, 151-2, 205; 1st Light Infantry 63, 75, 93, 108, 112, 132, 145, 151, 205; 2nd Grenadiers 63, 75, 86-8, 118, 126, 130, 132, 146, 151, 153, 157, 161, 205; 2nd Light Infantry 63, 74, 132, 146, 151, 206; 3rd Grenadiers 63, 74, 77, 93, 110-2, 118, 126, 132, 205; 3rd Light Infantry 63, 74, 76, 101, 108, 112, 206

Fletcher, Lieutenant Richard 68, 119, 134, 202
Forbes, Maj. David 162-3, 165
Ford, Commodore John 18
Fort Bourbon 37, 42, 60, 84, 106, 112-3, 189; see also Fort de la Convention, Fort Edward
Fort de la Convention; 42, 46, 50, 53, 65, 73, 79, 88, 92-4, 96-7, 99-102, 105-6, 108, 110-1; see also Fort Bourbon, Fort Edward
Fort de la République 42, 51, 84, 92, 94, 96-7, 99, 101-6, 108, 113; see also Fort Louis
Fort Edward 111, 173, 186; see also Fort Bourbon, Fort de la Convention
Fort Fleur d'Epée 129-130, 142-3, 149, 150-1, 155
Fort Louis 84, 113, 162; see also Fort de la République
Fort Matilda; 11, 133, 139, 161, 163, 167-170, 172-4
Fort Royal 42-3, 46, 60, 84-5, 89, 99, 104-5, 107, 159; see also République-ville
Fort Saint Charles 11, 129, 132-4, 164; see also Fort Matilda
Fort Saint-Louis 97, 131, 143
Fremantle, Lt. Col. Stephen 161, 190

Galion stream 11-2, 174
Gardner, Rear Admiral Alan 18, 32, 40, 49-51, 53
Garlies, Capt. George Stewart, Lord RN 63, 88, 105, 118, 129, 144, 227-8
Gell, Rear Admiral John 40
General Orders 67, 76, 94, 146, 173
Gibraltar 22, 33-4, 113, 138, 168, 181, 202
Gillespie, Surgeon Leonard 183, 191
Gimat, Governor Jean-Joseph, Chevalier de 44, 49-52
Gomm, Lt. Col. William 145, 150-1, 153, 179, 190
Gordon, Col. Sir Charles 57, 61, 66, 68, 71, 74, 79-80, 83, 85, 92, 100, 103, 118, 121, 124-5, 138-9, 155, 188, 195, 206
Gordon, Maj. William 54, 57

Graham, Brig. Gen. Colin 51, 155, 161-6, 170-1, 196
Grande Baie 129, 142
Grande-Terre 127, 129, 131-2, 143-5, 154-5, 228-9
Grant, Capt. John 161
Grenada 17, 43, 54, 57, 64, 68, 116, 119, 123, 140, 157, 159, 182, 181, 204
Grey, Capt. George RN 23, 37, 58, 115, 130, 195
Grey, Lt. Gen. Sir Charles 29, 32; early life 21-4; command in N. America 24-6; appointment to W. Indies command 28, 33-41, 53, 57; and capture of Martinique 58-79, 83-108, 110-113; and capture of Saint Lucia 114-6, 119-121, 125; and capture of Guadeloupe 126-134; consolidation and defence of conquests 123-5, 135-140, 142, 144-151, 153-5, 157-160, 164, 167, 169-170, 172-3; illness and return to Britain 168-9, 171-3; assessment, later life, and death 187-192, 194-5; and booty 36, 112, 121-3, 158-9, 174, 177-9; nepotism of 37, 112, 115-6, 121, 134, 195
Grey, Capt. Thomas 23, 37, 115, 121, 134
Grey, Edward 116
Grey, Capt. William 23, 37, 116, 121
Grey, Maj. Henry George 23, 112, 179, 195
Gros Morne (Morne des Olives) 66, 73, 76, 81, 83, 86, 98
Guadeloupe 11-12, 36-7, 42-5, 47-8, 65, 116, 121, 124, 179, 181, 183-193, 195-6, 198, 228; capture of 126-139; recapture of 142-176

Halifax, Nova Scotia 17, 39, 62, 100, 183, 204
Hoffman, Midshipman Frederick 61, 70, 89, 91, 105, 107-9, 111
Hugues, Victor 12, 196, 198-9; oversees recapture of Guadeloupe 141-3, 145, 147-9, 151, 155, 159-167, 169-174, 180, 192; and Jacobin rule in Antilles 181, 184-5, 188-190
Hunter, Maj. Gen. Peter 182

Hutton, Capt. Henry 162-3, 165

Irving Maj. Gen. Paulus Æmilius 186
Irving, Maj. Robert 67, 153, 164, 190
Islet aux Ramieres; see Pigeon Island

Jamaica 17-9, 29, 34, 36, 39, 42-4, 49, 65, 136-7, 177, 191, 226, 228-9
James, Lt. Bartholomew RN 70, 114-5, 126, 135
Jervis, Vice-Admiral Sir John; early life 29-32; assignment to W. Indies command 33, 36, 40-1, 44, 53, 58, 64, 66; and capture of Martinique 71, 74-5, 77-9, 84, 92, 95-6, 101-110, 112-3; and capture of Saint Lucia 114, 120; and capture of Guadeloupe 133-5; consolidation and defence of conquests 136, 138-140, 142, 144, 149, 154-5, 157, 164, 167-8, 170; illness and return to Britain 169, 173, 177; assessment, later life, and death 188-9, 192, 197-8; forces commanded by 226-229; quarrels with Prescott 121-4, 148-9, 169, 179; and booty 36, 158, 177-8
Johnstone, Lt. Col. Boulter 77-8

Keating, Lt. Henry 166

La Crosse, Jean-Baptiste-Raymond, Baron 46-8, 116
La Rochette, Commandant Jean Baptiste de 86
Laforey, Vice Admiral Sir John 18, 49, 54-5
Lake, Lt. Gen. Gerard 15, 168
Leeward Islands 17, 43-4, 38, 40-1, 44, 49, 65, 127, 157, 181, 187, 191, 193, 203, 208; see also Antigua, Dominica, Saint Kitts, Nevis, Guadeloupe
Leissègues, Capitaine de Vaisseau Corentin Urbain de 141
Lennox, Lt. Col. Charles 136-7
Lloyd, Lt. Col. Vaughan 55, 57
Lyon, Maj. William 85, 179

M'Dowall, Capt. John Alexander 142-3

INDEX

Mackewan, Capt. John 82
Magan, Lt. Col. Hugh 161, 165-6
Maitland, Capt. Charles 121
Maitland, Maj. Frederick 40, 55, 57, 86, 89, 191, 120-1, 125, 179, 193, 201
Malcolm, Capt. Robert 183
Manley, Maj. Orlando 63, 83, 197
Manningham, Maj. Coote 90
Marie Galante 48, 179, 191, 198
Marines 20, 55-6, 64, 73, 81, 83-6, 88, 90, 113, 129-130, 150, 154, 185; regulars acting as 20, 61, 182, 206
Markham, Capt. John RN 41, 226
Martinique 12, 36-8, 40, 42-53, 60, 65-6, 76-8, 193, 195, 199-201; capture of 70-113 190-1, 205-8; British administration of 114-6, 118, 120-5, 127, 129, 133-4, 136, 139, 141, 144-6, 148, 155, 157-161, 167, 170, 174, 176-7, 179, 181-2, 184, 186-7, 189
Mason, Maj. Finch 40, 74-5, 120
Meunier, Major Edouard 52, 73-4, 86, 90
Monteil, Lt. Col. Laroque de 56
Morne des Olives; see Gros Morne
Morne Fortuné 118-9, 185
Morne Le Brun 75, 81, 86, 88, 92, 94, 96
Morne Mascotte 130, 150-1
Morne Tartanson 105
Myers, Brig. Gen William 55, 57, 80, 85, 95, 114, 136, 179, 183, 196

Nares, Capt. George Strange 77-8, 85, 98, 102, 116
National Guard 50, 52, 56-7, 71, 75, 77-8, 80, 93, 107, 108, 110, 116, 119, 133
Nepean, Evan 38, 145, 153, 157
Nevis 17, 43
Nugent, Capt. Charles Edmund RN 89, 108

Ogle, Capt. William Newton 40, 116
Ostend, diversion of forces to 33-5
Oswald, Capt. John 63, 87, 200

Parker, Cdr. Christopher RN 120, 227
Paterson, Lt. Col. Robert 63, 118, 197
Paumier, Capt. Mungo 55, 85

Pélardy, Général de Brigade Mathieu 141, 152, 155, 161
Picton, Capt. Thomas 181
Pigeon Island (Islet de Ramieres) 66, 76-8, 83-5, 120, 185
Pitt, William 15, 33, 38, 66, 158, 173, 192, 198
Pointe-à-Pitre 127, 129-132, 142-6, 149-150, 152, 155, 162, 164, 169-170, 181, 191
Port au Prince 137
Powlett, Capt. Hon. Henry RN 112, 226
Pratt, Capt. John 145
Prescott, Lt. Gen. Robert 38, 59, 60, 63, 143; and capture of Martinique 71, 74, 85-6, 88, 93, 96, 113; Governor of Martinique 114-5, 121-4, 126, 138, 148-9, 155, 160, 188; and defence of Fort Matilda 12, 161, 163, 167-176; return to Britain and subsequent career 179, 195
Preston, Lt. D'Arcy RN 120
Prize Courts 122

Ramsay, Lt. Col. Hon. George 20, 61, 86-7, 182, 186, 200
Regiments & Corps, British; 7th Dragoon Guards 28; 7th Light Dragoons 63; 8th Light Dragoons 28; 10th Light Dragoons 63, 76, 99; 11th Light Dragoons 16; 15th Light Dragoons 63; 16th Light Dragoons 63; 17th Light Dragoons 37, 121; 18th Light Dragoons 112; 19th Light Dragoons 25; 20th (Jamaica) Light Dragoons 17; 1st Foot (Royals), 1st Bn. 17, 34, 2nd Bn. 34, 138; 2nd Foot (Queen's), 1st Bn. 20, 61, 81, 86-7, 200, 206 2nd Bn. 182, 186; 3rd Foot 34-5; 6th Foot 17, 21, 33-4, 60, 62-3, 74, 96, 99, 118, 121, 125-6, 135, 157, 182, 204-6; 7th Foot 37, 118; 8th Foot 38, 63, 163, 205; 9th Foot 33-4, 51, 54, 56-7, 62-3, 71, 73-4, 76, 82, 86-8, 93, 96, 118, 121, 125-6, 145, 157, 182, 184-5, 201, 202-3, 205-6; 10th Foot 17, 137; 12th Foot 38, 63, 80, 163, 205; 13th Foot 17, 34; 15th Foot 12, 17, 33-4, 51, 55, 61, 63, 68, 74, 77-8, 85, 92, 96, 99, 114, 126, 136, 145, 161, 169-70, 174, 182,

203, 205-6, 209; 16th Foot 17, 137; 17th Foot 38, 63, 163, 168, 191, 205; 18th Foot 34, 138; 20th Foot 17, 22, 34; 21st Foot 12, 33-4, 51-2, 63, 116, 145, 151, 155, 157, 169, 174-7, 203, 205-6; 22nd Foot 38, 63, 65, 85, 136, 145-7, 200, 205; 23rd Foot 38, 63, 163, 145, 205; 28th Foot 24, 34-5, 59; 31st Foot 38, 63, 150, 163, 168, 205-6; 32nd Foot 33, 137, 203-4; 33rd Foot 12, 24, 38, 63, 82, 86-7, 163, 166, 169, 205-6; 34th Foot 38, 63, 87, 163, 168, 182, 184, 186, 205-6; 35th Foot 12, 38, 63, 87, 136, 145, 161, 169-70, 182, 200, 205; 38th Foot 38, 63, 82, 163, 201, 205-6; 39th Foot 12, 34, 38, 61, 63, 68, 79, 114, 126, 145, 150, 161, 163, 165-6, 169, 182, 190, 202, 205-6; 40th Foot 38, 63, 86-7, 98, 163, 183, 205-6; 41st Foot 38, 57, 61, 63, 65, 136, 183, 205-6; 42nd Highlanders 24, 34-5; 43rd Foot 34, 38, 61, 63, 68, 79-80, 118, 126, 130, 132, 132-3, 150, 153, 161-3, 165-6, 170, 182, 190-1, 202, 205-6; 44th Foot 24, 38, 60, 63, 82, 87, 163, 205-6; 45th Foot 33, 51, 137, 182, 203-4; 46th Foot 168, 181, 184, 196; 48th Foot 33, 51, 67, 137, 203-4; 49th Foot 17, 137; 53rd Foot 35; 54th Foot 34-5, 183; 55th Foot 17, 38, 60, 63, 87, 90, 163, 205-6; 56th Foot 34, 38, 61, 63, 68, 145, 163, 167, 169, 176, 182, 190, 205-6, 209; 58th Foot 34, 37, 61, 63, 68, 81, 86, 89-90, 95, 114, 125-6, 136, 145, 161, 182, 190, 205-6, 209; 59th Foot 34-5, 183; 60th Foot 34, 40, 55, 125, 205-6, 3rd Bn. 34, 51, 137, 203-4, 4th Bn. 12, 34, 51, 54-7, 63, 145, 157, 169, 203-4; 61st Foot 161, 168, 184-6; 62nd Foot 17, 34; 64th Foot 24, 34, 38, 61, 63, 68, 61, 83, 86, 114, 126, 136, 145, 161, 170-1, 182, 190, 205-6, 209; 65th Foot 17, 33-4, 61, 63, 68, 75, 81-3, 86, 88, 95, 136, 145-6, 150-1, 157, 161, 163, 182, 190, 204-6; 66th Foot 17, 145; 67th Foot 33, 51, 137, 203-4; 68th Foot 168, 181, 184, 186; 70th Foot 34, 38, 62-3, 67-8, 74, 76-8, 85-6, 93, 96, 114, 116, 126, 136, 164, 171, 182, 190, 200, 205-6, 209; 79th Foot 183; 80th Foot 38-9, 62; 83rd Foot 182; 85th Foot 168; 98th Foot 23; Carolina Black Corps 61, 64, 76, 129, 161, 184, 209; Malcolm's Royal Rangers 183-4, 185; Myers' Regiment of Foot 183; Royal Martinico Volunteers 169; Soter's Island Rangers 169; Whyte's Regiment of Foot 183; see also Flank Battalions, Royal Artillery, Royal Engineers, Royal Irish Artillery, Royal Military Artificers

Regiments & Corps, French; 14e Régiment d'Infanterie 133; 31e Régiment d'Infanterie 56, 116, 119; 32e Régiment d'Infanterie 207; 37e Regiment d'Infanterie 73, 111, 207; 50e Régiment d'Infanterie 133; 52e Régiment d'Infanterie 207; Bataillons de Sans-Culottes de la Guadeloupe 141, 160, 162; Chasseurs de Martinique 42, 50, 79-80, 1er Bn. 73, 75, 81-2, 92-3, 98, 2e Bn. 73-4, 86, 3e Bn. 50, 73; see also National Guard

République-ville 40, 42-4, 48-50, 66, 73-4, 76-85, 90, 92-7, 99, 102, 104-6, 110, 112, 118, 120, 126, 157, 160, 176, 181, 207, 209, 227; see also Fort Royal

Ricard, Général de Brigade Nicolas Xavier de 116, 118-120, 133, 189-200

Riou, Capt. Edward RN 103, 105, 226

Rivière Salée (Guadeloupe) 127, 129, 145

Rivière Salée (Martinique) 76, 78, 85, 88

Riviere, Admiral Charles Joseph Mascarene de 49

Robertson, Capt. Lewis RN 146, 151-3, 155, 188

Robinson, Capt. Frederick Philipse 82, 201-2

Rochambeau, Lieutenant Général Donatien-Marie-Joseph de Vimeur, Vicomte de; arrival in W Indies 46-53, 116; defence of Martinique 73-4, 76-79, 81, 83-5, 88, 92-5, 97-99, 101-2, 104-6, 108, 114, 141; captivity and later life 110-113, 120, 158, 179, 189, 199

Rogers, Capt. Josias RN 41, 58, 64, 68, 71, 79, 84, 92, 100-2, 105-8, 129, 132, 135-6, 179, 188, 226, 228-9

INDEX 243

Rogers, Lt James RN 135
Rogers, Lt. Thomas RN 84, 108
Rouyer, Général de Brigade Charles Etienne 141-2, 159
Royal Artillery 17-18, 54-5, 63-4, 68, 81, 83, 98, 105, 118, 134, 142, 145, 150, 161, 165, 169, 173, 184, 188, 191, 197, 204-5; see also Royal Irish Artillery
Royal Engineers 12, 38, 55, 63, 68, 118-9, 129, 134, 143, 161, 164, 166, 169, 188, 191, 202, 205
Royal Irish Artillery 37, 63, 68, 98, 118, 145, 161-2, 204-5
Royal Military Artificers 37
Royalists, French 12, 15, 37, 40, 45-6, 48-54, 60, 65-6, 71, 73, 75, 94, 116, 141-3, 147, 149, 155-6, 158, 160-4, 166, 169, 173, 180, 184, 188, 199
Rutherford, Lt. William Cordon RN 77
Ruvijnes, Capt. Francis de 83, 105, 146, 150, 162

Saint Domingue 17, 36-7, 45-6, 49, 65, 136, 138-9, 141, 191, 196, 199
Saint Christopher's; see Saint Kitts
Saint Kitts 42-3, 54, 63, 68, 134, 144-5, 154, 146, 157, 159, 169
Saint Lucia 36-8, 43-6, 48-50, 65-6, 187, 189, 193, 195, 202; capture of, 114-127, 133, 141, 191; British occupation of 134, 139, 146-7, 158, 181, 184; recapture of 185-6
Saint Pierre 42, 46, 48, 50-2, 73-4, 80-1, 86-92, 95, 112, 114-5, 123, 155, 157, 160, 168-9, 173, 193, 207, 209
Saint Vincent 17, 43, 47, 51, 64, 146, 157-8, 169, 184, 186, 197
Sancé, Chevalier Jean-Louis Alexandre Gédéon Ridouet de 40, 66, 99, 199
Sawyer, Capt. Charles RN 146, 151, 229
Schank, Capt. John RN 41, 77, 79, 96
Scott, Sir William 158-9 173
Shadwell, Lt. James 99
Ships, British; *Asia* (64) 106, 227; *Assurance* (troop ship) 146, 164, 227, 229; *Beaulieu* (40) 75, 226; *Bellona* (74) 173; *Blanche* (32) 120, 134, 179, 185, 228; *Blonde* (32) 40-1, 61, 111-2, 226; *Boyne* (98) 36, 41, 58-9, 64, 69, 71, 95, 101, 103, 106, 108, 114, 118, 126, 130, 133, 135, 144, 148-9, 157, 164, 166, 177, 226, 228; *Bulldog* (16) 167, 229; *Ceres* (32) 129, 227-8; *Dromedary* (armed storeship) 79, 227; *Duke* (98) 51; *Europa* (50) 18; *Hero* (transport) 55; *Hind* (28) 55; *Intrepid* (64) 137; *Irresistible* (74) 64, 226, 228; *Leviathan* (74) 40; *London* (transport) 118; *Majestic* (74) 173, 183; *Monarch* (74) 51; *Nautilus* (16) 55, 144, 226, 229; *Quebec* (32) 41, 71, 88, 129, 132, 135, 226, 228; *Queen* (98) 51; *Ramillies* (74) 181; *Rattlesnake* (16) 118, 120, 226; *Roebuck* (hospital ship) 25, 161, 227, 229; *Rose* (28) 103, 107, 118, 129; *Santa Margarita* (36) 88, 90, 227-8; *Seaflower* (16) 131, 227; *Solebay* (32) 64, 88, 118, 146, 226, 228; *Terpsichore* (32) 174, 176, 226, 228; *Theseus* (74) 173; *Trusty* (50) 18, 55; *Undaunted* (28, ex-*Bienvenue*) 110; *Vanguard* (74) 146, 229; *Vengeance* (74) 64, 71, 118, 161, 226, 229; *Vesuvius* (bomb) 64, 89, 92, 101, 105, 227; *Veteran* (64) 64, 71, 118, 130, 144-6, 226, 228; *Victorious* (74) 109; *Winchelsea* (32) 63, 118, 129, 142, 144-6, 227-8; *Woolwich* (armed storeship) 75, 118, 167, 227, 229; *Zebra* (sloop) 75, 90, 101, 103, 106-7, 227, 229
Ships, French; *Bienvenue* (28) 73, 103, 109; *Pique* (32) 142, 179; *Prevoyante* (transport) 170; *Thétis* (36) 142
Sinclair, Capt. Charles, Lord 99
Skerrett, Maj. John 81, 83
Smyth, Lt. George Stracey 118
Sourrière, Heights of 81-2, 88, 92-6, 105
Sowerby, Lt. Col. John 54, 81
Stewart, Brig. Gen. James 184-6
Stewart, Capt. Hon. William 63, 80, 85, 99, 104, 111, 132, 147, 150, 152-4, 200
Stewart, Lt. Col. Robert 63, 108, 190
Stovin, Capt. Richard 162-3, 166, 191

Symes, Brig. Gen. Richard Mitchelbourne 39, 78, 89, 108, 110, 115, 130, 139, 146, 150-1, 153-4, 171, 179, 190

Thomas, Capt. John 174
Thompson, Rear Admiral Charles 41, 64, 71, 75, 103, 106, 110, 114, 118, 139, 146, 163, 174, 197-8
Tobago 17, 40, 45, 48, 54-7, 62, 64, 125, 140, 143, 202, 204
Toosey, Lt. Philip 150
Townshend, Ensign Lord William 102
Trinité 50, 66, 71, 73, 75-6, 81, 83, 86, 88, 112
Trois Rivieres 45, 71, 74

Vaughan, Lt. Gen. John 173-4, 181-6
Vipond, Capt. Joseph 67

Walker, Capt. Joseph 162

Wardle, Dr John 40
Watt, Lt. James 78
Wetherall, Capt. Frederick 104
Whitworth, Capt. Francis 87
Whyte, Brig. Gen. John 60, 62, 66, 68, 74, 76-8, 85, 114, 136, 139, 179, 183, 196, 206
Williamson, Maj. Gen. Adam 17, 65, 136
Willyams, Rev. Cooper 41, 84
Windward Islands 12, 17, 42-4, 46, 48, 55, 65, 73, 121, 142; see also Barbados, Grenada, Martinique, Saint Lucia, Saint Vincent, Tobago
Wolley, Lt. Isaac RN 88, 147, 151-3

Yellow Fever 20, 59, 64, 116, 134-5, 138, 143, 146, 159, 179, 185, 188-190
Yonge, Sir George 89
York, Gen. HRH Prince Frederick, Duke of 15, 34-5, 39, 146, 182

From Reason to Revolution series – Warfare 1721-1815

http://www.helion.co.uk/series/from-reason-to-revolution-1721-1815.php

The 'From Reason to Revolution' series covers the period of military history 1721–1815, an era in which fortress-based strategy and linear battles gave way to the nation-in-arms and the beginnings of total war.

This era saw the evolution and growth of light troops of all arms, and of increasingly flexible command systems to cope with the growing armies fielded by nations able to mobilise far greater proportions of their manpower than ever before. Many of these developments were fired by the great political upheavals of the era, with revolutions in America and France bringing about social change which in turn fed back into the military sphere as whole nations readied themselves for war. Only in the closing years of the period, as the reactionary powers began to regain the upper hand, did a military synthesis of the best of the old and the new become possible.

The series will examine the military and naval history of the period in a greater degree of detail than has hitherto been attempted, and has a very wide brief, with the intention of covering all aspects from the battles, campaigns, logistics, and tactics, to the personalities, armies, uniforms, and equipment.

Submissions

The publishers would be pleased to receive submissions for this series. Please contact series editor Andrew Bamford via email (andrewbamford@helion.co.uk), or in writing to Helion & Company Limited, Unit 8 Amherst Business Centre, Budbrooke Road, Warwick, CV34 5WE

Titles

No 1   *Lobositz to Leuthen: Horace St Paul and the Campaigns of the Austrian Army in the Seven Years War 1756-57* (Neil Cogswell)

No 2   *Glories to Useless Heroism: The Seven Years War in North America from the French journals of Comte Maurés de Malartic, 1755-1760* (William Raffle (ed.))

No 3   *Reminiscences 1808-1815 Under Wellington: The Peninsular and Waterloo Memoirs of William Hay* (Andrew Bamford (ed.))

No 4   *Far Distant Ships: The Royal Navy and the Blockade of Brest 1793-1815* (Quintin Barry)

No 5   *Godoy's Army: Spanish Regiments and Uniforms from the Estado Militar of 1800* (Charles Esdaile and Alan Perry)

No 6   *On Gladsmuir Shall the Battle Be! The Battle of Prestonpans 1745* (Arran Johnston)

No 7   *The French Army of the Orient 1798-1801: Napoleon's Beloved 'Egyptians'* (Yves Martin)

No 8   *The Autobiography, or Narrative of a Soldier: The Peninsular War Memoirs of William Brown of the 45th Foot* (Steve Brown (ed.))

No 9   *Recollections from the Ranks: Three Russian Soldiers' Autobiographies from the Napoleonic Wars* (Darrin Boland)

No 10 *By Fire and Bayonet: Grey's West Indies Campaign of 1794* (Steve Brown)

No 11 *Olmütz to Torgau: Horace St Paul and the Campaigns of the Austrian Army in the Seven Years War 1758-60* (Neil Cogswell)

No 12 *Murat's Army: The Army of the Kingdom of Naples 1806-1815* (Digby Smith)

No 13 *The Veteran or 40 Years' Service in the British Army: The Scurrilous Recollections of Paymaster John Harley 47th Foot – 1798-1838* (Gareth Glover (ed.))

No 14 *Narrative of the Eventful Life of Thomas Jackson: Militiaman and Coldstream Sergeant, 1803-15* (Eamonn O'Keeffe (ed.))

No.15 *For Orange and the States: The Army of the Dutch Republic 1713-1772 Part I: Infantry* (Marc Geerdinck-Schaftenaar)

No 16 *Men Who Are Determined to be Free: The American Assault on Stony Point, 15 July 1779* (David C. Bonk)

No 17 *Next to Wellington: General Sir George Murray: The Story of a Scottish Soldier and Statesman, Wellington's Quartermaster General* (John Harding-Edgar)

No 18 *Between Scylla and Charybdis: The Army of Elector Friedrich August of Saxony 1733-1763 Part I: Staff and Cavalry* (Marco Pagan)

No 19 *The Secret Expedition: The Anglo-Russian Invasion of Holland 1799* (Geert van Uythoven)

No 20 *'We Are Accustomed to do our Duty': German Auxiliaries with the British Army 1793-95* (Paul Demet)

No 21 *With the Guards in Flanders: The Diary of Captain Roger Morris 1793-95* (Peter Harington (ed.))

No 22 *The British Army in Egypt 1801: An Underrated Army Comes of Age* (Carole Divall)

No 23 *Better is the Proud Plaid: The Clothing, Weapons, and Accoutrements of the Jacobites in the '45* (Jenn Scott)

No 24 *The Lilies and the Thistle: French Troops in the Jacobite '45* (Andrew Bamford)

No 25 *A Light Infantryman With Wellington: The Letters of Captain George Ulrich Barlow 52nd and 69th Foot 1808-15* (Gareth Glover (ed.))

No 26 *Swiss Regiments in the Service of France 1798-1815: Uniforms, Organisation, Campaigns* (Stephen Ede-Borrett)

No 27 *For Orange and the States! The Army of the Dutch Republic 1713-1772: Part II: Cavalry and Specialist Troops* (Marc Geerdinck-Schaftenaar)

No 28 *Fashioning Regulation, Regulating Fashion: Uniforms and Dress of the British Army 1800-1815 Volume I* (Ben Townsend)

No 29 *Riflemen: The History of the 5th Battalion 60th (Royal American) Regiment, 1797-1818* (Robert Griffith)

No 30 *The Key to Lisbon: The Third French Invasion of Portugal, 1810-11* (Kenton White)

No 31 *Command and Leadership: Proceedings of the 2018 Helion & Company 'From Reason to Revolution' Conference* (Andrew Bamford (ed.))

No 32 *Waterloo After the Glory: Hospital Sketches and Reports on the Wounded After the Battle* (Michael Crumplin and Gareth Glover)

No 33 *Fluxes, Fevers, and Fighting Men: War and Disease in Ancien Regime Europe 1648-1789* (Pádraig Lenihan)

No 34 *'They Were Good Soldiers': African-Americans Serving in the Continental Army, 1775-1783* (John U. Rees)

No 35 *A Redcoat in America: The Diaries of Lieutenant William Bamford, 1757-1765 and 1776* (John B. Hattendorf (ed.))

No 36 *Between Scylla and Charybdis: The Army of Friedrich August II of Saxony, 1733-1763: Part II: Infantry and Artillery* (Marco Pagan)

No 37 *Québec Under Siege: French Eye-Witness Accounts from the Campaign of 1759* (Charles A. Mayhood (ed.))

No 38 *King George's Hangman: Henry Hawley and the Battle of Falkirk 1746* (Jonathan D. Oates)

No 39 *Zweybrücken in Command: The Reichsarmee in the Campaign of 1758* (Neil Cogswell)

No 40 *So Bloody a Day: The 16th Light Dragoons in the Waterloo Campaign* (David J. Blackmore)

No 41 *Northern Tars in Southern Waters: The Russian Fleet in the Mediterranean 1806-1810* (Vladimir Bogdanovich Bronevskiy / Darrin Boland)

No 42 *Royal Navy Officers of the Seven Years War: A Biographical Dictionary of Commissioned Officers 1748-1763* (Cy Harrison)

No 43 *All at Sea: Naval Support for the British Army During the American Revolutionary War* (John Dillon)

No 44 *Glory is Fleeting: New Scholarship on the Napoleonic Wars* (Andrew Bamford (ed.))

No 45 *Fashioning Regulation, Regulating Fashion: Uniforms and Dress of the British Army 1800-1815 Vol. II* (Ben Townsend)

No 46 *Revenge in the Name of Honour: The Royal Navy's Quest for Vengeance in the Single Ship Actions of the War of 1812* (Nicholas James Kaizer)

No 47 *They Fought With Extraordinary Bravery: The III German (Saxon) Army Corps in the Southern Netherlands 1814* (Geert van Uythoven)

No 48 *The Danish Army of the Napoleonic Wars 1801-1814, Organisation, Uniforms & Equipment: Volume 1: High Command, Line and Light Infantry* (David Wilson)

No 49 *Neither Up Nor Down: The British Army and the Flanders Campaign 1793-1895* (Phillip Ball)

No 50 *Guerra Fantástica: The Portuguese Army and the Seven Years War* (António Barrento)

No 51 *From Across the Sea: North Americans in Nelson's Navy* (Sean M. Heuvel and John A. Rodgaard)

No 52 *Rebellious Scots to Crush: The Military Response to the Jacobite '45* (Andrew Bamford (ed.))

No 53 *The Army of George II 1727-1760: The Soldiers who Forged an Empire* (Peter Brown)

No 54 *Wellington at Bay: The Battle of Villamuriel, 25 October 1812* (Garry David Wills)

No 55 *Life in the Red Coat: The British Soldier 1721-1815* (Andrew Bamford (ed.))

No 56 *Wellington's Favourite Engineer. John Burgoyne: Operations, Engineering, and the Making of a Field Marshal* (Mark S. Thompson)

No 57 *Scharnhorst: The Formative Years, 1755-1801* (Charles Edward White)

No 58 *At the Point of the Bayonet: The Peninsular War Battles of Arroyomolinos and Almaraz 1811-1812* (Robert Griffith)

No 59 *Sieges of the '45: Siege Warfare during the Jacobite Rebellion of 1745-1746* (Jonathan D. Oates)

No 60 *Austrian Cavalry of the Revolutionary and Napoleonic Wars, 1792–1815* (Enrico Acerbi, András K. Molnár)

No 61 *The Danish Army of the Napoleonic Wars 1801-1814, Organisation, Uniforms & Equipment: Volume 2: Cavalry and Artillery* (David Wilson)

No 62 *Napoleon's Stolen Army: How the Royal Navy Rescued a Spanish Army in the Baltic* (John Marsden)

No 63 *Crisis at the Chesapeake: The Royal Navy and the Struggle for America 1775-1783* (Quintin Barry)

No 64 *Bullocks, Grain, and Good Madeira: The Maratha and Jat Campaigns 1803-1806 and the emergence of an Indian Army* (Joshua Provan)

No 65 *Sir James McGrigor: The Adventurous Life of Wellington's Chief Medical Officer* (Tom Scotland)

No 66 *Fashioning Regulation, Regulating Fashion: Uniforms and Dress of the British Army 1800-1815 Volume I* (Ben Townsend) (paperback edition)

No 67 *Fashioning Regulation, Regulating Fashion: Uniforms and Dress of the British Army 1800-1815 Volume II* (Ben Townsend) (paperback edition)

No 68 *The Secret Expedition: The Anglo-Russian Invasion of Holland 1799* (Geert van Uythoven) (paperback edition)

No 69 *The Sea is My Element: The Eventful Life of Admiral Sir Pulteney Malcolm 1768-1838* (Paul Martinovich)

No 70 *The Sword and the Spirit: Proceedings of the first 'War & Peace in the Age of Napoleon' Conference* (Zack White (ed.))

No 71 *Lobositz to Leuthen: Horace St Paul and the Campaigns of the Austrian Army in the Seven Years War 1756-57* (Neil Cogswell) (paperback edition)

No 72 *For God and King. A History of the Damas Legion 1793-1798: A Case Study of the Military Emigration during the French Revolution* (Hughes de Bazouges and Alistair Nichols)

No 73 *'Their Infantry and Guns Will Astonish You': The Army of Hindustan and European Mercenaries in Maratha service 1780-1803* (Andy Copestake)

No 74 *Like A Brazen Wall: The Battle of Minden, 1759, and its Place in the Seven Years War* (Ewan Carmichael)

No 75 *Wellington and the Lines of Torres Vedras: The Defence of Lisbon during the Peninsular War* (Mark Thompson)

No 76 *French Light Infantry 1784-1815: From the Chasseurs of Louis XVI to Napoleon's Grande Armée* (Terry Crowdy)

No 77 *Riflemen: The History of the 5th Battalion 60th (Royal American) Regiment, 1797-1818* (Robert Griffith) (paperback edition)

No 78 *Hastenbeck 1757: The French Army and the Opening Campaign of the Seven Years War* (Olivier Lapray)

No 79 *Napoleonic French Military Uniforms: As Depicted by Horace and Carle Vernet and Eugène Lami* (Guy Dempsey (trans. and ed.))

No 80 *These Distinguished Corps: British Grenadier and Light Infantry Battalions in the American Revolution* (Don N. Hagist)

No 81 *Rebellion, Invasion, and Occupation: The British Army in Ireland, 1793 -1815* (Wayne Stack)

No 82 *You Have to Die in Piedmont! The Battle of Assietta, 19 July 1747. The War of the Austrian Succession in the Alps* (Giovanni Cerino Badone)

No 83 *A Very Fine Regiment: the 47th Foot in the American War of Independence, 1773–1783* (Paul Knight)

No 84 *By Fire and Bayonet: Grey's West Indies Campaign of 1794* (Steve Brown) (paperback edition)